1815 to the Present

Teachers Guide

With tremendous gratitude
we wish to acknowledge
and express our appreciation
to those who assisted in the
making of this manual:

Ned and Leslie Bustard
Eric VanDerhoof
Christi McCullars
Shea Foster
Emily Fischer
and Aaron Larsen

Dear Friends,

We hope this guide will be helpful as you study the period from 1815 to the Present this year. You are about to take a journey through the past where you can see God's providence, judgement, and provision for His people on a daily basis. This study should help build an understanding of the world in which we live and what sacrifices and battles occurred which resulted in the tremendous blessings we now know. God was faithful to His people through the years just as He is today. What a joy it is for young children to come to realize God's faithfulness as they learn from the past.

There are 32 events/people featured in the cards in this series. That is approximately one per week. A few of the cards have extra projects which may spread into the following week. The projects are only suggestions, so use your imagination and have fun with your group. You will note that the projects vary to appeal to different ages. You may choose the ones you think are appropriate for your student(s). We recommend singing the song daily for the first several weeks, after that three times a week is usually enough. Remember, the reason for the song is to help memorize the chronology of the events. It is also good to have the children recite events, in proper order, rather that singing it after the song has been memorized. A sample school week might be planned as follows:

MONDAY: Sing the song (you may want to have a student come to the front of the room and hold up the flashcards in order as the class sings). Present the new card. Read what it says on the back and discuss it. Allow different students to read it out loud if you can. Then allow the students to answer questions on the worksheet. The questions are based on information on the cards.

TUESDAY: Sing the song. Orally review questions from this card's worksheet and from previous events. Obviously you cannot review every questions every day, so do a sampling. Assign different children different sources from the resource list on the card and allow them to look up the information and share it with the class.

WEDNESDAY: Sing the song. Orally review questions from the worksheet. Do one of the projects.

THURSDAY: Sing the song. Orally review from this week and previous weeks. Discuss how this card relates to those before it. Do another project, if there is one.

FRIDAY: Give test. Use remaining time for class instruction and drill. If you have already studied any of the previous series we strongly encourage review and testing of those series. Appendix 1 is provided for testing the student(s) on four different cards each week. It is a good idea for the children to write out their chronology also.

Having fun makes it easy to learn. Using the cards for games is one way. Ask the children to shuffle them and then see who can get their cards in order the fastest. Or have four to six students mix up their cards and then play Go Fish. This allows them to get familiar with the titles. Or you can get in a large room and see who can make their own timeline the fastest. A good way to drill questions in a classroom is to divide the children into two teams and ask questions in order. Teams receive a point for each right answer.

We have found one of the best ways to file the cards is to laminate them, punch a hole in the top right corner, and keep them on a large ring. The children can add the newest card and also have the previous cards handy. Another idea is to laminate them, put a Velcro strip on the card and on the wall, and start a timeline that children can put up and take down over and over again. An extra set of cards mounted at the end of the room for a reference timeline is a good idea too.

In order to encourage children to read historical fiction related to classroom work, we suggest a book chart to show points earned for each book read by each student. After receiving a certain number of points we allow the child to have a special lunch with their teacher. You could have a mom bring in a special lunch or allow the winners to go out.

Each worksheet, test, or writing assignment should receive three grades, one each for Content, Grammar and Linguistics (Spelling).

GRADING: A grading scale you may find helpful is to count ten points for essay questions, five points for one sentence answers and two points for fill in the blank answers. The percentile grade will then be the total number of points achieved divided by the total number of points possible.

GRAMMAR: The child should answer the questions in a complete sentence in which they first restate the question. For example: What is the Scripture reference for Creation? The Scripture reference for Creation is Genesis 1-2. This grade should be applied to an application grade in grammar, but should not affect history content grades. We suggest application at twenty percent of the overall grade.

LINGUISTICS: The children should spell all words correctly. You should deduct for misspelled words once the rule for spelling a particular word has been mastered. For example: i before e except after c. Once this has been covered a child's grade would be reduced if they spelled receive as recieve. If they are using a history card to do their worksheet they should be taught that those words to be transcribed directly from the card should be spelled correctly. This grade would be applied towards a linguistics application grade. Again we suggest twenty percent, but not to affect their history grade.

When you look at the tests you will see that there are not the same number of questions on each test or worksheet. We assign five points per question, with the listings of the chronology receiving two points per item listed. Partial credit may be counted because the questions are essay and they may have portions correct. Some students may ask why they are receiving three grades on each paper. We believe that it is important for a student to realize that grammar and linguistics matter in history class as well as in grammar class. All three contribute to help make students understood by others, and are thus intertwined.

Finally we welcome your feedback and comments. We hope that his resource will enrich the education of those children entrusted to you, and will help them understand the comprehensive responsibility that God requires of them.

Sincerely,

Marlin Detweiler

Laurie Detweiler

Marlin and Laurie Detweiler
Veritas Press
September 15, 1998

1815 TO THE PRESENT
Teachers Guide

TABLE OF CONTENTS

Appendix

THE MONROE DOCTRINE
Worksheet

1. What is the date given for the Monroe Doctrine?

____

2. How many terms did President James Monroe serve? What were the dates?

____

____

3. President Monroe did not want _______________ nations to control countries in this hemisphere.

4. What concern did Monroe have about other countries control of this hemisphere?

____

____

5. About which countries was Monroe concerned?

____

____

6. Name two other presidents that followed the Monroe Doctrine.

____

____

MONROE'S INAUGURATION

The Monroe Doctrine
Project

Revolution in Latin America

At first we shall have to go back a great many years and take a look into the past. Spain had never allowed its colonies to trade with any other nation, but in spite of the laws Spanish-American colonies had always smuggled in a great many British goods.

When Napoleon conquered almost all of Europe, he conquered Spain, sent the king away, and put his own brother on the Spanish throne instead.

How do you suppose that the Spanish colonies liked this? You might perhaps expect that they would be glad to have a change, for they had been governed badly for centuries. But the Spanish people were true to their king. They would have nothing to do with Napoleon's brother.

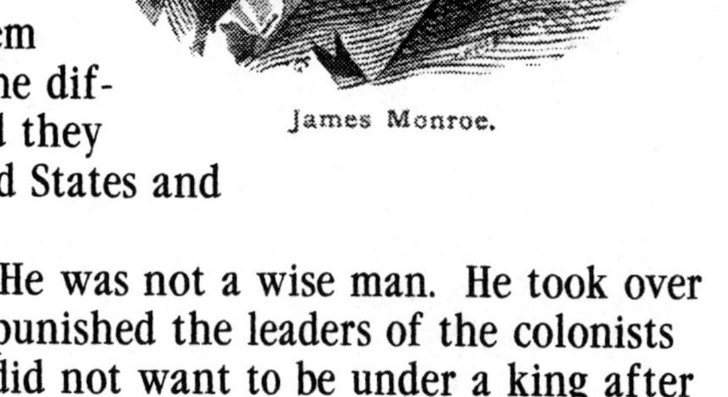
James Monroe.

The Spanish-American colonist even rose against him. They set up governments of their own all over Central and South America, and said that they would rule themselves until the true king could come back to his throne.

But the king did not come back for a number of years, and in the meantime his colonies had their first taste of liberty and independence. They traded freely with Great Britain. And British merchants supplied them with plenty of money. They could not help noticing the difference between self-government and Spanish rule, and they often thought about the great revolutions in the United States and France, which had made those countries independent.

At last the Spanish king came back to his throne. He was not a wise man. He took over his colonies and began once more to rule harshly. He punished the leaders of the colonists severely. So the Spanish Americans decided that they did not want to be under a king after all, and that they would be better off independent. Revolutions broke out in many places.

Success of San Martin in the South

The first successes were won in the district of the Argentine. There a man who had been an officer in the Spanish army made himself leader. His name was San Martin. After spending many months in collecting and drilling "the Army of the Andes," he accomplished one of the most difficult things ever attemped by any army. He led his troops over one of the highest and coldest mountain passes in the world, dragging his cannon and supplies after him. His soldiers came down on the other side of the mountains into Chile and soon put an end to Spanish rule there. Then San Martin marched them northward into Ecuador and Peru. He had to work slowly, for most of the South Americans were very ignorant. He had to teach them to want independence. But Argentina quickly declared itself an independent nation.

THE MONROE DOCTRINE
Project, Page 2

BOLIVAR'S SUCCESS IN THE NORTH

Meanwhile, what had been happening in the northern part of South America? The leader in the north, Bolivar, had founded two republics, Bolivia and Columbia. He had won the native cowboys over to his side, and his army had several times defeated the Spaniards. Venezuela also had declared its independence.

Then Bolivar moved south into Ecuador and met San Martin. Between them, they put an end to Spanish rule. Bolivar had hoped to unite all the Spanish-American countries into one, but he failed in this purpose. Nevertheless, he is given high honor, and is often called "the George Washington of South America." Many cities there have erected statues to his memory.

While these events had been taking place in South America, Mexico had freed itself from Spain, and the countries of Central America also had made themselves republics. At the same time Brazil had separated from Portugal and made itself an empire; later it too became a republic. As the nineteenth century drew to a close, all that Spain had left of her American possessions were the islands of Cuba and Puerto Rico.

A PROBLEM FOR THE POWERS

How would the older nations of the world treat these new Latin-American countries? Spain would not admit that they were independent and still claimed them as her colonies. No nation wanted to make an enemy of Spain. But, on the other hand, the Latin-American countries claimed that they were independent and wished to be considered so. All the European nations wanted their trade. Which side should they take? It was a hard problem to solve.

And what made it harder was that the new countries had very unsteady governments. They kept continually changing. One strong man would seize power from another only to be thrown down in turn by a third. Spain said, "You see, they cannot govern themselves."

The United States was at this same time trying to buy Florida from Spain, and did not want to do anything that would make Spain angry until after the treaty had been signed. It was not signed until 1819.

So the years passed, and no foreign power was willing to say that it considered the South Americans independent. But after 1819 the United States felt free to do so. Its people had always been in sympathy with their desire for liberty and independence. Henry Clay had spoken out strongly many times for the South Americans. So after the wars between Spain and the South Americans had been going on for more than ten years, our government decided that the Latin Americans had won the right to be considered separate states, and therefore recogonized them as independent.

PRESIDENT MONROE'S MESSAGE

But Spain had no idea of letting her colonies go so easily. A number of other kings in Europe were ready to assist the Spanish king; it seemed as if they were going to help him gain back his colonies.

This worried the United States, for the result might be that the European kings might seize parts of America as their reward for helping Spain. The United States did not want

The Monroe Doctrine
Project, Page 3

them as neighbors. Great Britian also was worried, for she wanted to keep her large South American trade, and she could not if the other kings were given parts of the New World or if Spain won in a war with the colonies.

So Great Britain prevented the Spanish king from getting the help promised by the other kings. And President Monroe, with the help of John Quincy Adams, who was then Secretary of State, sent a message to Congress, telling what he thought ought to be done. The message was sent to Congress in 1823. It was not a law, but only a message.

President Monroe believed that there was a natural separation of interests between the Old World and the New World, and that neither one should meddle in the affairs of the other. His message contained three main points: (1) That the United States would deny the right of any European power to plant any new colonies on the American continent; (2) That we were resolved not to meddle with the affairs of the nations of the Old Worlds; (3) That we were equally determined that they should not in any way meddle with the affairs of the New World.

That declaration is called the "Monroe Doctrine." It means that we should consider that "America is for Americans." We stand by the right of the different nations on both the American continents, North and South, to manage their own affairs in their own way, without interference from Europe.

Henry Clay

The Monroe Doctrine
Project

For discussion or answer in writing

1. What did the Spanish colonies think of Napoleon's brother?

____

____

2. Who won independence for South America in the South? In the North?

____

____

3. Why did President Monroe send his message to Congress?

____

____

4. What were the three main parts of the Monroe Doctrine?

____

____

For fun:

These expressions were used in the story. Make up sentences using the expressions, and choose teams to see which makes the fewest mistakes.

1823
Monroe Doctrine
San Martin
Bolivar

THE MONROE DOCTRINE
Project 2

Look at the map below. Color the Spanish possessions red and the Portuguese possessions yellow. Color the United States green. This will help you to see why President Monroe was so concerned.

The Monroe Doctrine
Project 3

Monroe's Seventh Annual Message to Congress

. . . At the proposal of the Russian Imperial Government, made through the minister of the Emperor residing here, a full power and instructions have been transmitted to the minister of the United States at St. Petersburg to arrange by amicable negotiation the respective rights and interests of the two nations on the northwest coast of this continent. A similar proposal has been made by His Imperial Majesty to the Government of Great Britain, which has likewise been acceded to. The Government of the United States has been desirous by this friendly proceeding of manifesting the great value which they have invariably attached to the friendship of the Emperor and their solicitude to cultivate the best understanding with his Government. In the discussions to which this interest has given rise and in the arrangements by which they may terminate the occasion has been judged proper for asserting, as a principle in which the rights and interests of the United States are involved, that the American continents, by the free and independent condition which they have assumed and maintain, are henceforth not to be considered as subjects for future colonization by any European powers. . .

It was stated at the commencement of the last session that a great effort was then making in Spain and Portugal to improve the condition of the people of those countries, and that it appeared to be conducted with extraordinary moderation. It need scarcely be remarked that the results have been so far very different from what was then anticipated. Of events in that quarter of the globe, with which we have so much intercourse and from which we derive our origin, we have always been anxious and interested spectators. The citizens of the United States cherish sentiments the most friendly in favor of the liberty and happiness of their fellow-men on that side of the Atlantic. In the wars of the European powers in matters relating to themselves we have never taken any part, nor does it comport with our policy to do so. It is only when our rights are invaded or seriously menaced that we resent injuries or make preparation for our defense. With the movements in this hemisphere we are of necessity more immediately connected, and by causes which must be obvious to all enlightened and impartial observers. The political system of the allied powers is essentially different in this respect from that of America. This difference proceeds from that which exists in their respective Governments; and to the defense of our own, which has been achieved by the loss of so much blood and treasure, and matured by the wisdom of their most enlightened citizens, and under which we have enjoyed unexampled felicity, this whole nation is devoted. We owe it, therefore, to candor and to the amicable relations existing between the United States and those powers to declare that we should consider any

The Monroe Doctrine
Project 3, Page 2

attempt on their part to extend their system to any portion of this hemisphere as dangerous to our peace and safety. With the existing colonies or dependencies of any European power we have not interfered and shall not interfere. But with the Governments who have declared their independence and maintain it, and whose independence we have, on gr at consideration and on just principles, acknowledged, we could not view any interposition for the purpose of oppressing them, or controlling in any other manner their destiny, by any European power in any other light than as the manifestation of an unfriendly disposition toward the United States. In the war between those new Governments and Spain we declared our neutrality at the time of their recognition, and to this we have adhered, and shall continue to adhere, provided no change shall occur which, in the judgement of the competent authorities of this Government, shall make a corresponding change on the part of the United States indispensable to their security.

The late events in Spain and Portugal shew that Europe is still unsettled. Of this important fact no stronger proof can be adduced than that the allied powers should have thought it proper, on any principle satisfactory to themselves, to have interposed by force in the internal concerns of Spain. To what extent such interposition may be carried, on the same principle, is a question in which all independent powers whose governments differ from theirs are interested, even those most remote, and surely none of them more so than the United States. Our policy in regard to Europe, which was adopted at an early stage of the wars which have so long agitated that quarter of the globe, nevertheless remains the same, which is, not to interfere in the internal concerns of any of its powers; to consider the government de facto as the legitimate government for us; to cultivate friendly relations with it, and to preserve those relations by a frank, firm, and manly policy, meeting in all instances the just claims of every power, submitting to injuries from none. But in regard to those continents circumstances are eminently and conspicuously different. It is impossible that the allied powers should extend their political system to any portion of either continent without endangering our peace and happiness; nor can anyone believe that our southern brethren, if left to themselves, would adopt it of their own accord. It is equally impossible, therefore, that we should behold such interposition in any form with indifference. If we look to the comparative strength and resources of Spain and those new Governments, and their distance from each other, it must be obvious that she can never subdue them. It is still the true policy of the United States to leave the parties to themselves, in hope that other powers will pursue the same course. . . .

THE MONROE DOCTRINE
Test

1. What is the date given for the Monroe Doctrine?

____

____

2. President James Monroe served ________ terms as president of the United States.

   He served from 1817 - __________.

3. What is the Monroe Doctrine?

____

____

____

____

____

4. Name two presidents who have followed the Monroe Doctrine.

____

____

____

5. Monroe especially did not want ______________________ countries to be controlled by Europe.

Traveling the Erie Canal
Worksheet

1. What is the date given for traveling the Erie Canal?

____

2. Up until 1800 how were roads made?

____

____

3. Businessmen and merchants had to pay a lot of _________ to transport wares.
4. What was the least expensive method to transport wares?

____

____

5. How was cargo carried across the ocean?

____

____

6. What was the Erie Canal?

____

____

7. How long did it take to build the Erie Canal?

____

8. What was the purpose of the Erie Canal?

____

____

9. Many ___________ and ___________

have been written about the Erie Canal.

The Erie Canal
Project

Engineering the Erie Canal

After reading the book *The Amazing Impossible Erie Canal,* and the reading provided, draw red arrows indicating the direction of water flow in each illustration. Then label the Main Gate and the Sluice Gate.

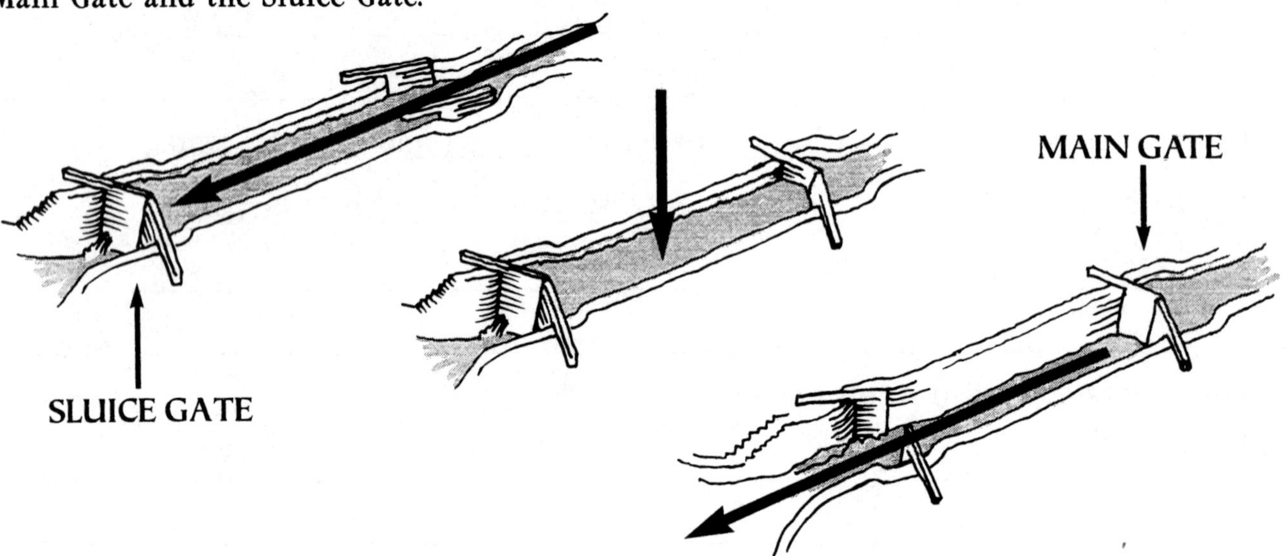

Below is an illustration of an *Aqueduct*.

What was it was used for?

An Aqueduct was used to carry the canal over rivers and valleys.

Identify what type of boat this is and label its parts.

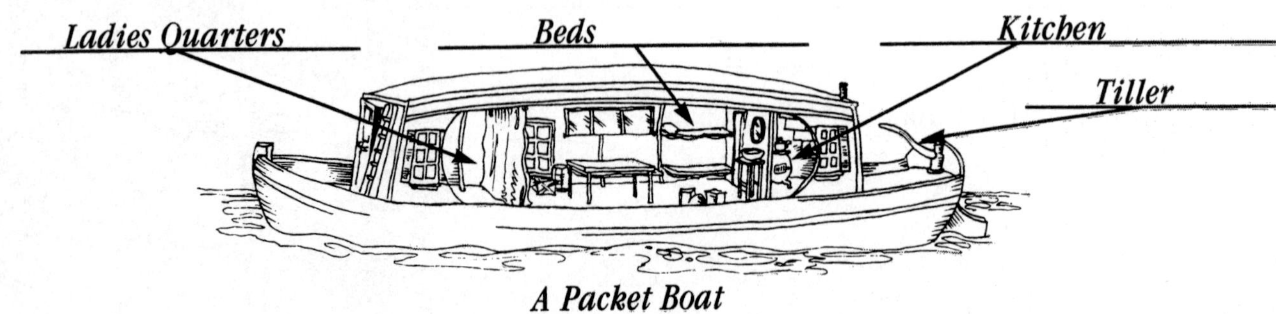

A Packet Boat

THE ERIE CANAL
Project

Engineering the Erie Canal

After reading the book *The Amazing Impossible Erie Canal,* and the reading provided, draw red arrows indicating the direction of water flow in each illustration. Then label the Main Gate and the Sluice Gate.

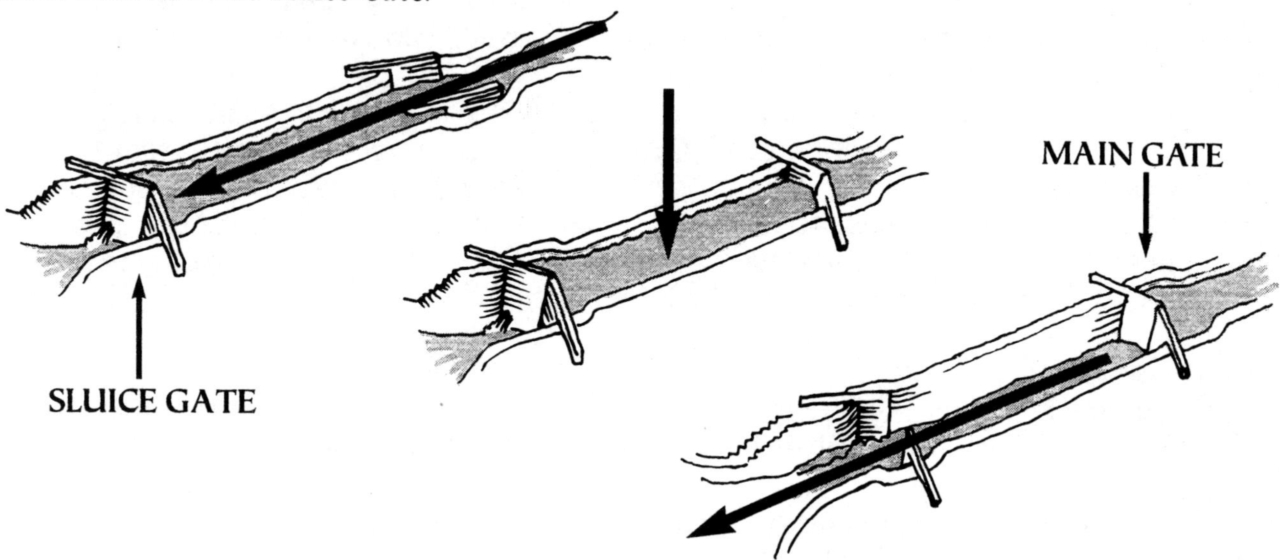

Below is an illustration of an *Aqueduct*.

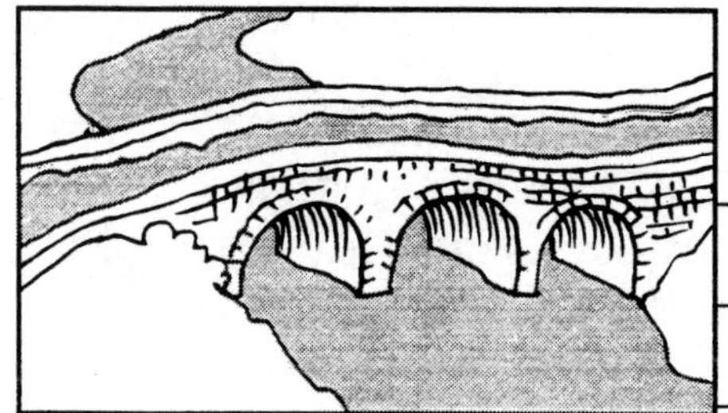

What was it was used for?

An Aqueduct was used to carry the canal over rivers and valleys.

Identify what type of boat this is and label its parts.

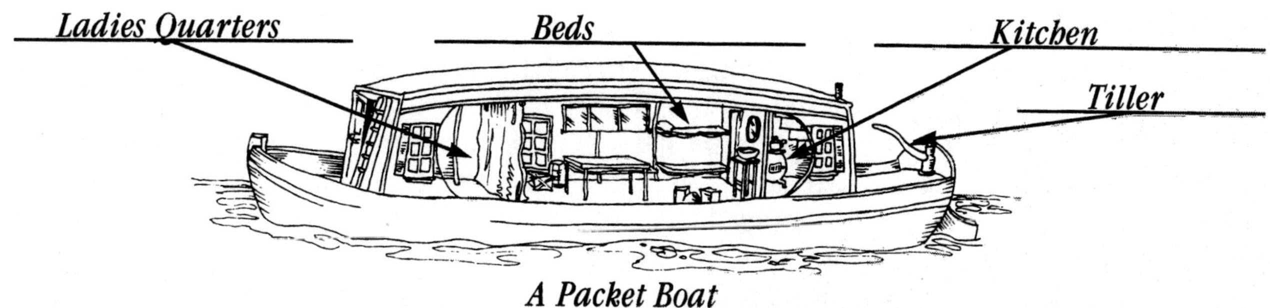

A Packet Boat

The Erie Canal
Project 2

The Importance of Erie

Before the steam engine was invented and railroads were built, cities and towns were found chiefly near the sea or along the rivers. The ancient nations that first became civilized inhabited regions about the big waters. Babylon was on the Euphrates, the Egyptians lived on the banks of the Nile and the Greeks inhabited the islands and the shores of the Aegean Sea. England surrounded by sea and water by rivers, was the first country in Northern Europe to become densely populated.

The reason is simple. In those days water was the only practical means of long-distance transportation. Manufacturing, even of a primitive kind, was impossible away from the water because the manufacturers could not ship their wares to the markets. For the same reason it did not pay the farmers to raise more produce than they themselves could consume. There were a few exceptions, such as the cattle-raisers; they could drive their cattle to market over long distances. Their produce transported itself.

Early Transportation by Water

The manufacturers and the farmers near the water could produce larger quantities, for they could load their wares and their produce on boats or ships at comparatively little expense, and send them even to other counties. Consequently all manufacturers and farmers wanted to be near the water. It was trade that developed civilization, but it was water transportation that made trade possible.

Railroads have since changed these condtions. Without railroads the interior of our vast country would still be wild prairie and forest. Freight cars serve on land as ships serve on water, but water has not lost all of its old-time importance. Even to-day there are few really big cities found inland.

But at the time the American colonies had freed themselves from England, and for long afterward, there was no thought of railways. Steam had not yet been put to practical use. The population of the new United States was then confined to the Atlantic seacoast and the river valleys. Boston, New York and Philadelphia had become the most important cities, because they had protected harbors for shipping.

Meanwhile there had been some migration westward throught the wilderness. The regions bordering on the shores of the Great Lakes and along the many rivers feeding them consist of low, rolling country, especially adapted to the raising of grains.

Men Look to the West

Very early in the history of the country there had been far-seeing men among the colonists who saw the tremendous advantages to the colonies that would follow, establishing some means of transportaion between the rich agricultural regions west of the Alleghenies and Atlantic seacoast. The lands along the coast were not adapted to wheat-growing, yet the population needed wheat. With easy transportation the farmers of the West would not only be able to supply this demand, but they would also be able to export their grains to Europe. Such a route would also render the wilderness between

THE ERIE CANAL
Project 2, Page 2

New York and the lake coutry inhabitable for the settlers along the way would also be able to ship their produce to market.

George Washington , practical surveyor and engineer, was one of the first to have his imagination roused by these possibilities. He had explored the country between Albany, on the Hudson, and Buffalo, on Lake Erie. Already much of this region was traversed by water routes. He became an enthusiastic advocate for connecting these waterways by canals so that boats might pass from New York to the interior. To him it was not only a question of trade. If the sturdy settlers who had cleared their little homesteads in the wildernesses were not offered a means of communication with the states in the East, they would turn toward the power which held the Mississippi. Give them an outlet to the Atlantic coast and they would naturally maintain their allegiance to the States. To Washington and many others a waterway from the Great Lakes to the Hudson was necessary to develop a great united nation.

Possibly it was only those of big, broad minds who saw it from this point of view. More numerous were the merchants and tradesmen of New York, who, for more selfish reasons, agitated the idea with much energy. They feared the commercial rivalry of Boston and Philadelphia. With western grain exported to Europe passing through New York, that city would become the great trade center of the country and its most important seaport. They finally compelled the state legislature to take action.

FIRST DISCUSSION OF A GREAT CANAL

In 1791 the legislature had ordered a survey made. Engineers were sent to study the country between Albany and Lake Erie and report on the possibility of digging a through waterway between those two points. Their report was warmly in favor of the undertaking. And so the first actual step was taken toward the digging of the Erie Canal.

The Erie Canal

Project 2, Page 3

Travelers of that period have left interesting records of the difficulties to be encountered on the way. From New York City they journeyed from two to five days on sailing boats up to Albany, thence overland seventeen miles to Schenectady. Here they embarked again on boats, propelled by oars and sail, and sometimes, over shallow stretches, by means of poles. After traveling 104 miles in this fashion, at the rate of about twenty miles a day, they would reach Utica, a small, log-hut settlement. Another nine days' journey by water and land brought them to Oswego, on Lake Ontario. Naturally very little merchandise was sent over this route, but such as was sent cost $100 a ton, or more, for freight.

Private Individuals Fail to Dig a Canal

At first there was an attempt to enourage private companies to undertake the vast work of cutting through the waterway. Some were organized and even began work; short sections of canal were dug, connecting some of the various rivers and lakes on the way. But in those days there were few rich men, and it was found impossible to raise enough capital to finance the whole undertaking.

One of the most enthusiastic advocates of the scheme was Gouverneur Morris, then representing New York in the United States Senate. "Some day," said he, "ships will sail from London bound for Buffalo, via the Hudson River." It was he who interested De Witt Clinton in the idea, the man whose determination and energy were yet to bring it to a complete realization.

It was nearly twenty years after the first survey had been made that the state again took action. By this time it was obvious that the private companies could not accomplish much. So in 1810 the legislature appointed a canal commission to go to Washington and lay the matter before the president and Congress. As George Washington had already said years before, an Erie Canal was of great national importance: it would unite the nation- the East with what was then the West. The cost had been estimated at $7 million. Private capitalists could not subscribe such an amount, but surely Congress could appropriate such a sum for a work of such importance.

De Witt Clinton and the Erie Canal

De Witt Clinton

But in those days Congress did not make $7 million in appropriations so readily as it does now. There was much discussion and powerful opposition. Then came the War of 1812 and the Federal Government had other matters to which it must devote its energy and funds. It was then that De Witt Clinton began publicly to encourage the digging of the canal. And finally, in 1816, the governor of New York appointed a new canal commission authorized to raise a loan which would be guaranteed by the state. At the head of this commission the governor placed De Witt Clinton.

To test the interest of the people of the state in the canal scheme Clinton made it a political issue; in the following year, 1817, he became a candidate for governor, promising that if he were chosen he would make the digging of the canal his chief business. He was elected by one of the biggest majorities that ever put an official into office. On July 1 he was inaugurated. Three days later, on Independence Day, he went up to Rome, on the Mohawk River, attended by his staff, and began the digging of the canal by turning up the first shovelful of earth.

According to the plans, the canal was to be 40 feet wide at the top, 28 feet at the bottom and 4 feet deep. The cost was to be about $7 million. It was the size of the work that was the most remarkable; as a feat of engineering skill it was then unusual, but, compared with the great works that are undertaken in the present time, it was not especially difficult.

Yet there were many supposedly well educated people in those days who thought the Erie Canal a wild dream. "You cannot make water run uphill," they said, though the theory of locks, by means of which barges could be lifted to higher levels, had already been put into practice in canals abroad. The digging began. In two years a section fifteen miles in length was finished, connecting Rome with Utica. The next year the canal reached the Seneca River.

When the Canal was Finally Completed

De Witt Clinton had said that the work would be completed in 1823, but this promise was not fulfilled. It went more slowly than had been expected. His political enemies made the most of this in the next gubernatorial campaign. In spite of this he had been re-elected to a second term, but by a very slender majority. Plainly the people were growing discouraged with the slow progress of the canal work. At the next election, in 1822, Clinton had not even been nominated as canidate. His opponents came into office, though he remained the head of the canal commission. And then the governor removed him from that office, which he had held since 1810, even while governor. His enemies, those who had been against the canal from the beginning, a political ring known as the "Albany Regency," seemed to have triumphed. After this humiliation it was thought that Clinton's public career was ended.

But the man who had transformed talk into action was not to be overcome so easily. Under the Albany Regency the work on the canal almost came to a standstill. This caused even more dissatisfaction than the slow progress. So two years later, in 1824, Clinton found himself with enough friends to be nominated as candidate for governor once more. And when the election came around he was again put into office by a great majority. Once more in office and at the head of his old canal commission, he began pushing the work with renewed energy. And a year later, October 26, 1825, the work was completed and the opening ceremony was celebrated.

Ceremonies When the Canal Was Completed

The first boat to enter the canal at Buffalo was the Seneca Chief, a luxurious passenger packet. On board were Governor Clinton, his family, his friends, and his official staff. A team of four powerful gray horses hauled it along, and as they began treading the towpath. A cannon at the entrance of the canal announced the official opening. A minute later another cannon boomed forth, some miles away, then a third, far off in the distance, almost beyond hearing.

The Erie Canal
Project 2, Page 5

These cannons were the first of a series of several hundred cannons stationed at intervals along the canal, reaching down along the Hudson to New York, each barely within sound of the other. And so the news of the opening was flashed down to New York as fast as the sound could be relayed, passing down the line in one hour and twenty minutes.

Following the Seneca Chief into the canal came a procession of barges, each gaily decorated with flags and flowers, crowded with people. One, called Noah's Ark, carried as passengers a bear, two fawns, two eagles, two raccoons and two Indians. And so the procession continued along the canal toward Albany. All along the route it was met with music and cheering crowds of farmers, most of whom had settled in anticipation of the benefits they would derive from the canal.

At Albany the barges were greeted with the booming of cannon, a grand military procession and a citizens' parade. Here the flotilla of barges glided into the Hudson and began its journey down the river to New York. The Washington, a new steamer, one of the first afloat on the Hudson, came up to meet them. "Where are you from and whither bound?" it signaled. "From Lake Erie, bound for Sandy Hook," replied the Seneca Chief. The Washington and the Seneca Chief leading, the procession passed New York to the sound of ringing bells and booming cannon, and continued down the harbor toward the Narrows. The journey from Buffalo had taken just nine days.

The Waters of Lake Erie Mingle With the Ocean

Outside the Narrows the flotilla paused. Then the governor lifted a keg containing water from Lake Erie which he poured into the Atlantic Ocean, to signify the union of the two waters. Another keg, containing a mixture of waters from all the great rivers of the world—from the Ganges, the Thames, the Nile, the Amazon—was also poured over, to indicate that commerce from all parts of the world would now pass that way. As the governor pronounced the official address, tears streamed from his eyes. For twenty years he had talked and worked for the canal, at times apparently on the verge of failure. Now he had triumphed.

The celebration that welcomed the governor and his companions in New York City exceeded anything of the kind that had ever taken place before. Military and citizens' parades thronged the streets. All the trades were represented, the fire department leading. Heading the marching printers was a wagon carrying a printing-press. As the procession marched, the press turned out leaflets bearing the printed verse:

"Tis done! Tis done! The mighty chain
Which joins bright Erie to the Main,
For ages shall perpetuate
The glories of our native state."

The Erie Canal more than realized the expectations of those who had advocated its contruction years before. Even as a mere

Canals by 1850

business enterprise it proved a success from the beginning. In 1825, the year in which the work was completed at a cost of $7,000,000, the tolls collected along the finished part of the route amounted to over half a million dollars. Five years later, in 1830, the state collected $1,000,000 in tolls. By the end of 1837, only twelve years after it had been opened, the Erie Canal had paid $15,000,000 into the treasury, which was more than the cost of digging and maintaining it in repair combined.

What the Canal did for New York City

For the business interests of New York it had done even more. In 1824, the year before traffic was opened along the whole canal, it cost $88 to send a ton of freight from Buffalo to Albany. Eleven years later, in 1835, it cost only $3. This meant that the people of New York and those along the coast would get their bread so much cheaper. It also enabled the poor people of Europe to get their bread cheaper, for now vast quantities of wheat were shipped down the canal and exported to Europe. Over half of all the wheat exported from America to Europe came by this route. It was the Erie Canal that made New York the biggest business center on the Atlantic coast, the most important seaport in the country.

How The Canal Helped the State

With a navigable waterway traversing it, it was only natural that New York State should develop. What was once a wilderness, through which the early settlers had passed to reach the Great Lakes region, now became covered with prosperous farming communities. Even before the canal was completed the immigrants had arrived to lay out their homesteads, in anticipation of the produce they would be able to raise for the New York, Boston and Philadelphia markets.

Already while the canal was being dug there was talk of wagons that would run on iron rails, drawn by steam engines, and in 1831 a railroad was actually built from Albany to Schenectady, a distance of seventeen miles. Ten years later the railroad had been extended to Buffalo. But the railroads did not have any great effect on the traffic on the canal. For the reason that it costs so much to build and maintain railroads and freight cars, water transportaion is, and always will be, cheaper.

Passenger Packet and Freight Barge in Canal Basin at the foot of Allegheny Portage Railroad

THE ERIE CANAL
Project 2, Page 7

THE CANAL WAS WIDENED AND DEEPENED

It is usually said that the Erie Canal was completed in 1825. But that is not quite true. It still required more work. Within ten years there was more freight than the canal barges could handle. Branches reaching out into districts were continually being dug, until there were over a thousand miles of canal. Then the main canal was widened to 70 feet, so that barges large enough to carry eight thousand bushels of wheat instead of only one thousand bushels could pass.

It was not long before the railroad companies began to show a bitter opposition toward the canal. Naturally the canal forced them to keep down their freight rates. In every way they tried to impede any improvements on what they called the "ditch." Through their efforts a law was passed abolishing tolls. Apparently this would make freight rates cheaper on the canal. And so it did. But it also abolished the source of revenue from which improvements could be made. This obliged the legislature to appropriate special sums of money for the purpose. And this again raised a strong sentiment against the canal among those who did not benefit directly from it and felt they were being taxed for the good of those who lived along its route. The consequence was that the canal was neglected. Again the Canal was improved at great expense

But finally, in 1903, the people awoke to the realization that the railroads were opposed to the canal only for reasons of self-interest. And then amends were made for the many years of neglect. The people voted in favor of spending over $1,000,000,000 to build what may be said to be a new canal, but a modern one, along which steamers may sail as they do up and down the Hudson. The cost to the state turned out to be double what had been voted. The new canal follows, for the most part, the line of the old, but many miles have been relocated for several different reasons. Great and costly though the changes were, the canal did not regain its former importance.

The system of locks along the new Erie Canal, or the New York State Barge Canal, as it is now generally called, surpasses even the Panama locks. In a dry, sloping pasture behind the little town of Waterford the engineers have built what looks like a flight of giant steps-huge concrete blocks, in each of which is one of five locks. Combined they will lift the freight steamers 184 feet, more than twice as high as the Panama locks. At Little Falls, where the new channel of the canal ascends a narrow ravine, there is one lock, the highest in the world, which will lift the steamers over forty feet in eight minutes, as though they were being hoisted by a giant derrick. There are fifty-seven locks in all.

SOME WONDERFUL FEATURES AND THE CANAL TODAY

Other wonderful features were the great movable dams, big steel girders and steel plates riveted together, which were hinged on gigantic bridge-like structures. When navigation ceased in the winter these dams are swung up so that the ice floes would sweep down unimpeded. There were eight of these great dams, and each cost $800,000.

The St. Lawrence Seaway replaced the Canal as a commercial waterway. The canal system today is only used for recreational boating as a sort of "water park."

THE ERIE CANAL
Test

1. What is the date given for the Erie Canal?

____

2. Up until 1800 how were roads made?

____

____

3. What problem did businessmen have in transporting goods?

____

____

4. Traveling and transporting wares by ___________ was cheaper.

5. ______________________ carried cargo quickly across the ocean.

6. What was the Erie Canal?

____

____

7. How many years did it take to build the Erie Canal?

____

____

8. What has been written over the years about the Erie Canal?

____

____

Jacksonian Democracy
Worksheet

1. What was Andrew Jackson's nickname?

2. Where did Jackson receive his schooling?

3. When did he become a hero?

4. What was unique about his election as president? How did the people regard him?

5. Who was able to vote? How was this different than previous elections?

6. How did Jackson encourage his supporters after his election?

7. How did Jackson control legislation he opposed?

JACKSONIAN DEMOCRACY

Worksheet, Page 2

8. What was Jackson willing to do to preserve a strong union?

9. Why did Jackson remove control of federal money?

10. Who were three important statesmen during this time?

11. At the end of Jackson's term in 1836, what two important events occurred?

Jacksonian Democracy
Project

Andrew Jackson, A Self-Made Man

A DETERMINED YOUNG REBEL.

In one of the last years of the Revolutionary War, a band of British soldiers in South Carolina was sent out to capture some troublesome patriots, who were in the neighborhood of Waxhaw Creek. After a good deal of difficulty and some sharp fighting, they succeeded in bringing in a few backwoodsmen who were known to be determined rebels. Among these prisoners were two boys, Andrew Jackson, age thirteen, and his brother Robert, who was a little older. "Desperate young fellows these are," said one of the British officers, "but we shall soon tame them," and he ordered Andrew to clean and polish his boots. The slender, pale-faced boy drew himself up proudly and answered, "Sir, I am a prisoner of war, and demand to be treated as such." "Indeed!" cried the officer. "We shall soon see what you are. Down with you, and do my bidding!" The boy's eyes blazed with fury as he answered, "I am an American, and will not be the slave of any Britisher that breathes." The angry officer struck at him with his sword. Andrew parried the blow, but received a severe cut on his arm. To the end of his life the scar from that wound continued to nourish his hatred toward the British.

READING LAW.

Robert Jackson died while in the British prison pen, and Andrew, when he was finally given his freedom, found himself alone in the world, and obliged to make his own way as best he could. He worked for a short time in a saddler's shop in Charleston, but that trade was not agreeable to one of his restless nature. He had learned, in some unexplained way, to read and write, and so he tried school teaching for a little while. The next thing heard of him, he was in Salisbury, North Carolina, trying to read law in the office of a noted judge whose name was John McNairy.

APPOINTED TO OFFICE.

He did not learn much law, but he was shrewd and self-confident, and had good judgment. And so, through the influence of his friend McNairy, he was appointed public prosecutor for the western district of North Carolina. He was then only twenty-one years of age.

On the following page, illustrate something from the experiences of Andrew Jackson listed above.

JACKSONIAN DEMOCRACY
Project, Page 2

Jacksonian Democracy
Project 2

Andrew Jackson's Nick-Name

They say that the way General Jackson came to be nicknamed "Old Hickory" is as follows: During the Creek War he had taken a severe cold, and his soldiers had made a shelter for him of hickory bark. The next morning, a tipsy soldier, not knowing what he was about, kicked at the bark shelter and over it went. Jackson, speechless with rage, sprang out of the hickory heap and rushed towards the drunken offender. "Why I didn't know you were in there, Old Hickory!" shouted the soldier. For an instant a shout of laughter broke from the camp but one soldier, quicker-witted than the others, called "Three cheers for Old Hickory." The drunken soldier was saved a punishment, Jackson's temper was quieted, his dignity maintained, and he receive a a new name.

Draw a picture illustrating the story above.

Jacksonian Democracy
Test

1. What was Andrew Jackson's nickname?

2. When did Andrew Jackson serve as President?

3. Where was Jackson educated?

4. What was unique about his election as president? How did the people regard him?

5. What changed regarding the voting process before he was elected?

6. What presidential right did Jackson use more than his predecessors?

7. What did Jackson do for his campaign supporters after the election?

Jacksonian Democracy
Test

Review

1. How many terms did Monroe serve as president? What were the beginning and ending years?

____

____

2. What did the Monroe Doctrine state?

____

____

____

____

3. How were roads made before 1800?

____

____

____

4. What was built to help transport goods westward? Why was this helpful?

____

____

____

5. The _____ Canal was completed in c. 1825 and stretched from _______________ to _______________.

The Cotton Gin Establishes the South

Worksheet

1. Who invented the cotton gin? When was it invented?

2. What did the cotton gin do? How was this accomplished before the cotton gin?

3. Why had the demand for cotton increased?

4. Where did laborers come from to meet the high demand of producing cotton? What problems resulted?

5. Describe the Industrial Revolution.

6. What marked the First Industrial Revolution? Where did it begin?

The Cotton Gin Establishes the South
Worksheet

7. What are royalties? Did Eli Whitney receive royalties for the cotton gin?

8. What did Eli Whitney produce later in life? What was significant about this?

Eli Whitney

The Cotton Gin Establishes the South
Project

Cotton Pickin'

Cotton Growing in the South

Cotton had been grown in the South for many years. It had been made on the plantations into a rough cloth. Very little had been sent away. The reason for this was that it took a very long time to separate the cotton fiber from the seed. One slave working for a whole day could hardly clean more than a pound of cotton. Still as time went on more cotton was grown. In 1784 a few bags of cotton were sent to England. The Englishmen promptly seized it because they did not believe that so much cotton could be grown in America. In 1791 nearly two hundred thousand pounds of cotton were exported from the South. Then came Whitney's great invention, which entirely changed the whole history of the country.

Whitney's Cotton Gin

Eli Whitney was a Conneticut schoolmaster. He went to Georgia to teach General Greene's children. He was very ingenious, and one day Mrs. Greene suggested to him that he might make a machine which would separate the cotton fiber from the cotton seed. Whitney set to work and soon made an engine or gin, as he called it, that would do this. The first machine was a rude affair. But even with it one slave could clean one hundred pounds of cotton in a day. Mrs. Greene's neighbors promptly broke into Whitney's shop and stole his machine. Whitney's cotton gin made the growing of cotton profitable. With the invention of the steam locomotive and the reaper, no invention has so tremendously influenced the history of the United States.

After reading the above have the children do the following project. This project explores what it was like to take the seeds out of cotton. The children will quickly realize that this was an unpleasant task and one that people would have been very happy to have a machine to do the work. After taking the cotton apart use the materials to make a wreath.

Supplies
cotton in its natural form
wreath (one per student)
other greens or flower
glue gun, glue sticks

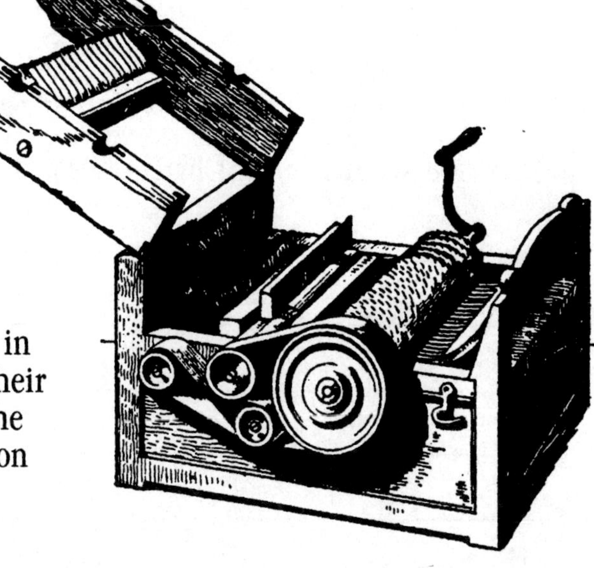

Directions
After talking to the students about the difficulty in removing the seeds from cotton have them try their hand at this. Then give them the materials for the wreath and allow them to arrange the materials on the wreath.

The Cotton Gin Establishes the South
Test

1, Who invented the cotton gin? When was it invented?

2. Why was the invention of the cotton gin so important?

3. Why had the demand for cotton increased?

4. What part of the country was producing the most cotton?

5. What illegal activity developed because of the demand for cotton?

6. Where did the Industrial Revolution begin?

   Describe what is meant by the term "Industrial Revolution."

The Cotton Gin Establishes the South

Test, Page 2

Review

1. What were the dates that Monroe served as president?

2. State the Monroe Doctrine?

3. What state did the Erie Canal stretch across? From where to where did it stretch?

4. What was the importance of the canal?

5. What presidential power did Andrew Jackson use more than any other previous president?

6. On the back write the events studied so far this year in chronological order and give dates for each.

Slavery in the South
Worksheet

1. Who were the first to take Africans from their homes and sell them into slavery?

2. Who did the Africans themselves sometimes sell into slavery?

3. When did Massachusetts legally recognize slavery?

4. What is an indentured servant? (You may need to look this up in a dictionary.)

5. When was slave trade outlawed?

6. List some of the reasons that slaves were sold illegally in the states?

Slavery in the South
Worksheet, Page 2

7. Why did only a few slaves learn to read and write?

8. In 1818 who had outlawed slavery?

9. What was the underground railroad?

10. What did the 13th amendment to the Constitution outlaw? When did this occur?

Slavery in the South
Project

Negro Spirituals by T. W. Higginson
—ABRIDGED FROM *ATLANTIC MONTHLY*, VOL. 19, JUNE, 1867

The war brought to some of us, besides its direct experiences, many a strange fulfilment of dreams of other days. For instance, the present writer had been a faithful student of the Scottish ballads, and had always envied Sir Walter the delight of tracing them out amid their own heather, and of writing them down piecemeal from the lips of aged crones. It was a strange enjoyment, therefore, to be suddenly brought into the midst of a kindred world of unwritten songs, as simple and indigenous as the Border Minstrelsy, more uniformly plaintive, almost always more quaint, and often as essentially poetic.

This interest was rather increased by the fact that I had for many years heard of this class of songs under the name of "Negro Spirituals," and had even heard some of them sung by friends from South Carolina. I could now gather on their own soil these strange plants, which I had before seen as in museums alone.

Often in the starlit evening I have returned, and, entering the camp, have silently approached some glimmering fire, round which the dusky figures moved in the rhythmical barbaric dance the negroes call a "shout," chanting, often harshly, but always in the most perfect time, some monotonous refrain. Writing down in the darkness, as I best could, —perhaps with my hand in the safe covert of my pocket,— the words of the song, I have afterwards carried it to my tent, like some captured bird or insect, and then, after examination, put it by. The music I could only retain by ear, and though the more common strains were repeated often enough to fix their impression, there were others that occurred only once or twice.

The words will be here given, as nearly as possible, in the original dialect; and if the spelling seems sometimes inconsistent, or the misspelling insufficient, it is because I could get no nearer.

The favorite song in camp was the following,—sung with no accompaniment but the measured clapping of hands and the clatter of many feet. It was sung perhaps twice as often as any other. This was partly due to the fact that it properly consisted of a chorus alone, with which the verses of other songs might be combined at random.

HOLD YOUR LIGHT.

"Hold your light, Brudder Robert, —
Hold your light,
Hold your light on Canaan's shore.

"What make ole Satan for follow me so?
Satan ain't got notin' for do wid me.
Hold your light,
Hold your light,
Hold your light on Canaan's shore."

This would be sung for half an hour at a time, perhaps, each person present being named in turn. It seemed the simplest primitive type of "spiritual." The next in popularity was almost as elementary, and, like this, named successively each one of the circle. It was, however, much more resounding and convivial in its music.

BOUND TO GO.

"Jordan River, I'm bound to go,
Bound to go, bound to go, —
Jordan River, I'm bound to go,
And bid 'em fare ye well.

"My Sister Lucy, I'm bound to go,
Bound to go, &c.

SLAVERY IN THE SOUTH
Project, Page 2

Sometimes it was "tink 'em" (think them) "fare ye well." The ye was so detached that I thought at first it was "very" or "vary well."

By this time every man within hearing, from oldest to youngest, would be wriggling and shuffling, as if through some magic piper's bewitchment; for even those who at first affected contemptuous indifference would be drawn into the vortex erelong.

Almost all their songs were thoroughly religious in their tone, however quaint in their expression, and were in a minor key, both as to words and music. The attitude is always the same, and, as a commentary on the life of the race, is infinitely pathetic. Nothing but patience for this life, – nothing but triumph in the next. Sometimes the present predominates, sometimes the future; but the combination is always implied. In the following, for instance, we hear simply the patience.

THIS WORLD ALMOST DONE.

"Brudder, keep your lamp trimmin' and a-burnin',
Keep your lamp trimmin' and a-burnin',
Keep your lamp trimmin' and a-burnin',
For dis world most done.
So keep your lamp, &c.
Dis world most done."

This next was a boat-song, and timed well with the tug of the oar. It begins with a startling affirmation, yet the last line quite outdoes the first.

ONE MORE RIVER.

O, Jordan bank was a great old bank!
Dere ain't but one more river to cross.
We have some valiant soldier here,
Dere ain't, &c.
O, Jordan stream will never run dry,
Dere ain't, &c.
Dere's a hill on my leff, and he catch on my right,
Dere ain't but one more river to cross."

I could get no explanation of this last riddle, except, "Dat mean, if you go on de leff, go to 'struction, and if you go on de right, go to God, for sure."

In others, more of spiritual conflict is implied, as in this next.

O THE DYING LAMB!

"I wants to go where Moses trod,
O de dying Lamb!
For Moses gone to de promised land,
O de dying Lamb!
To drink from springs dat never run dry,
O, &c.
Cry O my Lord!
O, &c.
Before I'll stay in hell one day,
O, &c.
I'm in hopes to pray my sins away,
O, &c.
Cry O my Lord!
O, &c.
Brudder Moses promised for be dar too,
O, &c.
To drink from streams dat never run dry,
O de dying Lamb!"

In the next, the conflict is at its height, and the lurid imagery of the Apocalypse is brought to bear. This book, with the books of Moses, constituted their Bible; all that lay between, even the narratives of the life of Jesus, they hardly cared to read or to hear.

SLAVERY IN THE SOUTH
Project, Page 3

DOWN IN THE VALLEY.

"We'll run and never tire,
We'll run and never tire,
We'll run and never tire,
Jesus set poor sinners free.
Way down in de valley,
Who will rise and go with me!
You've heern talk of Jesus,
Who set poor sinners free.

"De lightnin' and de flashin',
De lightnin' and de flashin',
De lightnin' and de flashin',
Jesus set poor sinners free.
I can't stand de fire. (Thrice.)
Jesus set poor sinners free,
De green trees a-flamin'. (Thrice.)
Jesus set poor sinners free,
Way down in de valley,
Who will rise and go with me?
You've heern talk of Jesus
Who set poor sinners free."

"De valley" and "de lonesome valley" were familiar words in their religious experience. One of the most singular pictures of future joys, and with a fine flavor of hospitality about it, was this: —

WALK 'EM EASY.

"O, walk 'em easy round de heaven,
Walk 'em easy round de heaven,
Walk 'em easy round de heaven,
Dat all de people may join de band.
Walk 'em easy round de heaven. (Thrice.)
O, shout glory till 'em join dat band!"

The chorus was usually the greater part of the song, and often came in paradoxically, thus: —

O YES, LORD.

"O, must I be like de foolish mans?
O yes, Lord!
Will build de house on de sandy hill.
O yes, Lord!
I'll build my house on Zion hill,
O yes, Lord!
No wind nor rain can blow me down
O yes, Lord!"

The next is one of the wildest and most striking of the whole series: there is a mystical effect and a passionate striving throughout the whole. The Scriptural struggle between Jacob and the angel, which is only dimly expressed in the words, seems all uttered in the music. I think it impressed my imagination more powerfully than any other of these songs.

WRESTLING JACOB.

"O wrestlin' Jacob, Jacob, day's a-breakin';
I will not let thee go!
O wrestlin' Jacob, Jacob, day's a-breakin';
He will not let me go!
O, I hold my brudder wid a tremblin' hand;
I would not let him go!
I hold my sister wid a tremblin' hand;
I would not let her go!

"O, Jacob do hang from a tremblin' limb,
He would not let him go!
O, Jacob do hang from a tremblin' limb;
De Lord will bless my soul.
O wrestlin' Jacob, Jacob," &c.

The [next song] contains one of those odd transformations of proper names with which their Scriptural citations were often enriched. It rivals their text, "Paul may plant, and may polish wid water," in which the sainted Apollos would hardly have recognized himself.

SLAVERY IN THE SOUTH

Project, Page 4

IN THE MORNING.

"In de mornin',
In de mornin',
Chil'en? Yes, my Lord!
Don't you hear de trumpet sound?
If I had a-died when I was young,
I never would had de race for run,
Don't you hear de trumpet sound?

"O Sam and Peter was fishin' in de sea,
And dey drop de net and follow my Lord.
Don't you hear de trumpet sound?

"Dere's a silver spade for to dig my grave
And a golden chain for to let me down.
Don't you hear de trumpet sound?
In de mornin',
In de mornin',
Chil'en? Yes, my Lord!
Don't you hear de trumpet sound?"

Some of the songs had played an historic part during the war. For singing the next, for instance, the negroes had been put in jail in Georgetown, S. C., at the outbreak of the Rebellion. *"We'll soon be free,"* was too dangerous an assertion; and though the chant was an old one, it was no doubt sung with redoubled emphasis during the new events. *"De Lord will call us home,"* was evidently thought to be a symbolical verse; for, as a little drummer-boy explained to me, showing all his white teeth as he sat in the moonlight by the door of my tent, "Dey tink de Lord mean for say de Yankees."

WE'LL SOON BE FREE.

"We'll soon be free,
We'll soon be free,
We'll soon be free,
When de Lord will call us home.
My brudder, how long,
My brudder, how long,
My brudder, how long,
'Fore we done sufferin' here?
It won't be long (Thrice.)
'For de Lord will call us home.
We'll walk de miry road (Thrice.)
Where pleasure never dies.
We'll walk de golden street (Thrice.)
Where pleasure never dies.
My brudder, how long (Thrice.)
'Fore we done sufferin' here?
We'll soon be free (Thrice.)
When Jesus sets me free.
We'll fight for liberty (Thrice.)
When de Lord will call us home."

One day when I was being rowed across from Beaufort to Ladies' Island, I found myself, with delight, on the actual trail of a song. One of the oarsmen, a brisk young fellow, not a soldier, on being asked for his theory of [the origin of negro spirituals], dropped out a coy confession. "Some good speritual," he said, "are start jess out o' curiosity. I been a-raise a sing, myself, once."

My dream was fulfilled, and I had traced out, not the poem alone, but the poet. I implored him to proceed.

"Once we boys," he said, "went for tote some rice, and de nigger-driver, he keep a-callin' on us; and I say, 'O, de ole nigger-driver!' Den anudder said, 'Fust ting my mammy tole me was, notin' so bad as nigger-driver.' Den I made a sing, just puttin' a word, and den anudder word."

Then he began singing, and the men, after listening a moment, joined in the chorus as if it were an old acquaintance, though they evidently had never heard it before. I saw how easily a new "sing" took root among them.

SLAVERY IN THE SOUTH
Project, Page 5

THE DRIVER.

"O, de ole nigger-driver!
O, gwine away!
Fust ting my mammy tell me,
O, gwine away!
Tell me 'bout de nigger-driver,
O, gwine away!
Nigger-driver second devil,
O, gwine away!
Best ting for do he driver,
O, gwine away!
Knock he down and spoil he labor,
O, gwine away!"

It will be observed that, although this song is quite secular in its character, its author yet called it a "spiritual." I heard but two songs among them, at any time, to which they would not, perhaps, have given this generic name. One of these consisted simply in the endless repetition of the mysterious line,

"Rain fall and wet Becky Martin."

But who Becky Martin was, and why she should or should not be wet, and whether the dryness was a reward or a penalty, none could say. I got the impression that, in either case, the event was posthumous, and that there was some tradition of grass not growing over the grave of a sinner; but even this was vague, and all else vaguer.

The other song I heard but once, on a morning when a squad of men came in from picket duty, and chanted it in the most rousing way.

HANGMAN JOHNNY.

"O, dey call me Hangman Johnny!
O, ho! O, ho!
But I never hang nobody,
O, hang, boys, hang!

"O, dey call me Hangman Johnny!
O, ho! O, ho!
But we'll all hang togedder,
O, hang, boys, hang!"

As they learned all their songs by ear, they often strayed into wholly new versions, which sometimes became popular, and entirely banished the others. "Hangman Johnny" remained always a myth as inscrutable as "Becky Martin."

These quaint religious songs were to the men more than a source of relaxation; they were a stimulus to courage and a tie to heaven. I never overheard in camp a profane or vulgar song. With the trifling exceptions given, all had a religious motive, while the most secular melody could not have been more exciting. They sang reluctantly, even on Sunday, the long and short metres of the hymnbooks, always gladly yielding to the more potent excitement of their own "spirituals." By these they could sing themselves, as had their fathers before them, out of the contemplation of their own low estate, into the sublime scenery of the Apocalypse. I remember that this minor-keyed pathos used to seem to me almost too sad to dwell upon, while slavery seemed destined to last for generations; but now that their patience has had its perfect work, history cannot afford to lose this portion of its record. There is no parallel instance of an oppressed race thus sustained by the religious sentiment alone. These songs are but the vocal expression of the simplicity of their faith and the sublimity of their long resignation.

Slavery in the South
Project 2

Letter from Mrs. A. M. Smythe to her cousin, Feb 17, 1837 concerning the sale of a family of slaves.

My Dear Cousin

I must beg a favor of you which I trust you will grant. at March court our little all will be sold for debt. You know how much I am attached to Sally and her children. attached to them because they are the best of slaves. I never knew so faithful and valuable a family of negroes. you have it in your power to pur chase them. if you do so I can leave the country with peace of mind. the first of April we will set out for the North Western territory, a howling Wilderness.

My Husband will be in Abingdon this week, he told me, he would visit you, his spirits are so low I fear he will not. if you see him, say every thing to cheer him.

My Mother is unable to raise the money at present to buy the family I speak of – Harry would I suppose but his Wife will sell a negro upon the most trivial offence. none can please her.

Martha the oldest of the children is 16 she has been afflicted with St. Vitus's dance 8 winters. in the Spring Summer, and Fall she is perfectly well, Doct. Floyd told me in the commencement of the disease that lime was the only cure, for several winters it has been gradually leaving her, this winter she has been confined only one day of course she will go lower in consequence of it. she does all kinds of work, that is usual about a house. and knits all the Woolen socks and stockings that are worn in the family – Mary is 13 she can sew very well – Madison is 10, a very capable and likely boy. there are three younger ones. Sally will have another in June.

I wish My Dear Cousin you would write as soon as you can –

My love to yourself and family

I am My Dear Cousin Yours truly and sincerely

A M S

SLAVERY IN THE SOUTH

Project 3

Slavery in the States in 1800, 1821 and 1850

Color the slave states of the thirteen original states in red. Color the slave states added in 1800 in blue. Color the free states green.

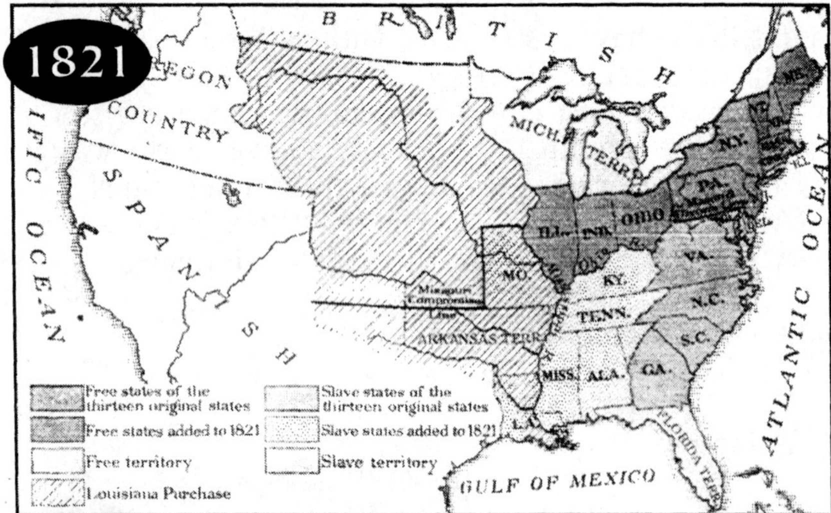

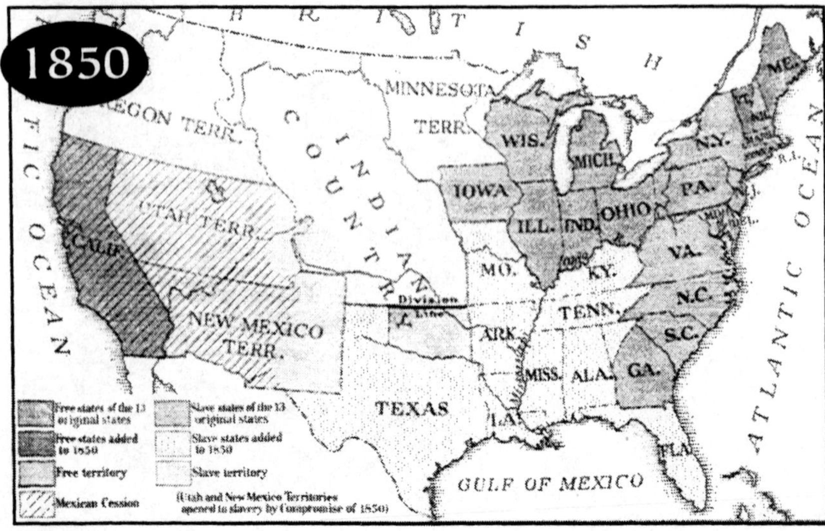

Color the slave states red. Color the free states blue.

Slavery in the South
Test

1. What was an indentured servant?

2. Who were the first people to sell Africans into slavery?

3. When was slave trade outlawed?

4. Why were slaves sold illegally in the states?

5. When did the northern states outlaw slavery?

6. What was the purpose of the underground railroad?

   Who was a famous conductor on the "Railroad"?

7. What amendment to the Constitution outlawed slavery in the entire United States?

Slavery in the South

Test, Page 2

Review

1. What did Monroe state in the Monroe Doctrine?

2. What was the purpose of the Erie Canal?

3. What presidential power did Andrew Jackson use more than any other president before him?

4. What was the purpose of Eli Whitney's cotton gin?

5. List in chronological order the events studied to date and the dates that correspond with them.

The Cherokee Trail of Tears

Worksheet

1. What was the Indian Settlement Act of 1830?

2. What Indian tribe refused to obey the Indian Settlement Act of 1830?

   What did the government offer to give them?

3. Why did people want to own the Cherokee land?

4. What did the government eventually force the Cherokees to do?

   What is this event called?

5. Approximately how many Indians died on their journey?

THE CHEROKEE TRAIL OF TEARS
Project

Wampum Necklace

Wampum were small beads made from polished shells, such as clam shells. They were strung together into belts or strands and used by the Indians as money or jewelry in ceremonies. Below you can see a picture of a wampum belt used as an early token of agreement between the United States and Cherokees regarding the exchange of eastern and western lands.

We will be making a paper wampum necklace. You may want to have some mothers make some cookies and brownies and give each child a certain amount of wampum. They could then purchase the goodies with wampum. During the week you might also want to have some extra credit projects in order to earn more wampum.

Supplies

wallpaper, gift wrap
scissors
glue
skewer sticks (sold in packages at grocery stores)
pencil or pen
wampum pattern
elastic thread

Instructions

Have the students trace the wampum bead pattern onto the back of the paper. Cut out the taced patterns. Wrap the cut out paper around the skewer, glue the end of the paper to form a bead. Remove skewer and allow to dry. After making about twenty beads, string them on the elastic thread. Tie a knot in the ends to form the neclace.

THE CHEROKEE TRAIL OF TEARS

Project 2

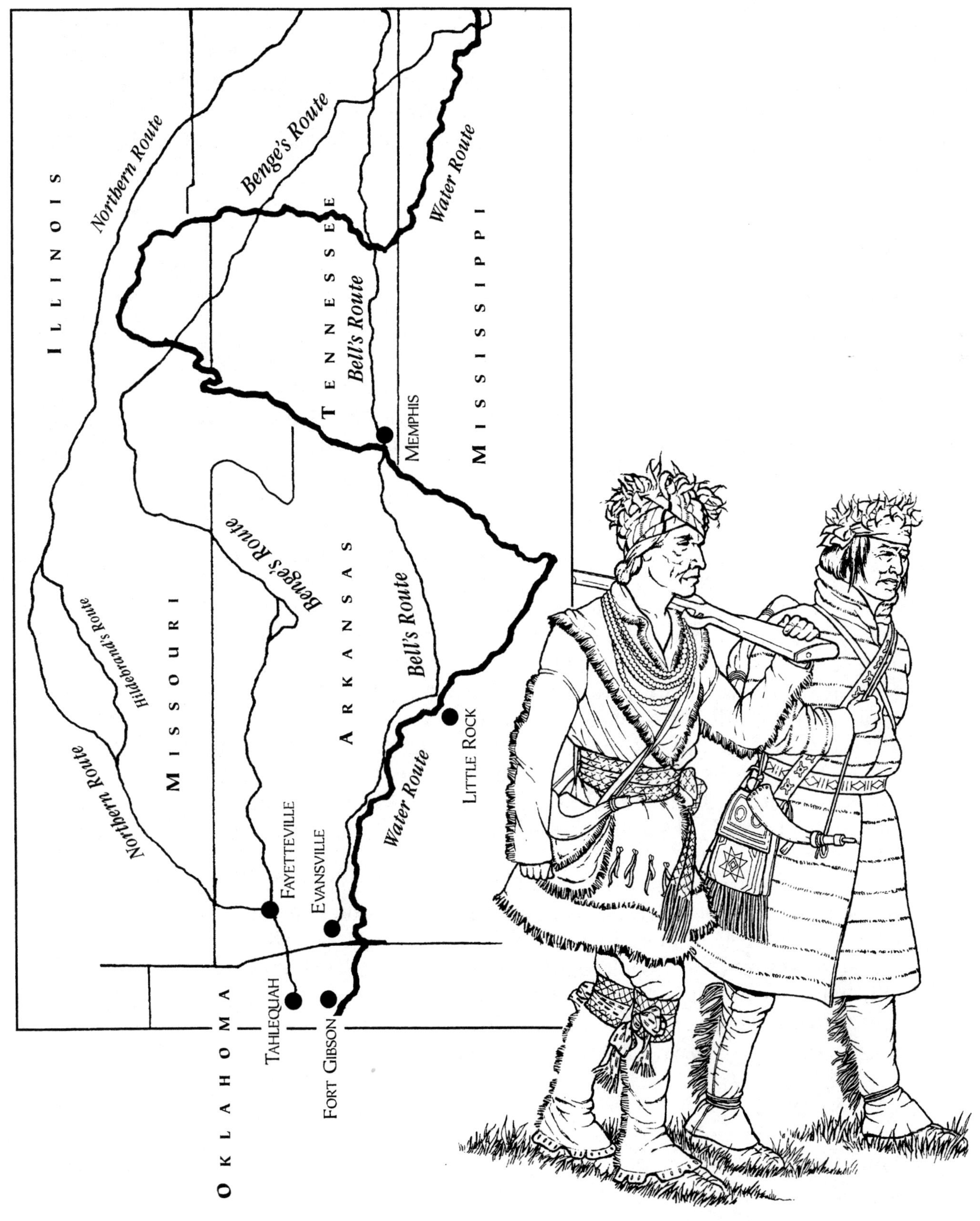

THE CHEROKEE TRAIL OF TEARS
Project 2, Page 2

Below you will read two different sources of information on the Cherokee "Trail of Tears." The first is a letter written by a young Indian girl, written to her friend as she awaited being moved from her home. The second is an article written in the Register by Theodore Pease Russell. When he was 19 the Cherokee Trail of Tears touched his life as Indians were driven from their towns in the Southeast United States to Indian Territory. He later wrote down his encounters in the register a half century later.

Red Clay Cherokee Nation
March 10, 1838

Beloved Martha, I have delayed writing to you so long I expect you have relinquished all thought of receiving anything from me. But my Dear Martha I have not forgotten my promise. I have often wished to enjoy your company once more but it is very uncertain whether I shall ever again have that pleasure.

If we Cherokees are to be driven to the west by the cruel hand of oppression to seek a new home in the west, it will be impossible. My father is now in Washington City. He was one of the delegates who went to Florida last October. We do not know when he will return.

Not long since Mr. Stephen Forman received a letter from Father. He was absent when the letter came home and before he arrived the troops had been there and taken it to the Agency, given it to General Smith and he handed it around for all to read. It is thus all our rights are invaded.

About two months ago my youngest brother died. He was sick almost two months. I was not at home when he died but they sent for me to attend his funeral. He was burnt very badly last fall and it is very likely his death was occasioned by it, however we do not exactly know.

It will not be long before our next (school) vacation. Then we expect to go home. Perhaps it may be the last time we shall have the privilege of attending school in this nation. But we are not certain. If we should remove to the Arkansas I should still hope to continue our correspondence. Please to present my best respects to your father & family, Miss E. Jones and Miss Betsey Tirtle. Write with me in love to you.

Your Sincere friend,

Jane Bushyhead

The Cherokee Trail of Tears

Project 2, Page 3

From The Register—

The government removed the Cherokee Indians from Georgia to the Indian Reservation (Territory in Oklahoma) in 1839. I remember February of that year, a division of the Ross party came through this valley and camped on Knob Creek, a camp extending from the Half-Way House along the west bank of the creek at the foot of Shepherd Mountain for nearly a mile. It was a muddy time.

There were about 2,000 Indians in this division. All of the others had gone by way of Farmington, but the roads were so bad that htis last division had come this way along the Fredericktown road and such a road at that time! A few days before the Indians came a man arrived to find suitable camping spots and supplies such as corn, oats, and fodder for their teams. There were so few people in the Arcadia Valley then there was only one man who had much to spare. But Abram Buford had a large crib of old corn, oats and fodder which were to be delivered at the place now owned by Judge Emerson. Mr. Buford hired father to send me with a team to haul oats and fodder, while his team hauled corn.

As the Indians came in they were furnished rations by lodges, each lodge to receive so much corn, oats and fodder, after which they camped at the place assigned them. They received no other rations; the hunters supplied meat out of the woods. Each morning when the Indians broke camp they were told how far they had to go and in what direction. The hunters spread out like a fan and started through the woods toward the next camping place, about ten miles ahead, and swept everything before them in the way of game. During the day deer could be seen running as if Old Scratch was after them across fields and roads.

About four o'clock I had finished hauling, so the Commissary Agent asked me if I did not want to go see the Indians in camp; he told me to let one of the boys take my team home, and he would show me how Indians lived. When we reached camp we found the first lodge close by what was to be Half-Way House. As each lodge came in to camp it went on beyond earlier arrivals until the last arrival was furthest in advance and so the first to move on in the morning.

As we came to each lodge, the commissary officer would explain everything. I saw families cooking supper, and noticed at each lodge a large tree had been felled by the body of which they had built their fire. On the butts of the logs I saw square holes that would hold about four quarts.

"Do you know what that is for?" the officer asked. "That is their grist mill; they shell corn into the hole, take that big pounder you see there, and pound the corn until it is fine enough, then they sift it and make bread."

We went along until we came to a squaw pounding corn. She soon dipped out the grain into a sieve, sifted out the finest of the meal, then put the rest back to be pounded again. It did not take long to make enough meal for bread for all the lodge.

The officer called my attention to girls dressed in silks and satins, their ears loaded with jewelry, their hair done up. I said "Surely these are not Indians; these are white ladies."

"These are Indians," said the officer. "Those negroes doing the cooking are their slaves."

The Cherokee girls were just as handsome as any girls and had fine forms, straight as an arrow.

THE CHEROKEE TRAIL OF TEARS
Project 2, Page 4

As we walked on, we saw hunters coming from every direction, loaded down with game; some used guns but the most that I saw had bows and arrows. We met one Indian with a string of fox squirrels, every one of them with a hole through its neck made by an arrow. Some hunters had deer, some turkeys or small game. The officer asked an Indian to let me see his bow and arrows. I would have liked to buy them, but I did not feel that I cared to talk to him much.

I saw a group of boys at play, but did not know what some of their games were. Some were pitching arrows, while some of the larger were shooting at a target on a tree with their bows; it was surprising how close they shot. I was shown how they make bows, how they fashioned arrows to the shafts, and how the points were fastened on.

I saw a group of girls playing at a short of battledore. When I heard the laughter of the boys and girls, I could hardly realise I was in an Indian camp, among people who had been called savages. But I also noticed that many of the old men and women did wear a savage look and seemed as though their hearts were full of hate toward the white race, and they would be glad to take your scalp if it were in their power to do so.

After strolling the length of the camp, with all the lodges up and it being after dark, we loitered back on a return trip. It was the duty of the officer to see to all the camp affairs just like a policeman in the city; for the Cherokee were under regulation as strict as if they were white. Some of the families were at super, and their tables were set with just as nice dishes; the fooded looked as good and smelt as good as any white folks. I felt I would like to sit down at one of their tables and be an Indian.

Back at our starting point the officer took my hand and said, "Now you have seen the Indians in camp, if you would like to be one, or join them, we will take you along and you can marry one of these girls; they will make a chief of you for Indian girls think it an honor to have a white husband. What do you say? Will you go?"

I finally told him I would go home and ask my ma, and see what she said. And as it was against the rules for anyone who did not belong to the company to be found inside the camp after 9 o'clock, I bade my conductor goodbye and started for home through the mud and darkness, tired, hungry and sleepy.

After reading the above use the map provided to trace the journey the Indians took on their trail of tears.

The Cherokee Trail of Tears

Project 3

Indian clothing

The Indian's suit was usually made of buckskin. It always consisted of leggings and a shirt or coat. He also wore moccasins and a war bonnet to match his suit. The suit is easily imitated by using yellow cambric. The shirt and leggings can be cut to fit the particular boy or girl. By folding the cloth, the leggings (picture 1) may be made with a single seam, as shown. The outer edges should be fringed. It is easier to let the cloth project about 2 inches beyond this seam. This may be cut into fringe with a pair of scissors, as shown in the illustration.

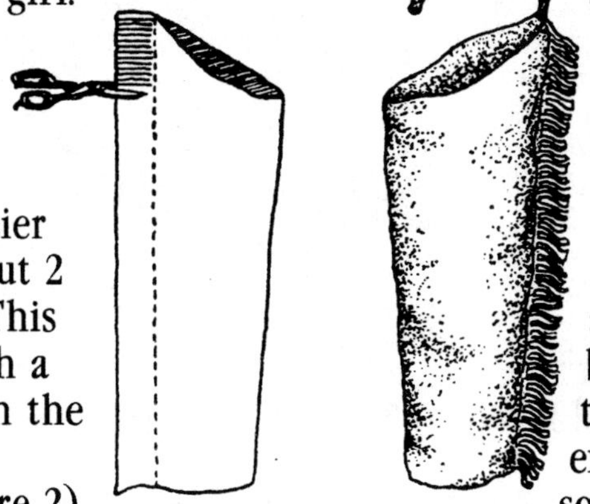

1. Fringed leggings.

The shirt or coat (picture 2) is a simple garment. It is made to open from the neck over the shoulders. It may be fringed both at the sides and under the arms. The leggings and shirt are drawn over the other clothing and fastened with safety pins. The Indian way was to lace the shirt at the shoulders and fasten each legging to the belt with a strap as shown in picture 1. A bright-colored blanket can be used for a girl's costume. It should be thrown over the shoulders and fastened about the waist with a belt.

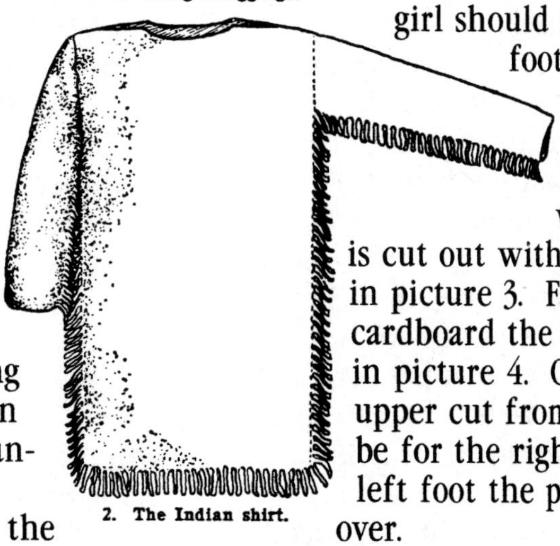

2. The Indian shirt.

When this costume is used, the face may be painted. This is done by first rubbing the skin well with vaseline and then using Venetian red. The whole of the boy's face is painted but only the cheeks of the girls are decorated. Indians did not paint the face or body for mere ornament, as each color had a meaning pertaining to their religious thoughts.

There are several forms of moccasins, or Indian shoes. Those used by the prairie tribes had three parts, namely the sole, the upper and the tongue. The soles were usually made of thick rawhide, while the tongues and uppers were made of buckskin. As an imitation to leather, white canvas may be used for the tongue and upper, while the sole may be cut from a piece of very thick felt. To determine the exact size of the pattern for the soles of the moccasins the bo or girl should first place the right foot, with the shoe removed, upon a piece of cardboard. The outline is drawn with a pencil and this is cut out with a pair of scissors as in picture 3. From another piece of cardboard the upper may be cut as in picture 4. Of course the sole and upper cut from these patterns will be for the right foot only. For the left foot the patterns are turned over.

To fit a normal sized child seven years of age the length of the sole, AB (picture 3), should be about 8 inches; the width, CD, about 3« inches; and the width of heel, EF, about 2« inches. The upper (picture 4) should measure about 9 inches at GH; and the width , IJ, about 4« inches. Then make the cuts KL and MH with a pair of

The Cherokee Trail of Tears

Project 3, Page 2

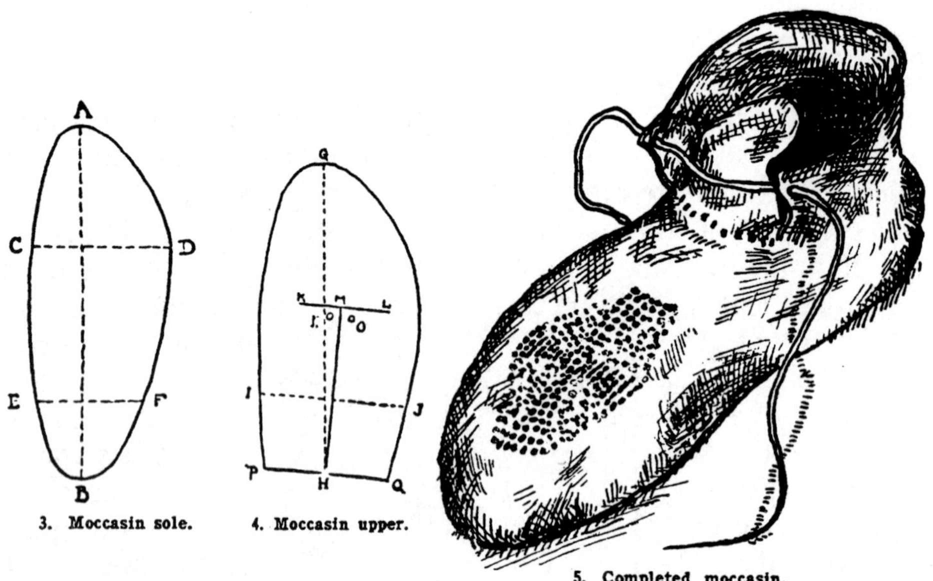

3. Moccasin sole.

4. Moccasin upper.

5. Completed moccasin.

scissors. The first, which is halfway between the toe and heel should be about 3 inches in length, In the corners N and O pierce two holes. In these, place a small leather string for lacing.

Now sew the upper on the sole beginning at the toe. The heel is made by sewing HP and HQ together. If the moccasin is turned wrong side out before sewing, the seams will be neater. Next cut out the tongue from piece of canvas. This should be about 3« inches long and 3 inches at the bottom. This is sewed to the upper so that the bottom will join KL. The completed moccasin is shown in picture 5.

The Indians often embroidered their moccasins beautiful headwork. A pretty effect, not unlike embroidery, may be had by using thick velvet instead of canvas for the uppers. These may be blue, red or yellow, or any favorite color. When canvas is used, beadwork may be imitated by cutting out designs in bright colored cloth and sewing, or even gluing, to the uppers.

The war bonnet, or ceremonial headdress, was always made of eagles' feathers. These were fastened to a cap of buffaloskin in the form of a circle. A good imitation of a native war bonnet can easily be made by taking an old hat of soft felt, cutting off the brim, and removing the band. Then secure about a dozen or more tail feathers of a turkey or rooster and cut the shaft of each feather to a point. With a penknife pierce two small openings above the rim (see A, picture 6). Then put the point of the quill through the openings (see B, picture 6), and double the point back into the hollow shaft (see C, picture 6). This secures the feather to the felt crown. Now sew or tie a bit of red flannel around the base of the quill (see D and E, picture 6).

This process is continued until the felt crown is surrounded with a circlet of feathers (picture 7). These are fixed in place with a thread, which is drawn through the shafts of the feathers with a needle to hold them in place as shown in the finished war bonnet.

The Indian outfit is finally ready for use and any boy or girl may be proud to wear it.

The Cherokee Trail of Tears

Project 3, Page 3

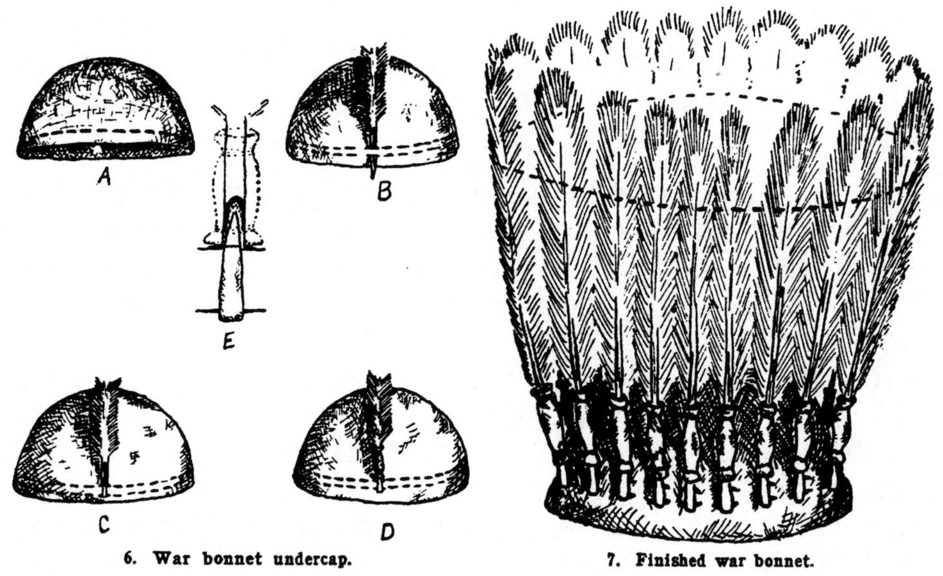

6. War bonnet undercap.

7. Finished war bonnet.

This play suit ought to interest the wearer in the clothing that was worn by the Indians before the white man came. The hide of the buffalo was worn for robes by tribes of the plains, but the leather was too harsh for clothing generally. Elk and moose skins, though soft , were too thick; so, as a rule, the tanned skin of the deer became the most used material. Other materials were made from bark, hair, fur, mountain-sheep wool, feathers and cotton. Sinew from tendons of the larger animals was used for thread, and bone awls served as needles. Men and women were equally skillful in sewing and men and boys made their own clothing. Belts of different materials were worn to support pouches, trinket-bags and so forth. Necklaces, ear-rings, charms and bracelets formed a part of the dress. In cold weather robes or capes of animal skins with the hair left on were added to the wardrobe of the red man.

Ceremonial costume was much more elaborate than everyday costume just as it has always been with white men. Moccasins and leggings were beaded with great skill and cunning design to attract attention to the owner. The great feathered war bonnets of big chiefs often trailed to the ground and were among the sights of a powwow.

THE CHEROKEE TRAIL OF TEARS
Project 4

Cherokee Nation v. State of Georgia (1831)

Mr. Chief Justice Marshall delivered the opinion of the Court:

This bill is brought by the Cherokee Nation, praying an injunction to restrain the state of Georgia from the execution of certain laws of that state, which as is alleged, go directly to annihilate the Cherokees as a political society, and to seize, for the use of Georgia, the lands of the nation which have been assured to them by the United States in solemn treaties repeatedly made and still in force.

If courts were permitted to indulge their sympathies, a case better calculated to excite them can scarcely be imagined. A people once numerous, powerful, and truly independent, found by our ancestors in the quiet and uncontrolled possession of an ample domain, gradually sinking beneath our superior policy, our arts, and our arms, have yielded their lands by successive treaties, each of which contains a solemn guarantee of the residue, until they retain no more of their formerly extensive territory than is deemed necessary to their comfortable subsistence. To preserve this remnant the present application is made.

Before we can look into the merits of the case, a preliminary inquiry presents itself. Has this Court jurisdiction of the cause?

The 3rd Article of the Constitution describes the extent of the judicial power. The 2nd Section closes an enumeration of the cases to which it is extended, with controversies between a state or the citizens thereof, and foreign states, citizens, or subjects. A subsequent clause of the same section gives the Supreme Court original jurisdiction in all cases in which a state shall be a party. The party defendant may then unquestionably be sued in this Court. May the plaintiff sue in it? Is the Cherokee Nation a foreign state in the sense in which that term is used in the Constitution?

The counsel for the plaintiffs have maintained the affirmative of this proposition with great earnestness and ability. So much of the argument as was intended to prove the character of the Cherokees as a state, as a distinct political society separated from others, capable of managing its own affairs and governing itself, has, in the opinion of a majority of the judges, been completely successful. They have been uniformly treated as a state from the settlement of our country. The numerous treaties made with them by the United States recognize them as a people capable of maintaining the relations of peace and war, of being responsible in their political character for any violation of their engagements, or for any aggression committed on the citizens of the United States by any individual of their community. Laws have been enacted in the spirit of these treaties. The acts of our government plainly recognize the Cherokee Nation as a state, and the courts are bound by those acts.

A question of much more difficulty remains. Do the Cherokees constitute a foreign state in the sense of the Constitution?

The counsel have shown conclusively that they are not a state of the Union, and have insisted that individually they are aliens, not owing allegiance to the United States. An aggregate of aliens composing a state must, they say, be a foreign state. Each individual being foreign, the whole must be foreign.

THE CHEROKEE TRAIL OF TEARS
Project 4, Page 2

This argument is imposing, but we must examine it more closely before we yield to it. The condition of the Indians in relation to the United States is perhaps unlike that of any other two people in existence. In the general, nations not owing a common allegiance are foreign to each other. The term foreign nation is, with strict propriety, applicable by either to the other. But the relation of the Indians to the United States is marked by peculiar and cardinal distinctions which exist nowhere else.

The Indian Territory is admitted to compose part of the United States. In all our maps, geographical treatises, histories, and laws, it is so considered. In all our intercourse with foreign nations, in our commercial regulations, in any attempt at intercourse between Indians and foreign nations, they are considered as within the jurisdictional limits of the United States, subject to many of those restraints which are imposed upon our own citizens. They acknowledge themselves in their treaties to be under the protection of the United States; they admit that the United States shall have the sole and exclusive right of regulating the trade with them and managing all their affairs as they think proper; and the Cherokees in particular were allowed by the Treaty of Hopewell, which preceded the Constitution, to send a deputy of their choice, whenever they think fit, to Congress. Treaties were made with some tribes by the state of New York under a then unsettled construction of the Confederation, by which they ceded all their lands to that state, taking back a limited grant to themselves in which they admit their dependence.

Though the Indians are acknowledged to have an unquestionable and, heretofore, unquestioned right to the lands they occupy until that right shall be extinguished by a voluntary cession to our government, yet it may well be doubted whether those tribes which reside within the acknowledged boundaries of the United States can, with strict accuracy, be denominated foreign nations. They may more correctly, perhaps, be denominated domestic dependent nations. They occupy a territory to which we assert a title independent of their will, which must take effect in point of possession when their right of possession ceases. Meanwhile, they are in a state of pupilage. Their relation to the United States resembles that of a ward to his guardian.

They look to our government for protection; rely upon its kindness and its power; appeal to it for relief to their wants; and address the President as their great father. They and their country are considered by foreign nations, as well as by ourselves, as being so completely under the sovereignty and dominion of the United States that any attempt to acquire their lands or to form a political connection with them would be considered by all as an invasion of our territory and an act of hostility.

These considerations go far to support the opinion that the framers of our Constitution had not the Indian tribes in view when they opened the courts of the Union to controversies between a state or the citizens thereof and foreign states.

In considering this subject, the habits and usages of the Indians in their intercourse with their white neighbors ought not to be entirely disregarded. At the time the Constitution was framed, the idea of appealing to an American court of justice for an assertion of right or a redress of wrong had perhaps never entered the mind of an Indian or of his tribe. Their appeal was to the tomahawk, or to the government. This was well understood by the statesmen who framed the Constitution of the United States, and might furnish some reason for omitting to enumerate them among the parties who might sue in the courts of the Union. Be this as it may, the peculiar relations between the United States and the Indians occupying our territory are such that we should feel much difficulty in considering them as designated by the term foreign state were there no other part of the Constitution which might shed light on the meaning of these words. But we think that in construing them, considerable aid is furnished by that clause in the 8th Section of the 3rd Article, which empowers Congress to regulate commerce with foreign nations, and among the several states, and with the Indian tribes.

In this clause they are as clearly contradistinguished by a name appropriate to themselves from foreign nations as from the several states composing the Union. They are designated by a distinct appellation; and as this appellation can be applied to neither of the others, neither can the appellation distinguishing either of the others be in fair construction applied to them. The objects to which the power of regulating commerce might be directed are divided into three distinct classes: foreign nations, the several states, and Indian tribes. When forming this article, the Convention considered them as entirely distinct. We cannot assume that the distinction was lost in framing a subsequent article, unless there be something in its language to authorize the assumption.

Foreign nations is a general term, the application of which to Indian tribes, when used in the American Constitution, is at best extremely questionable. In one article in which a power is given to be exercised in regard to foreign nations generally, and to the Indian tribes particularly, they are mentioned as separate in terms clearly contradistinguishing them from each other. We perceive plainly that the Constitution in this article does not comprehend Indian tribes in the general term foreign nations; not, we presume, because a tribe may not be a nation but because it is not foreign to the United States. When, afterward, the term foreign state is introduced, we cannot impute to the Convention the intention to desert its former meaning and to comprehend Indian tribes within it, unless the context force that construction on us. We find nothing in the context and nothing in the subject of the article which leads to it.

The Court has bestowed its best attention on this question and, after mature deliberation, the majority is of opinion that an Indian tribe or nation within the United States is not a foreign state in the sense of the Constitution, and cannot maintain an action in the courts of the United States.

A serious additional objection exists to the jurisdiction of the Court. Is the matter of the bill the proper subject for judicial inquiry and decision? It seeks to restrain a state from the forcible exercise of legislative power over a neighboring people, asserting their independence; their right to which the state denies. On several of the matters alleged in the bill, for example on the laws making it criminal to exercise the usual powers of self-government in their own country by the Cherokee Nation, this Court cannot interpose, at least in the form in which those matters are presented.

That part of the bill which respects the land occupied by the Indians, and prays the aid of the Court to protect their possession, may be more doubtful. The mere question of right might perhaps be decided by this Court in a proper case with proper parties. But the Court is asked to do more than decide on the title. The bill requires us to control the legislature of Georgia, and to restrain the exertion of its physical force. The propriety of such an interposition by the Court may be well questioned. It savors too much of the exercise of political power to be within the proper province of the Judicial Department But the opinion on the point respecting parties makes it unnecessary to decide this question.

If it be true that the Cherokee Nation have rights, this is not the tribunal in which those rights are to be asserted. If it be true that wrongs have been inflicted and that still greater are to be apprehended, this is not the tribunal which can redress the past or prevent the future.

The motion for an injunction is denied.

THE CHEROKEE TRAIL OF TEARS
Test

1. What is the approximate date of The Cherokee Trail of Tears?

2. What was the Indian Settlement Act of 1830?

3. Why were the Cherokees offered $5.7 million dollars?

4. Why did many people want to own the Cherokee land?

5. How many people began the difficult journey west? How many completed the journey?

6. Why was this journey called by the Cherokee people "The Trail of Tears"?

The Cherokee Trail of Tears
Test, Page 2

Review

1. How many terms did Monroe serve as president? What were the dates?

2. What was the purpose of the Erie Canal?

3. Who invented the cotton gin? What was its purpose?

4. What was the underground railroad?

5. List in chronological order all events studied to date.

Remember the Alamo
Worksheet

1. Who owned Texas in 1835? How many Americans lived there?

2. Who was the dictator of Mexico during this time?
   What did the Americans think of him?

3. What did they call the state of Texas when the Americans declared Independence from Mexico?

4. Who fought the battle at the Alamo? What was the outcome?

5. List some of the famous Americans killed at the Alamo?

6. In what year did Texas win its independence?

Remember the Alamo
Project

Remember the Alamo
by Theodore Roosevelt

"Thermopylae had its messengers of death, but the Alamo had none." These were the words with which a United States senator referred to one of the most resolute and effective fights ever waged by brave men against overwhelming odds in the face of certain death.

Soon after the close of the second war with Great Britain, parties of American settlers began to press forward into the rich, sparsely settled territory of Texas, then a portion of Mexico. At first these immigrants were well received, but the Mexicans speedily grew jealous of them, and oppressed them in various ways. In consequence , when the settlers felt themselves strong enough, they revolted against Mexican rule, and declared Texas to be an independent republic. Immediately Santa Anna, the Dictator of Mexico, gathered a large army, and invaded Texas. The slender forces of the settlers were unable to meet his hosts. They were pressed back by the Mexicans, and dreadful atrocities were committed by Santa Anna and his lieutenants.

In the United States there was great enthusiasm for the struggling Texans, and many bold backwoodsmen and Indian-fighters swarmed to their help. Among them the two famous were Sam Houston and David Crockett. Houston was the younger man, and had already led an extraordinary and varied career. When a mere lad he had run away from home and joined the Cherokees, living among them for some years; then he returned home. He had fought under Andrew Jackson in his campaign against the Creeks, and had been severely wounded at the battle of the Horse-shoe Bend. He had risen to the highest political honors in his State, becoming governor of Tennessee; and then suddenly, in a fit of moody longing for the life of the wilderness, he gave up his governorship, left the State, and crossed the Mississippi, going to join his old comrades, the Cherokees, in their new home along the waters of the Arkansas. Here he dressed, lived, fought, hunted, and drank precisely like any Indian, becoming one of the chiefs.

David Crockett was born soon after the Revolutionary War. He, too, had taken the part under Jackson in the campaigns against the Creeks, and had afterward become a man of mark in Tennessee, and gone to Congress as a Whig; but he had quarreled with Jackson, and been beaten for Congress, and in his disgust he left the State and decided to join the Texans. He was the most famous rifle-shot in all the United States, and the most successful hunter, so that his skill was a proverb all along the border.

David Crockett journeyed south, by boat and horse, making his way steadily toward the distant plains where the Texans were waging their life-and-death fight. Texas was a wild place in those days, and the old hunter had more than one hair-breadth escape from Indians, desperadoes, and savage beasts, ere he got to the neighborhood of San Antonio, and joined another adventurer, a bee-hunter, bent on the same errand as himself. The two had been in ignorance of exactly what the situation in Texas was; but they soon found that the Mexican army was marching toward San Antonio, whither they were going. Near the town was an old Spanish fort, the Alamo, in which the hundred and fifty American defenders of the place had gathered. Santa Anna had four thousand troops with him. The Alamo was a mere shell, utterly unable to withstand either a bombardment or a regular assault. It was evident, therefore, that those within it would be in the uttermost jeopardy if the place were seriously assaulted, but old Crockett and his companion never wavered. They were fearless and resolute, and masters of woodcraft, and they managed to slip through the Mexican lines and join the defenders within the walls. The bravest, the hardiest, the most reckless men of the border were there; among them were Colonel Travis, the commander of the fort, and Bowie, the inventor of the famous bowie-knife. They were a wild and ill-disciplined band, little used to restraint or control, but they were men of iron courage and great bodily powers, skilled in the use of their weapons, and ready to meet with stern and uncomplaining indifference whatever doom fate might have in store for them.

Soon Santa Anna approached with his army, took possession of the town, and besieged the fort. The defenders knew there was scarcely a chance of rescue, and that it was hopeless to expect that one hundred and fifty men, behind defenses so weak, could beat off four thousand trained soldiers, well armed and provided with heavy artillery; but they had no idea of flinching, and made a desperate defense. The days went by, and no help came, while Santa Anna got ready his lines, and began a furious cannonade. His gunners were unskilled, however, and he had to serve the guns from a distance; for when they were pushed nearer, the American riflemen crept forward under cover, and picked off the artillerymen. Old Crockett thus killed five men at one gun. But, by degrees, the bombardment told. The walls of the Alamo were battered and riddled; and when they had been breached so as to afford no obstacle to the rush of his soldiers, Santa Anna commanded that they be stormed.

The storm took place on March 6, 1836. The Mexican troops came on well and steadily, breaking through the outer defenses at every point, for the lines were too long to be manned by the few Americans. The few frontiersmen then retreated to the inner building, and a desperate hand-to-hand conflict followed, the Mexicans thronging in, shooting the Americans with their muskets, and thrusting at them with lance and bayonet, while the Americans, after firing their long rifles, clubbed them, and fought desperately, one against many; and they also used their Bowie knives and revolvers with deadly effect. The fight reeled to and fro between the shattered walls, each American the center of a group of foes; but, for all their strength and their wild fighting courage, the defenders were too few, and the struggle could have but one end. One by one the tall riflemen succumbed, after repeated thrusts with bayonet and lance, until but three or four were left. Colonel Travis, the commander, was among them; and so was Bowie, who was sick and weak from a wasting disease, but who rallied all his strength to die fighting, and who, in the final struggle, slew several Mexicans with his revolver, and with his big knife, of the kind to which he had given his name. Then these fell too, and the last man stood at bay. It was old Davy Crockett. Wounded in a dozen places, he faced his foes with his back to the wall, ringed around by the bodies of the men he had slain. So desperate was the fight he waged, that the Mexicans who thronged round about him were beaten back for the moment, and no one dared to run in upon him. Accordingly, while the lancers held him where he was, for, weakened by wounds and loss of blood, he could not break through them, the musketeers loaded their carbines and shot him down. Santa Anna declined to give him

REMEMBER THE ALAMO
Project, Page 3

mercy. Some say that when Crockett fell from his wounds, he was taken alive , and was then shot by Sant Anna's order; but his fate cannot be told with certainty, for not a single American was left alive. At any rate, after Crockett fell the fight was over . Every one of the hardy men who had held the Alamo lay still in death. Yet they died well avenged, for four times their number fell at their hands in the battle.

Santa Anna had but a short while in which to exult over his bloody and hard-won victory. Already a rider from the rolling Texas plains, going north through the Indian Territory, had told Houston that the Texans were up and were striving for their liberty. At once in Houston's mind there kindled a longing to return to the men of his race at the time of their need. Mounting his horse, he rode south by night and day, and was hailed by the Texans as a heaven-sent leader. He took command of their forces, eleven hundred stark riflemen, and at the battle of San Jacinto, he and his men charged the Mexican hosts with the cry of "Remember the Alamo." Almost immediately, the Mexicans were overthrown with the terrible slaughter; Santa Anna himself was captured, and the freedom of Texas was won at a blow.

After reading the above story of the Alamo have the children choose from the list below and write a one to two page report on the following people.

Davy Crockett
Jim Bowie
W. B. Travis
Santa Anna
Sam Houston
Juan Seguin
Susannah Dickinson and other women at the Alamo

Remember the Alamo
Project 2

Have your class, or family view the movie *The Alamo* starring John Wayne. After viewing it have the students compare the facts to the movie version in a discussion with them or in a written report.

David Crockett

REMEMBER THE ALAMO

Test

1. In what year did the battle of the Alamo take place?

2. Who owned Texas before the battle at the Alamo? How many Americans lived there?

3. What did the Americans call Texas after they declared it an independant state?

4. Who was Santa Anna and what was his response to the people of Texas declaring their independence?

5. What occurred at the battle at the Alamo?

6. When did Texas win its Independence?

Remember the Alamo

Test, Page 2

Review

1. What was the Monroe Doctrine?

2. What were Andrew Jackson's beliefs about the union?

3. Who were the first to take Africans from their homes and sell them into slavery?

4. What was the 13th amendment to the Constitution?

5. List the events studied to date in chronological order.

WESTWARD EXPANSION
Worksheet

1. Why did settlers who went west to California and the Oregon Territory consider themselves emigrants?

2. Why did many people go west?

3. Where did the emigrants buy their supplies before beginning the journey?

4. List the four main trails known to have been traveled. Next to each trail list why people generally went there.

5. What conditions did the travelers encounter on the trails?

Westward Expansion
Worksheet, Page 2

6. What were the groups called in which they traveled?

____

____

7. Within each wagon train community, ____________ were often made by the people to govern themselves.

8. When did westward expansion occur over these four trails?

____

____

____

____

Westward Expansion

Project

Making a Covered Wagon

Horse drawn wagons were the most common transportation west at the time of first expansion on the four trails that developed. Two wagons types developed for hauling both freight and people; the Conestoga Wagon and the Prairie Schooner.

The Conestoga was first built in the Lancaster, PA area. The wheels were big and the body sat high so it could clear underbrush and tree stumps. The ends curved up to keep the weight of the cargo centered and to allow it to double as a boat to cross streams and rivers when the wheels were removed. It was typically pulled by four to six oxen, horses or mules.

The Prairie Schooner was so named because the white top looked like the sails of a ship from a distance. Although quite sturdy, it was simply a standard farm wagon.

Both wagon types had smaller front wheels than back enabling sharp turns when necessary.

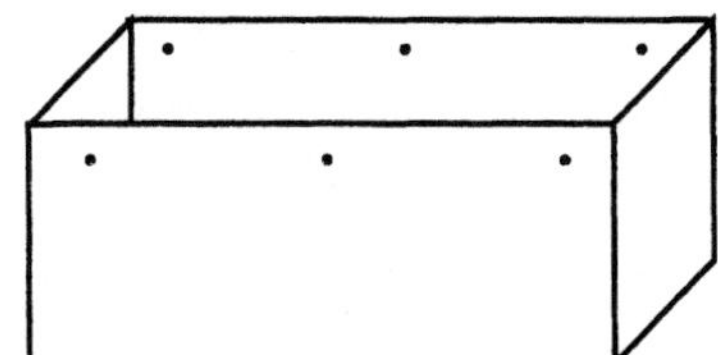

Supplies

Shoe box (one per student)
Cardboard (from which to cut wheels)
Pipe cleaners or floral wire
white cloth
Scissors or knife (to cut cardboard)
Glue (hot glue gun preferred)
Tempera paint
Ice pick or sharp pencil (to poke holes in the cardboard box)

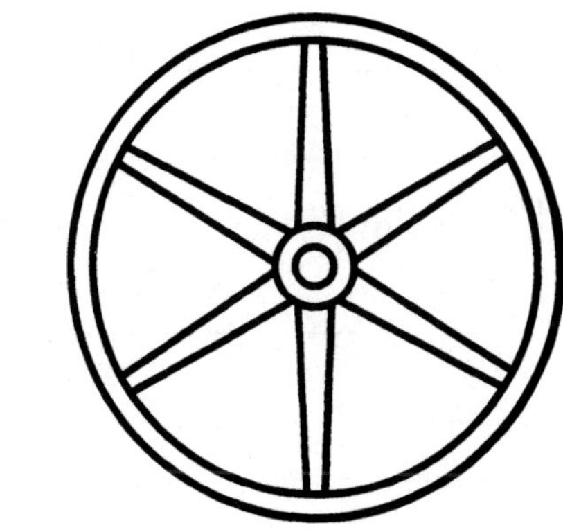

Directions

Discard the shoe box lid and paint the box (inside and out) blue, red, or brown. Allow to dry. Draw wheels on cardboard from pattern. Cut them out.
Paint spokes red. Allow to dry.
Poke holes in box as illustrated to fasten wire for support of cloth. Glue wire in place on one side bend in smooth curve and glue to the corresponding hole on the other side of box.
Glue cloth onto wire.
Glue wheels onto box.

Westward Expansion
Project 2–Literature Unit

The Way West: Journal of a Pioneer Woman

Saturday, April 9, 1853 How many miles did they travel on the first day?

Thursday, April 14, 1853 How many wagons are crossing the creek?

Thursday, April 21, 1853 What did they have to feed the stock? Why?

What are the weather conditions?

Monday, May 2, 1853 Why did the Indians come to the camp?

Saturday, May 7, 1853 How did they cross the creek?

Saturday, May 8, 1853 How many wagons were in sight?

Westward Expansion
Project 3—Literature Unit

The Pioneers Go West—Comprehension questions

Chapter 1

1. How long was the wagon trail from Missouri to California?

2. How large was the group of people that traveled the trail with Elisha Stevens?

3. What two things should be remembered about Mose Schallenberger?

4. Why were oxen better suited than horses for the trip to California?

5. Where was the "jumping-off place" for the journey west?

Chapter 2

1. How many wagons at a time could cross the river on the ferry?

2. What shape did the oxen form in the middle of the river?

Westward Expansion
Project 3, Page 2–Literature Unit

3. How were the settlers finally able to get the oxen across the river?

4. Which Indian tribe lived directly west of the Missouri River?

5. Why did Mose and John play a joke on John Sullivan?

Chapter 3

1. What speckled the countryside with "red and blue and yellow"?

2. How far could the wagon train travel on a good day?

3. What had to be done to the wagons in order to cross Elkhorn River?

4. What had weakened the powerful and warlike Pawnee tribe?

Westward Expansion

Project 3, Page 3–Literature Unit

5. Why shouldn't Mose and John feel proud of killing their first buffalo?

Chapter 4

1. What marked the end of the first stage of the journey for the emigrants?

2. What caused the boards and spokes of the wagons to shrink and get loose?

3. Why did Mose take his pistols on the buffalo hunt?

4. Why were Mose and John unable to shoot a buffalo?

5. What three things were lost by Mose and John?

Chapter 5

1. Where did the emigrant party stop for a few days to shoot some buffalo?

WESTWARD EXPANSION
Project 3, Page 4—Literature Unit

2. What did Mose and Allen see when they looked over the mound of rocks?

3. How many buffaloes were Allen and Mose able to shoot?

4. Why were Allen and Mose unable to sleep as they guarded the buffalo meat?

5. What is the altitude of the South Pass?

CHAPTER 6

1. What segment of Indians were the emigrants likely to meet west of the mountains?

2. What was old man Hitchcock's plan to save the party of emigrants hundreds of miles?

3. What vital resource had the party failed to take with them across the "shortcut"?

WESTWARD EXPANSION
Project 3, Page 5—Literature Unit

4. Where did the search party find the herd of lost cattle?

5. How was the search party able to stop the charging Indians of the Snake tribe?

CHAPTER 7

1. At what location did the California and Oregon parties part company?

2. How many wagons traveled in the California party?

3. What was the nickname given to the Paiute Indians? Why?

4. What was strange about the Humboldt River?

5. Give two reasons why the Steven's party stopped at Humboldt Sink even though it was "in most ways such a bad spot".

Westward Expansion
Project 3, Page 6—Literature Unit

Chapter 8

1. From whom did the Steven's party seek advise about the trail to California?

2. How were the emigrants able to confirm the accuracy of the Indian map?

3. What act caused a fight to almost break out between the emigrants and the Indians?

4. What happened to the oxen that drank the water from the hot springs?

5. Why did the Steven's party give Truckee River its name?

Chapter 9

1. Why did the people have to cross the Truckee River ten times within one mile?

2. How did the country change as the wagon train entered the canyon again?

3. Which fork of the river did the Stevens party decide to follow when they reached the California Mountains?

4. What almost caused the wagons to be abandoned?

5. What did Captain Stevens credit for the "miraculous" crossing of the Sierra Nevada?

Chapter 10

1. What was the size of the cabin which Mose and his party built?

2. Why was it good to hang the cow meat on the north side of the cabin?

3. What did the men use to make the snowshoes?

WESTWARD EXPANSION

Project 3, Page 8—Literature Unit

4. How deep was the snow by the time Mose and his party left the cabin?

____

____

5. Why was Mose unable to continue on the journey?

____

____

CHAPTER 11

1. How was Mose able to use to get some meat to eat?

____

____

2. What tasted as bad as the coyote meat?

____

____

3. What special treat did Mose have to celebrate Christmas?

____

____

4. What did Mose decide to do if he no longer caught any foxes in his traps?

____

____

5. What was Mose able to do in order to pass the time in the cabin?

____

____

____

WESTWARD EXPANSION
Project 3, Page 9—Literature Unit

CHAPTER 12

1. Who helped Mose get safely to California?

____

____

2. What good news did Mose receive from his Canadian friend?

____

____

3. Why was the Stevens party larger when it arrived in California than when it had begun?

____

____

4. Why did the Indians not take the guns and ammunition from the abandoned wagons?

____

____

5. How was Mose able to make good money when gold was discovered?

____

____

____

Westward Expansion
Project 3, Page 10—Literature Unit

Answers

Chapter one
1. at least 2000 miles
2. 50 people
3. he knew something about trapping; he knew nothing about snowshoes
4. they endure more hardship and live better on grass
5. Council Bluffs

Chapter two
1. one
2. a circle
3. tied a rope around the horns of a gentle ox and led it across with a canoe
4. Otoes
5. Sullivan had a fear of Indians

Chapter three
1. The first wildflowers
2. 15 miles
3. they had to be dismantled
4. an outbreak of smallpox
5. they had wasted a lot of powder and lead, and the meat wasn't fit to eat

Chapter four
1. Fort Laramie
2. the dry air of the plains
3. there was a chance of meeting Indians
4. they were scented by the bull buffalo and the herd ran away
5. dead antelope, rifles, pistols

Chapter five
1. Independence Rock
2. a bull buffalo fast asleep
3. 8 (7 + one more bull)
4. the wolves snarled and howled loudly over the dead buffaloes
5. a mile and a half above sea level

Chapter six
1. war parties
2. go straight west over the cutoff
3. water
4. at Big Sandy Creek
5. they threw up their hand to show that they wanted to talk

Chapter seven
1. Fort Hall
2. eleven
3. Diggers; they dug for roots
4. it got smaller instead of bigger and it suddenly disappeared
5. to feed and rest the oxen; they didn't know which direction to go

Chapter eight
1. Truckee, the Digger chief
2. a scouting party went out with the Indian chief to explore the trail
3. Mose lost his temper over a stolen halter
4. they became sick
5. in thanks to the Indian who had told them of it

Chapter nine
1. the river swung back and forth from side to side in the narrow passageway
2. mountains were covered with pine trees instead of being bare and ugly
3. both; the party divided and each followed a different fork of the river
4. a cliff about ten feet high
5. answered prayer

WESTWARD EXPANSION

Project 3, Page 11—Literature Unit

CHAPTER TEN

1. 12 feet wide and 14 feet long
2. no sun shone, and the meat stayed frozen
3. hickory strips from the wagons and rawhide
4. ten feet deep
5. his legs cramped up

CHAPTER ELEVEN

1. the steel traps Capt. Stevens had left behind
2. crow meat
3. a cup of coffee
4. try to get over the pass on his snowshoes
5. read books

CHAPTER TWELVE

1. Dennis Martin
2. everyone in the Stevens party had made it to California
3. two babies had been born along the trail
4. they were afraid of them
5. he took goods to the mines and sold them at high prices

WESTWARD EXPANSION
Test

1. What term was used for those settlers who headed for California and the Oregon Territory?

2. What caused many people to go west?

3. List the four main trails and next to each one why people generally went there.

4. What conditions did travelers endure as they traveled over the trails?

5. In what did many of the people travel? What were groups of these called?

Review

1. When was the Erie canal begun? How long did it take to complete?

WESTWARD EXPANSION
Test, Page 2

2. What changed regarding the voting process leading to the election of Andrew Jackson?

3. Why was the invention of the Cotton Gin so important?

4. What Indian tribe refused to obey the Indian Settlement Act of 1830?

   What did the federal government offer to give them?

5. List the events studied to date in chronological order.

War with Mexico
Worksheet

1. During what years was War with Mexico prevalent?

2. Who was president in 1846? What did he want from Mexico?

3. Name six American military leaders who helped defeat the Mexicans during this period.

4. When a peace treaty was finally signed what present day states were added the United States?

WINFIELD SCOTT ZACHARY TAYLOR

War with Mexico
Project

Map

At the time that Texas was annexed, (as you read about in card number seven) the Mexican boundary line had not been decided. Texas claimed that the boundary dividing the two was the Rio Grande; Mexico claimed that it was a river farther north, the Nueces River. The country between these rivers was without inhabitants; it was so wild and barren that no one thought it could ever be colonized, and yet neither Mexico nor the United States would consent to give it up.

President Polk sent an army under General Zachary Taylor to occupy the east bank of the Rio Grande. A Mexican army crossed the river. Two battles were fought, and the Mexicans were driven back with great loss. There was now no way to settle the question but by war.

Captain Lee with his corps of engineers was sent first to the Rio Grande, but his stay there was short. Another American army under General Winfield Scott was dispatched by way of Vera Cruz to capture the city of Mexico, and Lee was assigned to a place on General Scott's staff

By the end of this war the United States had wrestled from Mexico not only the disputed strip of land between the Nueces and the Rio Grande, but all that region now composing Utah, Nevada, and California, and most of New Mexico and Arizona, besides a part of Colorado and Wyoming.

On the map on the following page locate the the Rio Grande and the Nueces River. Color the land the United States obtained from Mexico in 1848 in red. Color the remainder of Mexico in yellow.

WAR WITH MEXICO
Project, Page 2

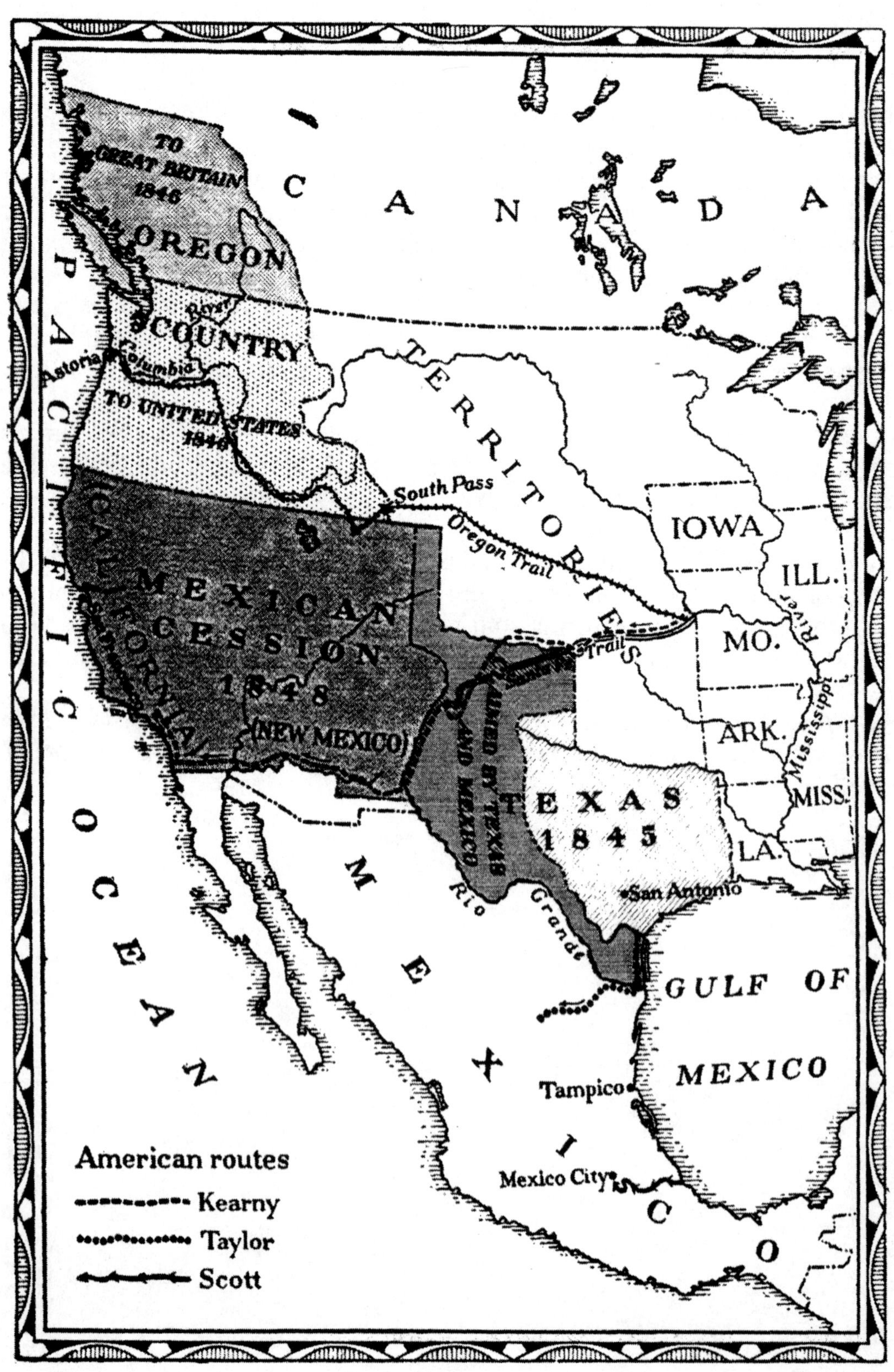

WAR WITH MEXICO

Test

1. During what years was the United States at war with Mexico?

____

____

____

2. In _____(year), President ________ wanted to buy the land that is now _____________ from Mexico, but Mexico refused to sell.

3. What action did the president mentioned above take that angered Mexico?

____

____

____

____

4. When did the U.S. finally obtain a peace treaty?

   What present day states became part of the holdings of the United States?

____

____

____

____

5. Name four Americans who fought against Mexico during this period.

____

____

____

____

WAR WITH MEXICO
Test, Page 2

Review

1. What was the Monroe Doctrine?

2. What illegal activity developed before the cotton gin because of the demand for cotton?

3. What was the Cherokee Trail of Tears?

4. Who was Santa Anna and what was his response to the people of Texas declaring their independence?

5. List the events studied to date in chronogical order. List dates next to each one.

'49ERS AND THE CALIFORNIA GOLD RUSH
Worksheet

1. Who first discovered gold in California? When?

____

____

2. Approximately how many Americans came looking for gold?

   Why were they called the "49ers?"

____

____

3. What route did those who came by boat take from the eastern United States?

____

____

4. Name the two predominant ways prospectors tried to find gold.

____

____

5. Why did California become a state quickly? When?

____

____

6. What city prospered as a result of the gold rush?

____

____

7. What happened to the man who first discovered gold there?

____

____

____

____

SUTTER'S FORT

'49ERS AND THE CALIFORNIA GOLD RUSH
Project

Gold in California

The country bordering the Pacific was a wilderness long after the eastern part of our country was well settled. As late as 1848 there were but a few thousand people in all California. The scattered inhabitants were a strange mixture of Yankees, Mormons, Mexicans, and Indians. There were also a few negroes and Spaniards. Most of the people lived in log huts, or adobe houses, which were made of clay. Their humble dwellings were scattered about through the wilderness near cattle ranches or mission stations. In some places clusters of huts later grew into towns or cities.

There was a rude village at San Francisco. Northeast from this village lay the beautiful valley of the Sacramento River, one of whose early settlers was a man in whom we shall be very much interested. He was a Swiss, named John A. Sutter. Sutter had come to California in 1839 and had taken up several thousand acres of land along the American River, a branch of the Sacramento River Near the mouth of the American River he had built a fort which people far and near called Sutter's Fort, and which became a center for all the settlements in this region. Sutter was a wealthy man. He owned twelve thousand cattle, fifteen thousand sheep, and much other property. To care for this stock he employed several hundred men. He was truly a prince in this western wilderness.

In Sutter's employ was a man named James W. Marshall, a carpenter who had emigrated from New Jersey. As there was a wealth of timber upon the surrounding mountains, Sutter decided to build a saw-mill. He chose Marshall to manage its construction. They selected a site on the south fork of the American River about fourty miles east of Sutter's Fort and near the foothills of the Sierra Nevada Mountains. The exact place they called Coloma. Marshall collected a few Indians and white men and began to build a sawmill here in 1848, just before the Mexicans were forced to cede California to Uncle Sam. It was necessary to dig a millrace, and in doing this they used a strong current of water to wash away the loose earth.

One afternoon in January, as Marshall was walking about the millrace, he noticed glittering yellow particles in the sand. It looked like gold. So he mounted a horse and made haste to Sutter's Fort. He found Sutter alone and displayed his nuggets. They tested the yellow metal in every way they could. When they had hammered it thin and tested it with acid they were certain that it was gold.

It seemed best to keep the matter a secret for a time, but such secrets are hard to keep. It was not long until all the settlers in the valley had heard of Marshall's discovery, though most people refused to believe it. They were anxious, however, to go up into the valley and see for themselves, and they made all sorts of excuses for going.

More than three months passed by before the people of California became fully alive to the great discovery. In the following May some thirty miners from the American River came to San Francisco carrying bottles, tin cans, and buckskin bags filled with the precious gold. One man, holding up a bottle of the yellow dust in one hand and swinging his hat in the other, walked along through the streets shouting, "Gold! Gold! Gold from the American River!" The people no longer doubted it.

'49ERS AND THE CALIFORNIA GOLD RUSH

Project, Page 2

Now no story was to big to be believed and everybody began to rush for the gold fields. Many sold their property and set off at once. Business in San Fransisco came to a standstill. There were two newspapers at that time, but there were no editions printed, because their printers had departed for the gold fields. In a few weeks three-fourths of all the men in town had gone to the mines. As everybody wanted tools, the price of shovels, pickaxes, blankets, and other supplies rose in value in a few days to six times their former price. The town council could not hold its meetings, the church was closed, farms were deserted, and waving fields of grain were allowed to go to waste. The doctor deserted his patients, and officers neglected their duties. The exciting news gradually spread down the coast to Monterey, Los Angeles, and San Diego. Everywhere the people went wild over the report, and the one cry along the whole coast was "Gold! Gold!"

The discovery of these rich gold mines soon changed the appearance of northern California. People no longer wished to care for horses and cattle on great ranches, or to cultivate small patches of ground. All hurried to the mines, and townspeople, who wished to hire a carpenter or other mechanic, had to pay him more than he could get at the camp. Carpenters were paid fifteen and twenty dollars a day, and a cook was sometimes paid three hundred dollars a month. Sailors deserted their ships and soldiers left the garrisons for the mines. Four or five ships belonging to Uncle Sam, which arrived in the harbor off Monterey, dared not land because the moment a sailor set foot on shore he deserted and hurried after gold. Before the summer was over there were four thousand men in the Sacramento Valley searching diligently for the nuggets of gold. California was not yet connected with the east by telegraph or railway, or even by wagon road, so the news traveled slowly to the eastern states. But the following year seventy-five thousand gold seekers had reached San Francisco and passed on to the gold valley. As this was the year 1849, the first gold seekers were called "forty-niners." The news spread over the world until there were men from all parts of the globe headed for the Pacific coast. From the eastern states great caravans of wagons called “prairie schooners” began to move across the western plains, bound for California.

Many from the east sailed around Cape Horn on a long weary voyage to California. A large number went by water to the Isthmus of Panama and journeyed overland through the tropical jungles for fifty miles to the City of Panama, where they took ship for San Francisco. Some arriving at Panama found that the boats which had sailed for San Francisco had been deserted by their crews at the Golden Gate and could not return. For weeks and months thousands of these people, unable to go farther, were forced to remain on the isthmus, where the deadly

climate sent many to their graves.

Many a gold seeker winding his way across the western plains found a nameless grave, for a terrible disease, known as cholera, spread among the emigrants. But in spite of the dangers of the journey and the dread disease, great numbers continued to risk the trip overland to the west. Sometimes there was a line of wagons unbroken for miles and at night numerous camp fires were grouped like a city. Some of these travelers brought their families with them, but most of the men were unmarried, or had left their families in the east, hoping to return to them loaded with wealth. Large numbers died of starvation or of thirst in passing through the terrible deserts.

Such was the mad rush for California that within three years after gold was discovered, there were one hundred thousand men at work in the gold mines. For a time Coloma, where the yellow metal was first found, remained the center of the gold-seeking country. However, as large numbers continued to enter the field, they spread out until they had covered most of the Sacramento Valley and the western slopes of the Sierra Nevada Mountains. Then they overflowed to the south and spread out through the valley of the San Joaquin. One writer said, "The people were running over the country and picking gold out of the earth just as a hog let loose in a forest would root up the ground nuts." One man employed sixty Indians and made a dollar a minute. Seven men, with fifty Indians, gathered in seven weeks two hundred and seventy-five pounds of pure gold.

In some places there were found very rich gold deposits. On a claim a few feet square there was taken out ten thousand dollars worth of the precious metal. They found gold in all forms, in seams in the rock, in scales, pellets, and in grains in the sand. Occasionally, a man would pick up a nugget weighing a pound or more. The largest piece of gold ever found in California was discovered by five poor men in 1854. It weighed one hundred and sixty-one pounds, as much as a grown man. The gold in it was about seven eighths pure and brought the men thirty-five thousand dollars. We are told that gold to the amount of sixty-five million dollars was obtained in California in one year, and in eight years it amounted to five hundred million.

From this immense sum you might imagine that every miner became wealthy, but this is not true. A few were wise enough after finding rich ore to gather up their wealth and leave the country before they spent or wasted what they had found. Some steady men, who had left their families in the east, worked hard gathering gold dust until they were well-to-do, and then returned to their homes. Most of the miners, however, wasted all the wealth they secured, always hoping to find more. Large numbers died from exposure and others went home, defeated and disappointed.

Marshall, who first discovered the precious metal, proved to be most unsteady. He went hither and thither among the mines, always looking for some unusually rich treasure. He became discouraged over his poor luck and despondent over his failure. He passed away all alone in his cabin, poor and almost unnoticed. Some years later the State of California gave five thousand dollars to erect a monument to his memory. It is placed on a hill near the place where gold was first discovered. On the monument stands a figure of a man with outstretched hand, the finger of which points to the very spot where Marshall picked up the first shining nugget of gold. Sutter also was a failure. When he gave up cattle raising

'49ERS AND THE CALIFORNIA GOLD RUSH
Project, Page 4

and tried to hunt gold, he lost all his property, land, and cattle, and his laborers were scattered.

Many of the miners were shiftless men, who hastened to the drinking and gambling dens as soon as they received their week's income, and stayed there until every penny was gone. One miner, who had searched in vain for many weeks, found at last a pocket of gold in a river bank from which he took out in a few hours several thousand dollars' worth of the metal. But success got the better of him, and before the first night passed he was drunk and penniless.

The gold miner dressed in a woolen or checked cotton shirt, with loose trousers tucked into high wrinkled boots. He wore a slouch hat and a belt about the waist in which he kept his knife and pistols. When too far from camp to return at night, he slept under the open sky on a bed of leaves or wrapped in his blanket. Men living this way became rude in manners and habits. They lived after a time very much like the Indians. Anybody who undertook to dress well, or to display polite manners, was quickly hooted and ridiculed. The miner's hair went untrimmed and fell about his shoulders, and his unshaven beard was wild and shaggy. The average miner was honest and faithful to his friends, but when any one took advantage of him, he looked to his knife and pistol for protection.

As most of these men were unmarried, or had left their families in the east, there was no family life in the mining field. The gentle influence of woman was greatly missed. It is said that these rough pioneers would often walk ten miles or more simply to see a woman without even expecting to become acquainted with her. Sometimes a miner would meet a little girl in the street of a mining town and would catch her up in his arms and kiss her repeatedly, and as he let her go would fill her little hand with gold dust. For several years there were far from enough women on the Pacific coast to make homes for the men. It is said that a woman in those days might commit any sort of crime in California and no jury could be found to convict her.

After the first wild rush was over, great numbers of people continued to come to California to make that land their permanent home, and to build up the Golden State. Sites that were fortunately located were quickly covered with buildings and the towns grew into cities. San Francisco was growing very rapidly. Long wharves were built. The hulks of abandoned ships were moored along the shore and used as shops and dwellings. Houses had been built on piles and the people had begun filling in with earth. Streets were soon cut through the hills and seven miles of streets graded. Along most of the way plank sidewalks were laid. San Francisco suffered dreadful fires, but nothing could stop her growth. People came in great numbers from Mexico and Chile, from China, England, France, and Germany, while thousands of Americans crossed the continent to make their homes in the Golden State. Soon California was eager to become a state of our great Union, and to have a star upon our flag to represent her.

Discussion

1. Tell the story of Sutter.
2. Let one pupil pretend he had gone to California by way of Panama, and give a talk to the class describing his journey.
3. Let another do likewise with the overland journey.

'49ERS AND THE CALIFORNIA GOLD RUSH

Project 2

Mining for Gold

Miners first began searching for gold in rivers by "panning" for it. A person would scoop up dirt from a riverbed into a round pan (like a pie pan) with a flat bottom and gently swirl the water in the pan. In doing this the dirt was washed over the edge leaving the heavier gold dust and gold flakes behind. People eventually realized that there had to be a more efficient way and invented different kinds of simple machines to do this. Many miners used a cradle, or rocker. The cradle was a wooden box with another box attached to the bottom that had a screen on it. The two were rocked back and forth and the rocking motion caused the heavier gold to fall through to the bottom where it was collected by the screen. Many other things were developed over the years, but it usually required hard labor and lots of it.

In order for your students to experience gold mining you may want to simulate panning for gold. Bring in some large wash tubs filled with sand and "gold." You can make gold nuggets by spray painting rocks. In order to make gold dust you may want to spray paint metal shavings (These can be found at local foundries). Be careful that these are not sharp. Allow the students to each take a turn searching for the nuggets, using a pie plate. Make sure you do not put in too many nuggets. Have fun!

'49ERS AND THE CALIFORNIA GOLD RUSH
Test

1. When was gold first discovered in California? By whom?

2. Why were the people who came looking for gold called the "49ers?"
   How many Americans were estimated to have come?

3. What route did those who came by boat take from the eastern United States?

4. How did prospectors try to find gold?

5. What was the reason California became a state quickly? When?

6. A nearby city prospered as a result of the gold rush. Name it.

7. What happened to the man who first discovered gold there?

'49ERS AND THE CALIFORNIA GOLD RUSH
Test

Review

1. Who invented the cotton gin? When was it invented?

2. Name two presidents who continued to follow the Monroe Doctrine.

3. What presidential right did Jackson use more than his predecessors?

4. In what year did Texas win its independence?

5. List in chronological order the cards studied to date. Include dates.

OPENING THE OREGON TERRITORY

Worksheet

1. What did the U.S. and Great Britain agree upon about the Oregon Country in 1846?

____

____

2. The U.S. portion of Oregon Country, which includes present day states of

______________, __________, ____________, and parts of ______________

and ______________, became a territory in 1848.

3. What profession was common among the first to settle the northwest?

____

____

4. Who established a trading company at the mouth of the Columbia River?

____

____

5. Who was Marcus Whitman?

____

____

6. What was the Pony Express?

____

____

7. What eventually replaced the Pony Express?

____

____

____

____

____

Opening the Oregon Territory

Project—Literature Unit

...If You Travelled West in a Covered Wagon

Instructions

Have students read the book *"...If You Traveled West in a Covered Wagon."* Supply each student with a copy of the cover on this page and of the following pages of this project.

Have them create their own book by answering the questions and illustrating the events. The pages should then be cut apart and stapled together along the left side to form a booklet.

1. What was the Oregon Territory?

2. Why did some people want to travel all the way to Oregon?

3. What was a covered wagon?

4. What was a wagon train?

5. Did anybody lead the wagon train?

6. What was a trail guide?

7. What kind of people traveled West?

8. What would your family bring
in their covered wagon?

9. What was the best time
of year to start the trip?

10. How would you cross rivers
when there were no bridges?

11. How far would you
travel in a day?

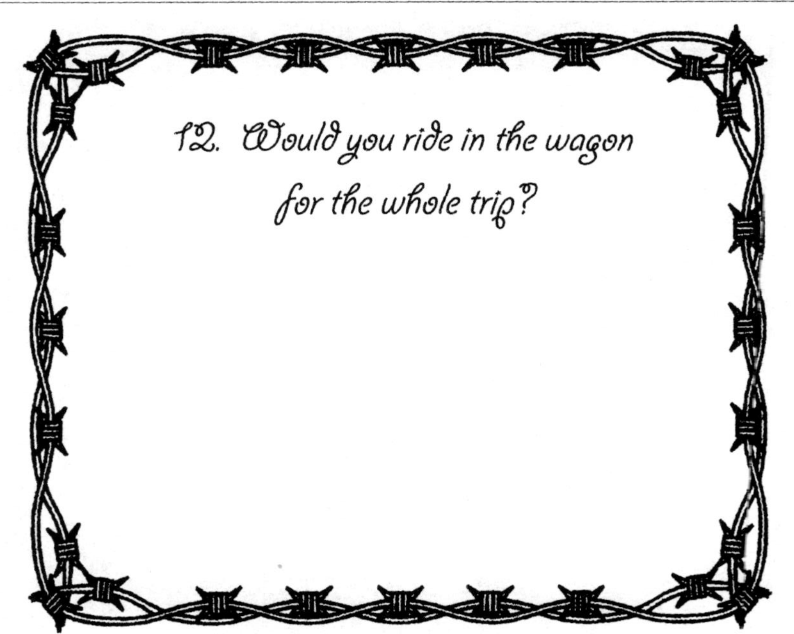
12. Would you ride in the wagon
for the whole trip?

13. What were the dangers
and difficulties of the trip?

14. Where would you sleep?

15. What kind of clothes
did people wear?

16. What would you eat?

17. How did you make buffalo meat last a long time?

18. How would you build a fire if you didn't have any wood?

19. What happened if you met Indians on the trail?

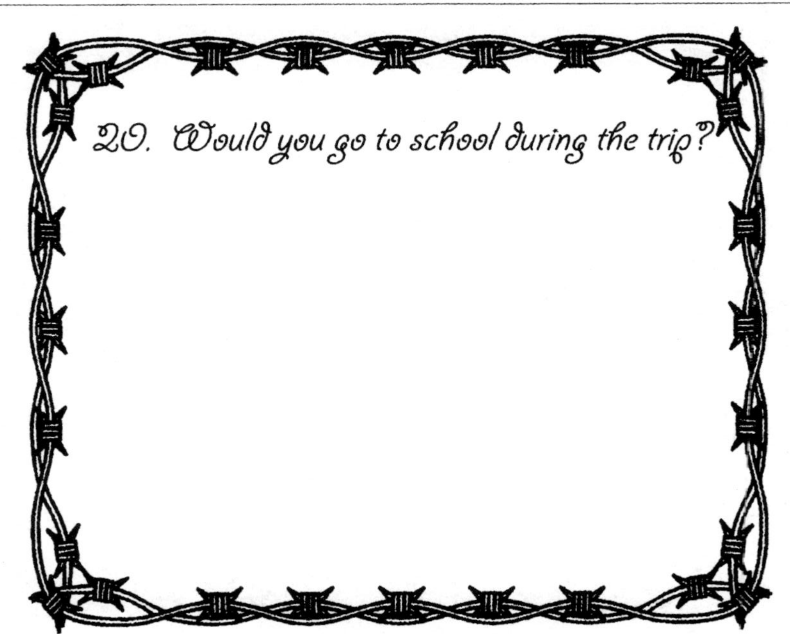

20. Would you go to school during the trip?

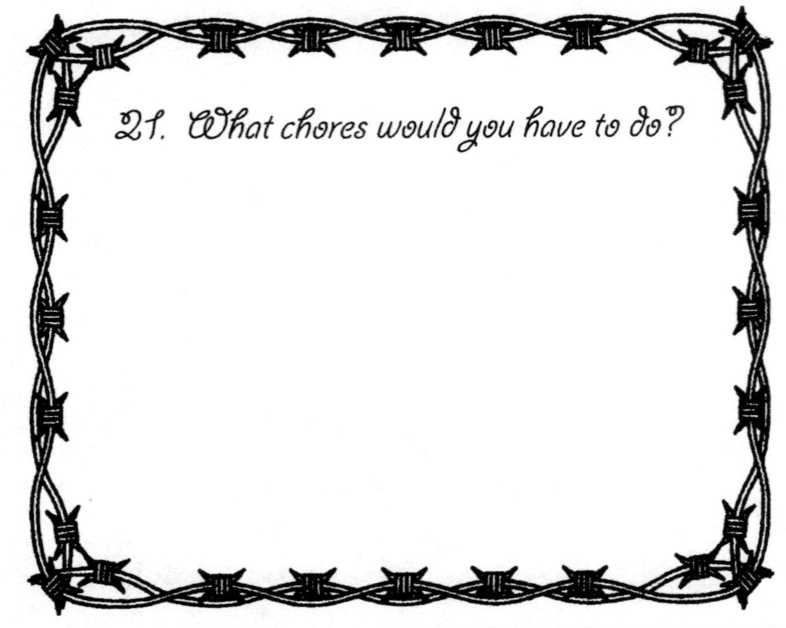
21. What chores would you have to do?

22. Would you see any wild animals?

23. Could you send a letter or receive one?

24. If you ran out of supplies
could you get more?

25. Was it hard driving the wagon's over mountains?

26. Without road signs, how would you know where you were?

27. What is the Continental Divide?

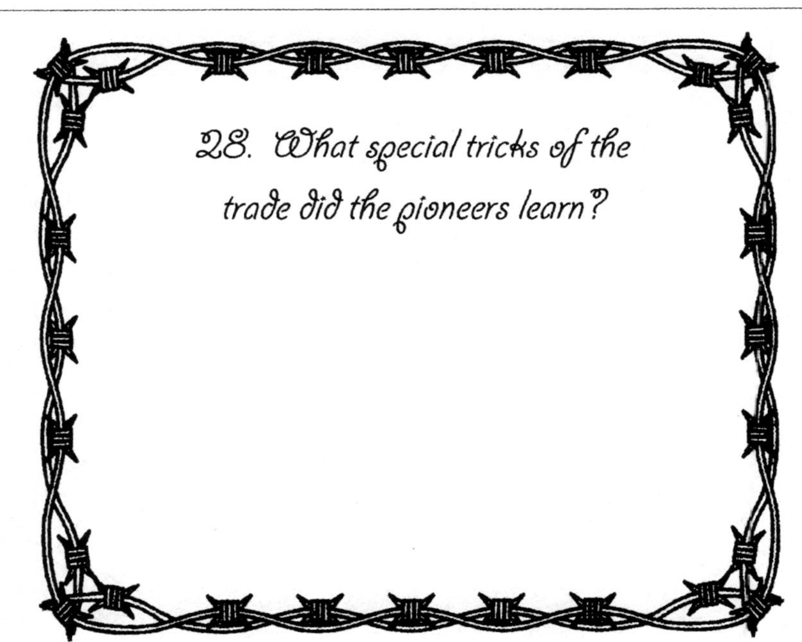

28. What special tricks of the trade did the pioneers learn?

29. How do we know what it was like to travel west in a covered wagon?

30. Is there anything left of the old Oregon Trail?

Opening the Oregon Territory

Project 2

After reading the book *They're off!, the Story of the Pony Express* by Cheryl Harness, use the following page to write a letter to a friend detailing your fictitious experiences as a rider carrying mail on the Pony Express.

Opening the Oregon Territory
Test

1. What is the approximate date of the Opening of the Oregon Territory?

2. In 1846 where did the U.S. and Great Britain agree to divide the Oregon Country?

3. Who were among the first to settle the northwest?

4. Who was John Astor? What did he establish?

5. Who was the Christian doctor who went to preach and doctor the Cayuse?
   What happened to him?

6. How was mail transported in the early 1860's?

7. Who invented the first transcontinental telegraph?

OPENING THE OREGON TERRITORY

Test, Page 2

Review

1. Who invented the cotton gin? When was it invented?

2. Name two presidents who continued to follow the Monroe Doctrine.

3. What was the Cherokee Trail of Tears?

4. In what year did Texas win its independence?

5. List in chronological order all cards studied to date.

   Next to each one give the approximate date.

LINCOLN, THE 16TH PRESIDENT
Worksheet

1. Why was Abraham Lincoln called a "Log cabin president?"

____

____

2. Abraham Lincoln grew to be ________ tall and was considered to be ______________, ____________, and ________________. He often read the ______________. He married ______________ ____________. They had _________ sons.

3. Describe Lincoln's political career.

____

____

____

4. When and why did Lincoln give the Gettysburg address?

____

____

5. What was the Emancipation Proclamation and when was it issued?

____

____

____

6. How did Lincoln believe the South should be treated after the War Between the States?

____

____

7. When and how did Abraham Lincoln die?

____

____

____

LINCOLN, THE 16TH PRESIDENT

Project

A Pictorial Depiction of Lincoln's Life

Materials

Poster board (one per student)
Glue
Scissors
Pencil
Resources (see the resources listed on the card)

Instructions

After reading the card, the attached autobiographies, and any other resources you have available, write a brief statement about each of the illustrations. Cut them apart. Glue them to a poster board along with the title page.

LINCOLN, THE 16TH PRESIDENT

Project, Page 2

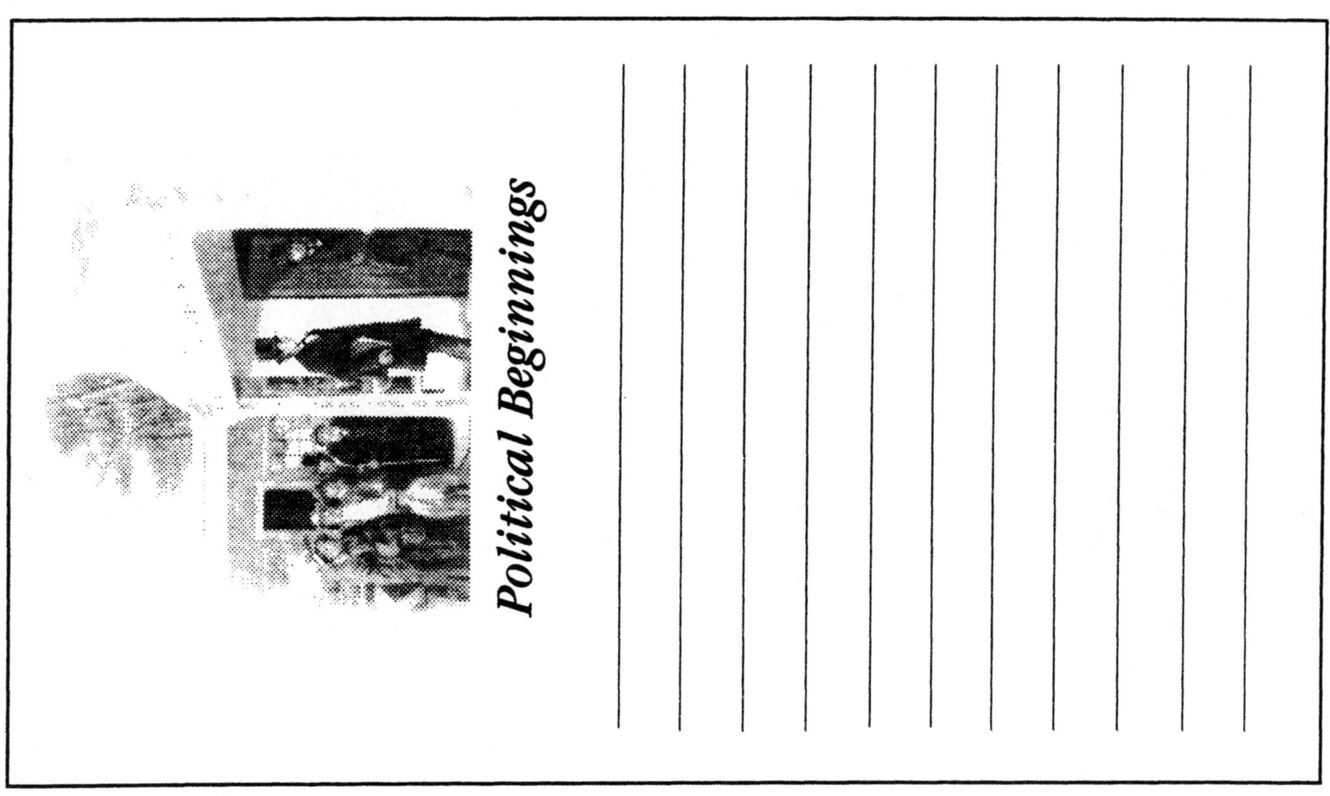

As a Boy

LINCOLN, THE 16TH PRESIDENT

Project, Page 3

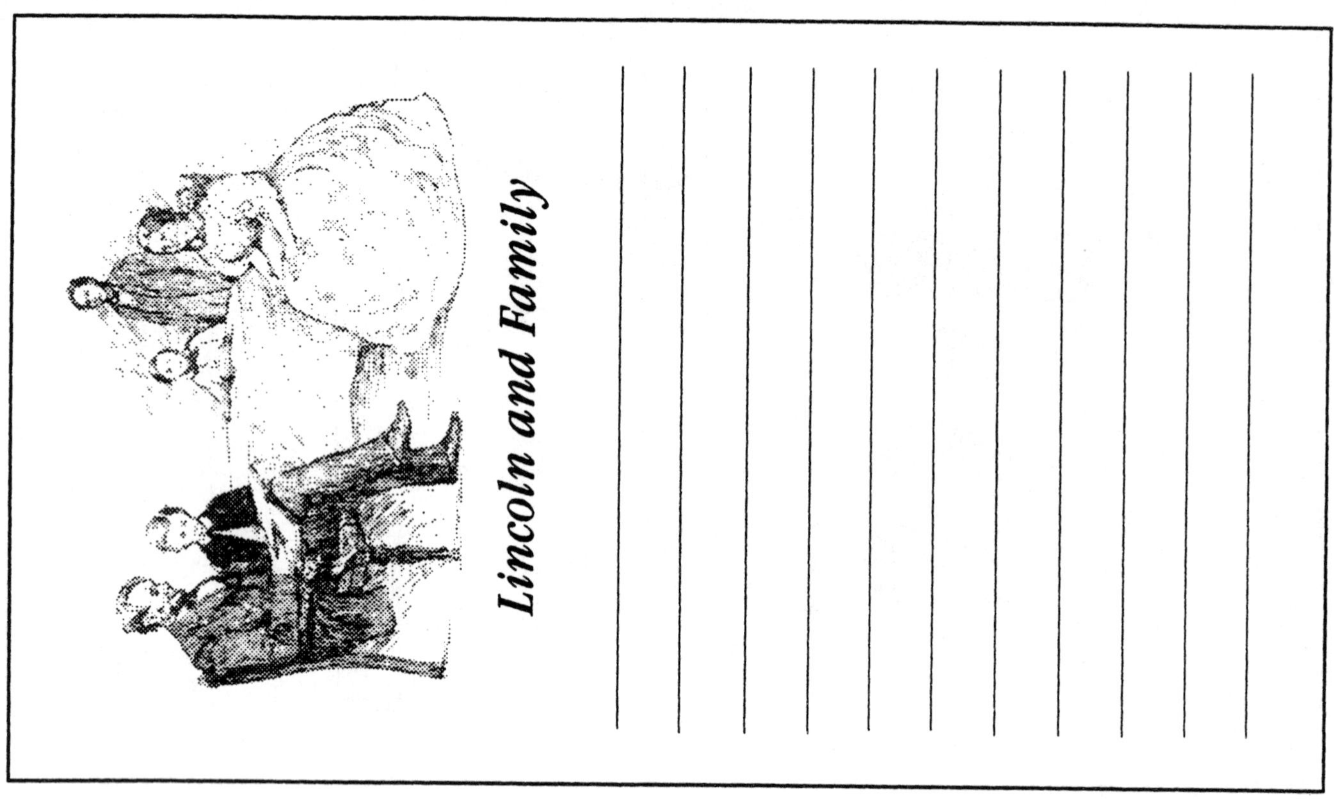

Lincoln and Family

Presidential Inauguration

LINCOLN, THE 16TH PRESIDENT

Project, Page 4

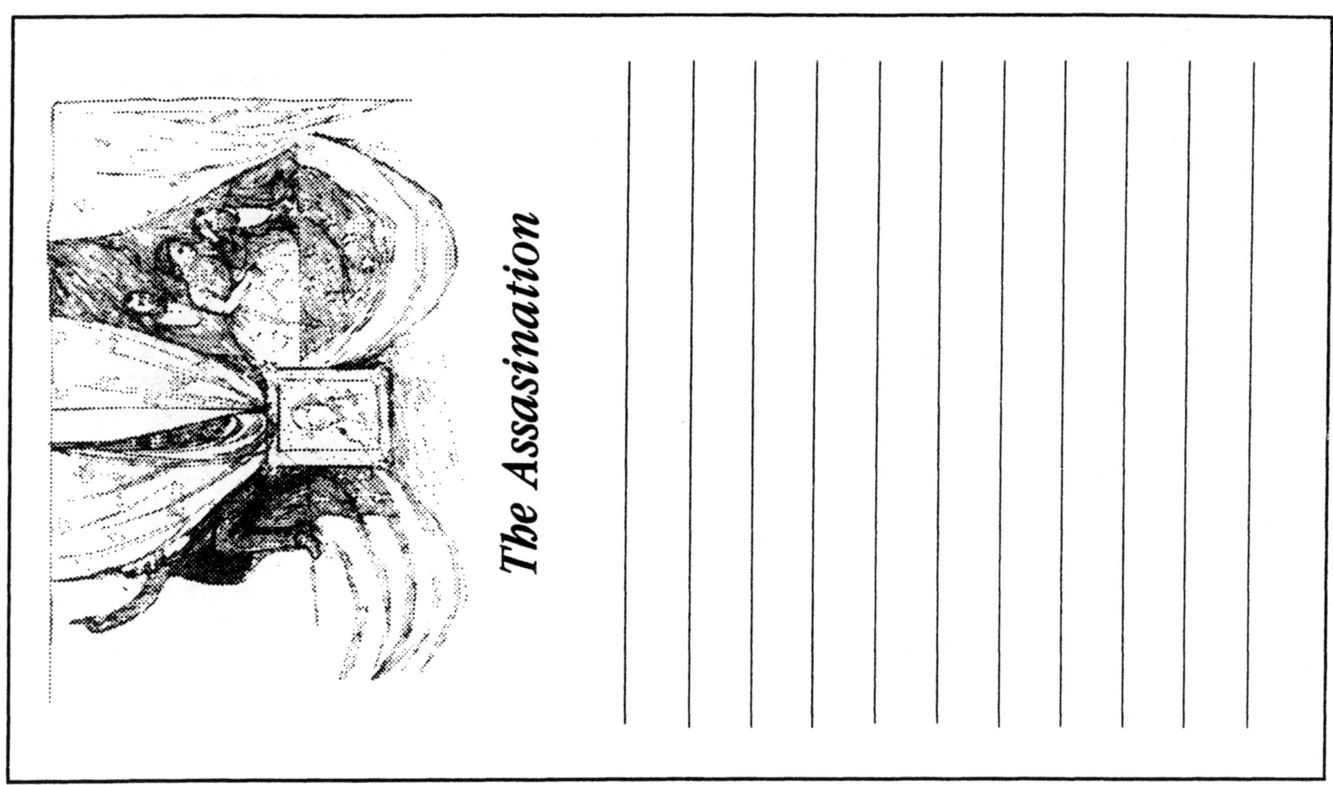

The Assasination

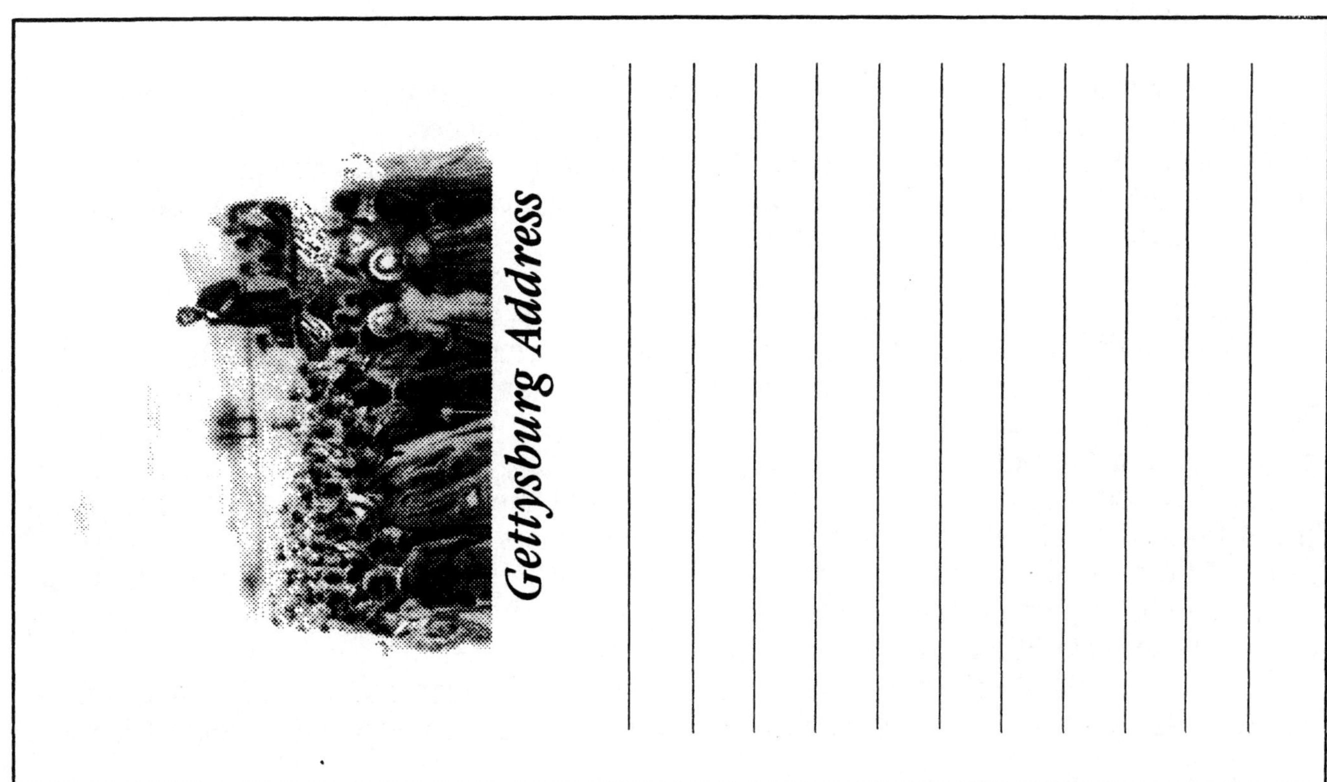

Gettysburg Address

Lincoln, the 16th President
Project 2

Lincoln's Autobiography

Below are two of three autobiographies written by Lincoln between 1858 and 1860.

June 1858

Lincoln wrote three autobiographies in a two year period. This first, terse effort was prepared at the request of Charles Lanman, who was compiling the Dictionary of Congress.

Born, February 12, 1809, in Hardin County, Kentucky.
Education defective.
Profession, a lawyer.
Have been a captain of volunteers in Black Hawk war.
Postmaster at a very small office.
Four times a member of the Illinois legislature, and was a member of the lower house of Congress.

December 20, 1859

Lincoln wrote this second autobiography for Jesse Fell, a longtime Illinois Republican friend who was a native of Pennsylvania. Fell used his influence to get the piece incorporated in an article appearing in a Pennsylvania newspaper on February 11, 1860. Lincoln enclosed the autobiography in a letter to Fell which said, "There is not much of it, for the reason, I suppose, that there is not much of me."

I was born Feb. 12, 1809, in Hardin County, Kentucky. My parents were both born in Virginia, of undistinguished families--second families, perhaps I should say. My mother, who died in my tenth year, was of a family of the name of Hanks, some of whom now reside in Adams, and others in Macon Counties, Illinois. My paternal grandfather, Abraham Lincoln, emigrated from Rockingham County, Virginia, to Kentucky, about 1781 or 2, where, a year or two later, he was killed by Indians, not in battle, but by stealth, when he was laboring to open a farm in the forest. His ancestors, who were Quakers, went to Virginia from Berks County, Pennsylvania. An effort to identify them with the New England family of the same name ended in nothing more definite, than a similarity of Christian names in both families, such as Enoch, Levi, Mordecai, Solomon, Abraham, and the like.

My father, at the death of his father, was but six years of age; and he grew up, litterally [sic] without education. He removed from Kentucky to what is now Spencer County, Indiana,

LINCOLN, THE 16TH PRESIDENT
Project 2, Page 2

in my eighth year. We reached our new home about the time the State came into the Union. It was a wild region, with many bears and other wild animals, still in the woods. There I grew up. There were some schools, so called; but no qualification was ever required of a teacher beyond "readin, writin, and cipherin" to the Rule of Three. If a straggler supposed to understand latin happened to sojourn in the neighborhood, he was looked upon as a wizzard [sic]. There was absolutely nothing to excite ambition for education. Of course when I came of age I did not know much. Still somehow, I could read, write, and cipher to the Rule of Three; but that was all. I have not been to school since. The little advance I now have upon this store of education, I have picked up from time to time under the pressure of necessity.

I was raised to farm work, which I continued till I was twenty-two. At twenty one I came to Illinois, and passed the first year in Macon County. Then I got to New Salem (at that time in Sangamon, now in Menard County), where I remained a year as a sort of Clerk in a store. Then came the Black Hawk war; and I was elected a Captain of Volunteers--a success which gave me more pleasure than any I have had since. I went the campaign, was elated, ran for the Legislature the same year (1832) and was beaten--the only time I ever have been beaten by the people. The next, and three succeeding biennial elections, I was elected to the Legislature. I was not a candidate afterwards. During this Legislative period I had studied law, and removed to Springfield to practise (sic) it. In 1846 I was once elected to the lower House of Congress. Was not a candidate for reelection. From 1849 to 1854, both inclusive, practiced law more assiduously than ever before. Always a whig in politics, and generally on the whig electoral tickets, making active canvasses I was losing interest in politics, when the repeal of the Missouri Compromise aroused me again. What I have done since then is pretty well known.

If any personal description of me is thought desirable, it may be said, I am, in height, six feet, four inches, nearly; lean in flesh, weighing on an average one hundred and eighty pounds; dark complexion, with coarse black hair, and grey eyes no other marks or brands recollected.

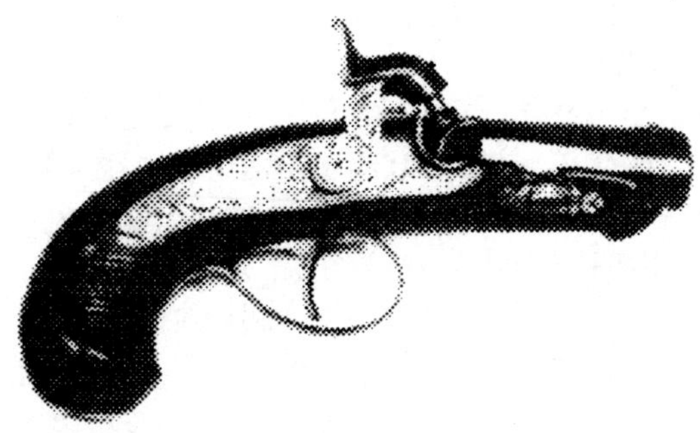

The pistol of John Wilkes Booth

LINCOLN, THE 16TH PRESIDENT
Project 3

The Emancipation Proclamation—A Transcription

January 1, 1863

By the President of the United States of America:
A Proclamation.

Whereas, on the twenty-second day of September, in the year of our Lord one thousand eight hundred and sixty-two, a proclamation was issued by the President of the United States, containing, among other things, the following, to wit:

"That on the first day of January, in the year of our Lord one thousand eight hundred and sixty-three, all persons held as slaves within any State or designated part of a State, the people whereof shall then be in rebellion against the United States, shall be then, thenceforward, and forever free; and the Executive Government of the United States, including the military and naval authority thereof, will recognize and maintain the freedom of such persons, and will do no act or acts to repress such persons, or any of them, in any efforts they may make for their actual freedom."

That the Executive will, on the first day of January aforesaid, by proclamation, designate the States and parts of States, if any, in which the people thereof, respectively, shall then be in rebellion against the United States; and the fact that any State, or the people thereof, shall on that day be, in good faith, represented in the Congress of the United States by members chosen thereto at elections wherein a majority of the qualified voters of such State shall have participated, shall, in the absence of strong countervailing testimony, be deemed conclusive evidence that such State, and the people thereof, are not then in rebellion against the United States.

"Now, therefore I, Abraham Lincoln, President of the United States, by virtue of the power in me vested as Commander-in-Chief, of the Army and Navy of the United States in time of actual armed rebellion against the authority and government of the United States, and as a fit and necessary war measure for suppressing said rebellion, do, on this first day of January, in the year of our Lord one thousand eight hundred and sixty-three, and in accordance with my purpose so to do publicly proclaimed for the full period of one hundred days, from the day first above mentioned, order and designate as the States and parts of States wherein the people thereof respectively, are this day in rebellion against the United States, the following, to wit:

Arkansas, Texas, Louisiana, (except the Parishes of St. Bernard, Plaquemines, Jefferson, St. John, St. Charles, St. James Ascension, Assumption, Terrebonne, Lafourche, St. Mary,

LINCOLN, THE 16TH PRESIDENT
Project 3, Page 2

St. Martin, and Orleans, including the City of New Orleans) Mississippi, Alabama, Florida, Georgia, South Carolina, North Carolina, and Virginia, (except the forty-eight counties designated as West Virginia, and also the counties of Berkley, Accomac, Northampton, Elizabeth City, York, Princess Ann, and Norfolk, including the cities of Norfolk and Portsmouth[)], and which excepted parts, are for the present, left precisely as if this proclamation were not issued.

And by virtue of the power, and for the purpose aforesaid, I do order and declare that all persons held as slaves within said designated States, and parts of States, are, and henceforward shall be free; and that the Executive government of the United States, including the military and naval authorities thereof, will recognize and maintain the freedom of said persons.

And I hereby enjoin upon the people so declared to be free to abstain from all violence, unless in necessary self-defence; and I recommend to them that, in all cases when allowed, they labor faithfully for reasonable wages.

And I further declare and make known, that such persons of suitable condition, will be received into the armed service of the United States to garrison forts, positions, stations, and other places, and to man vessels of all sorts in said service.

And upon this act, sincerely believed to be an act of justice, warranted by the Constitution, upon military necessity, I invoke the considerate judgment of mankind, and the gracious favor of Almighty God.

In witness whereof, I have hereunto set my hand and caused the seal of the United States to be affixed.

Done at the City of Washington, this first day of January, in the year of our Lord one thousand eight hundred and sixty three, and of the Independence of the United States of America the eighty-seventh.

By the President: ABRAHAM LINCOLN
WILLIAM H. SEWARD, Secretary of State.

Lincoln, the 16th President

Project 2, Page 3

Note: As you answer the discussion questions below remember that the "War Between the States" has not been studied yet by your students. Referring back to these pages on the Emancipation Proclamation may be helpful when you cover the next two "cards."

For now, help the student understand that these were Lincoln's convictions going into the war even though the document was issued after the war.

Discussion Questions:

1. What was the purpose of the Emancipation Proclamation?
2. Why was it issued?
3. Why were certain states specifically mentioned as being in rebellion?
4. What authority was cited in the document justifying the declarations of it?

Ole Abe has Gone 'an Did It, Boys.

Oh, ye niggers come along,
For I's qwine to sing a song,
An' I warn you dat you keep it mighty still;
But dis darky heard dem say,
His own self dis berry day,
Dat Ole Abe had went, an' gone and sign'd de bill.

Chorus
Ole Abe has Gone 'an Did It, Boys.
Glory, hallelujerum!
Ole Abe has Gone 'an Did It, Boys, Oh! Glory!
Ole Abe has Gone 'an Did It, Boys,
He's signed de confiscation laws,
Liberty an' freedom's ours, Oh! Glory!

Massa Burnside take de view
Dat de niggers am as true
As de white folks, or as any oder man;
So he nebber dribe us back,
When de hound was on our track,
An' de Lord stan' by him ebry time he plan.

LINCOLN, THE 16TH PRESIDENT
Test

1. What was a nickname that some had for Abraham Lincoln? Why?

____

____

2. Identify three personal characteristics of Abraham Lincoln?

____

____

____

3. Describe Lincoln's political career.

____

____

____

____

4. When and why did Lincoln give the Gettysburg Address?

____

____

5. What was the Emancipation Proclamation? When was it issued and by whom?

____

____

____

____

6. How did Lincoln die and when?

____

____

____

Lincoln, the 16th President

Test, Page 2

Review

1. Where did the Industrial Revolution begin? Describe what is meant by the term "Industrial Revolution."

2. What was the Indian Settlement Act of 1830?

3. When did Texas win its independence?

4. Who first discovered gold in California? When?

5. In chronological order list all the cards studied to date. Next to each place the appropriate date.

WAR BETWEEN THE STATES
Worksheet

1. What are the dates of the War Between the States?

2. What did the election of Abraham Lincoln in 1860 cause to happen?

3. What were the differences between the North and the South regarding state and federal government?

4. After Lincoln was elected how many southern states seceded?
   What did they become and who was their president?

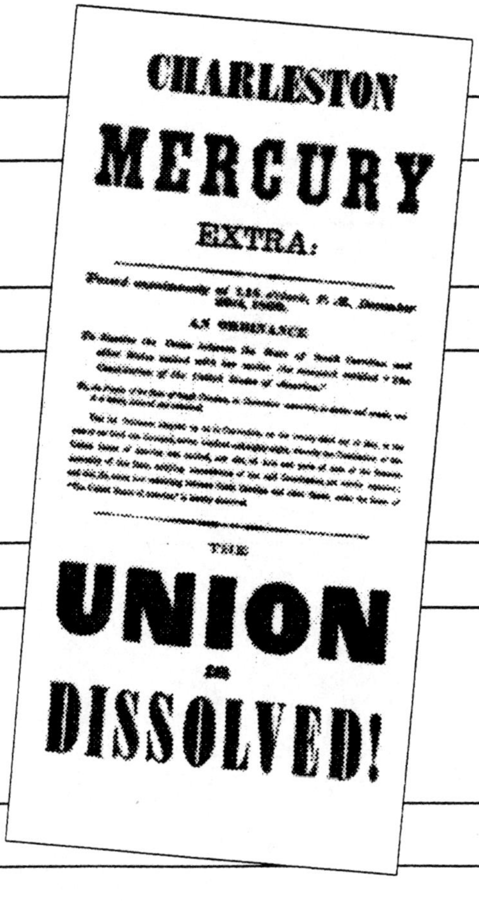

5. Define seceded.

6. What were the northern soldiers called?
   What were the southern soldiers called?

7. Did the north want to keep the union together or have it split apart?

WAR BETWEEN THE STATES
Worksheet

8. When and where were the first shots of the War between the States fired?

9. What occurred in April 1865?

10. What was the cause of the majority of deaths caused during the war?

WAR BETWEEN THE STATES
Project

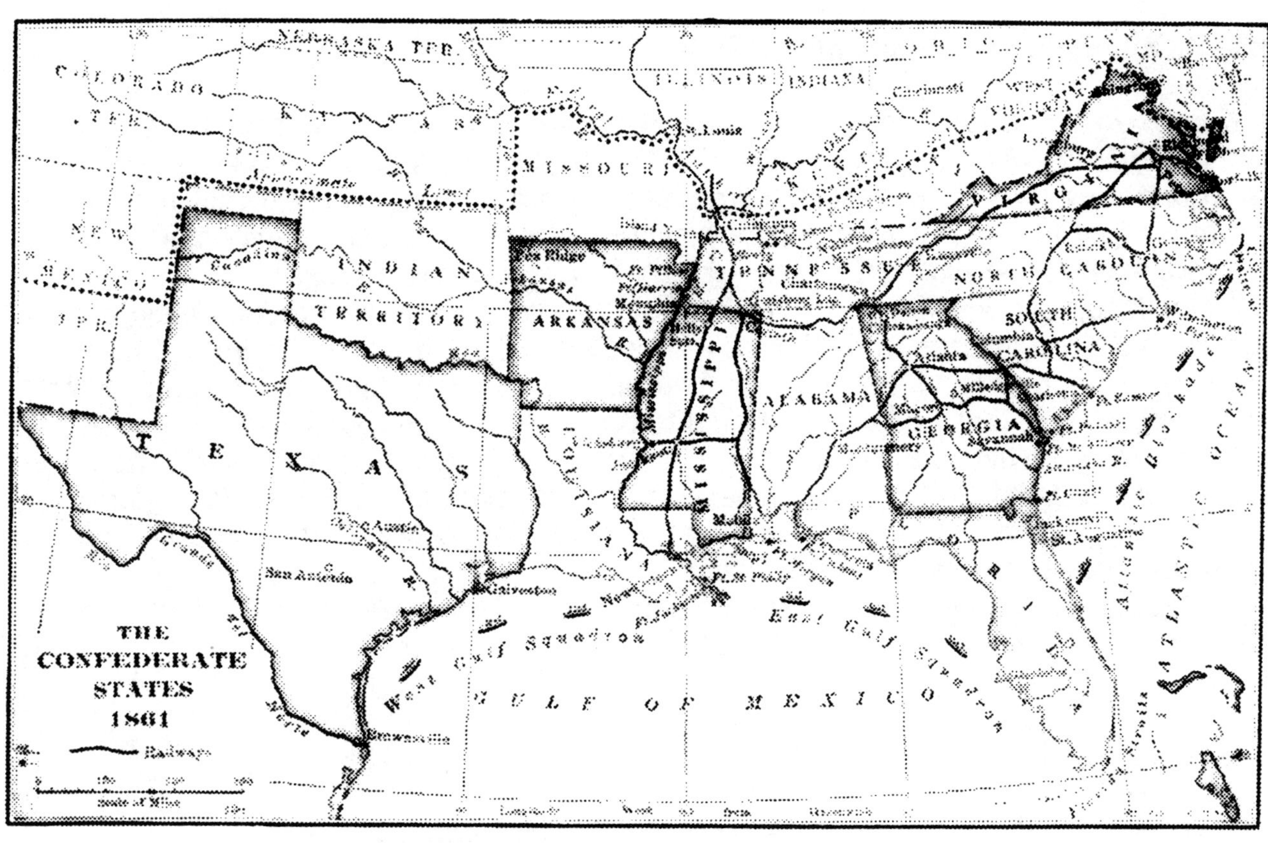

Below write the names of the eleven states that seceded from the Union by the middle of June, 1861.

______________________	______________________
______________________	______________________
______________________	______________________
______________________	______________________
______________________	______________________
______________________	

WAR BETWEEN THE STATES
Project 2

The Republican Party in Power

ABRAHAM LINCOLN (REPUBLICAN) AND ANDREW JOHNSON (WAR DEMOCRAT)

1. Lincoln and Johnson's Administrations (Sixteenth and Seventeenth Presidents, Two Terms, 1861-1869); the President's Arrival at Washington; his Inaugural Address; his Intentions toward the Seceded States. President Lincoln's friends believed that it would not be safe for him to make the last part of his journey to Washington publicly; and he therefore reached the national capital secretly by a special night train.

At his inauguration (March 4, 1861) he said: "I have no purpose, directly or indirectly, to interfere with the institution of slavery in the states where it exists. I believe I have no lawful right to do so ; and I have no inclination to do so." But the President also declared in the same speech that he held the Union to be perpetual, and that he should do his utmost to keep the oath he had just taken "to preserve, protect, and defend it". He furthermore declared that the government had no intention of beginning war against the seceded states, but would only use its power to retake the forts and other national property which had been seized by the Confederacy.

At this time the general feeling throughout the northern states was a strong desire for peace and a willingness to assure the southern states that their constitutional right to hold slaves should not be interfered with.

FIRST YEAR OF THE WAR (APRIL, 1861 - APRIL,1862)

2. Major Anderson's Condition at Fort Sumter; the First Gun of the War; Surrender of the Fort. Major Anderson now sent a message to the President, stating that he could not long continue to hold Fort Sumter unless provisions were sent to him. His entire garrison, aside from some laborers, consisted of eighty-five officers and men; the Confederate force in Charleston was about 7000. The government immediately made arrangements to send the needed supplies. As soon as Jefferson Davis heard of it he

ordered General Beauregard, in command of the Confederate army at Charleston, to demand the surrender of the fort.

Major Anderson declined to surrender, and at daybreak, April 12, 1861, the Confederates fired the first gun at the fort. It was answered by one from Sumter. War had begun. For thirty-four hours nineteen batteries rained shot and shell against the fort, which continued to fire back. Notwithstanding this tremendous cannonade, no one was killed on either side. But Major Anderson, finding that his ammunition was nearly exhausted, and having, nothing but pork to eat, decided to give up the fort. On Sunday (April 14) he, with his garrison, left the fort and embarked for New York; he carried with him the shot-torn flag under which he and his men had fought.

3. *President Lincoln's Call for Volunteers; the Rising of the North.* The next day (April 15, 1861) President Lincoln called for 75,000 volunteers for three months' service, for few then supposed that the war, if there was really to be a war, would last longer than that. In response to the President's call the whole North seemed to rise. Men of all parties forgot their political quarrels, and hastened to the defense of the capital. The heart of the people stood by the Union, and by the old flag. Within thirty-six hours several companies from Pennsylvania had reached Washington. They were speedily followed by the Sixth Massachusetts Regiment—the first full regiment to march. They had to fight their way through a mob at Baltimore. There, on April 19, 1861, the day on which the Revolutionary battles of Lexington and Concord were fought, the first Union soldiers gave their lives for the preservation of the nation.

Many of the volunteers were lads under twenty, and some of them had never left home before. There were many affecting scenes when the "boys in blue" started for Washington. Anxious mothers took tearful leave of sons, whom they feared they should never see again. The peril of the republic touched men in all conditions of life as nothing ever had before. Farmers left their plows, mechanics dropped their tools, clerks said farewell to their employers, college students threw down their books--all hurried to take their places in the ranks, and even lads of fifteen begged to go as drummer boys.

On the Southern side there were the same anxious leave-takings, for it should be borne in mind that while the people of the North were eager to offer their lives for the defense of the Union, the people of the South were just as eager to give theirs to repel what they considered invasion.

4. *Secession of Four More States; General Butler's "Contrabands."* President Lincoln's call for troops made it necessary for the remaining slave states to decide at once whether they would remain in the Union or go out. Virginia joined the Confederacy but the western part of the state had voted against secession, and later it became a separate state (1863) under the name of West Virginia. The Confederate capital was soon removed from Montgomery to Richmond. Arkansas, Tennessee, and North Carolina followed the example of Virginia; but Delaware, Maryland, Kentucky, and Missouri did not secede. By the middle of June the Confederacy consisted of eleven states; no more were added.

General Butler of Massachusetts held command of Fort Monroe in eastern Virginia. It

War Between the States

Project 2, Page 3

was the only Union stronghold in the state, and was of the very highest importance. A number of slaves came to the general and begged him to set them free. He had no authority to give them their liberty. On the other hand, he was certain that if he returned these slaves to their masters they would use them in carrying on the war against the Union. Finally, General Butler got out of the difficulty by saying, These negroes are; then putting spades in the hands of the "contrabands," as they were henceforth called, he set them to work to strengthen the fort. General Butler's action was the first decided blow struck at the existence of slavery after the commencement of the war.

After reading the above write several paragraphs about what happened at Fort Sumter and Lincoln's call for volunteers.

War Between the States

Project 3

Watch the movie *The Great Civil War Debate.* Rev. Steve Wilkins, Presbyterian pastor (PCA) presents the Southern side and Rev. Peter Marshal, Presbyterian minister (PCUSA) presents the Northern side. This video is an exellent way to view both sides of this controversial issue.

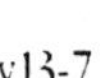

WAR BETWEEN THE STATES
Project 4

Following are two letters writen by soldiers during the War. The first is by Newton Robert Scott, Private, Company A, of the 36th Infantry, Iowa Volunteers to his neighborhood friend and future wife. The second is the convicted spy David O. Dodd on the morning of his hanging.

CAMP LINCOLN KEOKUK IOWA, OCTOBER THE 24TH, 1862
TO MISS HANNAH CONE

Dear Miss

I will Inform you that I am well at this time & that our Co. is all well Except two or three Persons. Our Mess is all well at the Present & I hope that when this Reaches you that it may find you & Friends well... I was Glad to Hear from you & that you was well But I Had about given up getting any answer from you. But Better Late than Never for Indeed Miss Hannah I do love to get News from Home for it looks as if that is all the consolation that us Soldiers Have... It is & Has Bin verry cold & Disagreeable to Day We cook & Eat out Doors & we Run to the Table & Eat But nearly Freeze our Fingers While Eating We Have one Stove in our Barracks Which Does a great Deal of good But one stove is a small make Shift for 80 or 90 men. It is verry cold Standing guard Especialy of nights But If we are Spared to get through the war & Return to our Homes all will be well...

Indeed Dear Miss there is thousands of Poor Soldiers that will see Home & Friends no more in this World If you was in Keokuk & See the number of Sick & Disabled Soldiers it would make your Heart Ache. they are Dieing [illegible] Every Day. But anough of the Hard Side of a Soldiers Life I would tell you the good Side If I know it But don't think that I am Home Sick or Disheartend for such is not the case. I am only telling you a few simple Facts of a Soldiers campaign Indeed I wish never to Return Home Permantly untill this Wicked & God Forsaken Rebellion is Destroyed—

If we had our choices of course we would Be at Home for we are not in the army for fun nor money & Furthermore we wish never to fill a cowards grave & Dear Miss we Have no Fears But that we will Ever Have the good will of those Kind Friends Left at Home. Success to the union Armys & Ere Long may we all Be permitted to Return to our Homes & Live a quiet & Peaceable Lives

Give my love & Respects to all Friends & Reserve a Share for yourself Please write Soon & tell all to Remember & write to the Soldiers for it gives them great Pleasure to hear from Home

In Friendship
Love & Truth
I am Truly yours

Newton Scott

CAMP LINCOLN KEOKUK IOWA, OCTOBER THE 24TH, 1862
MY DEAR PARENTS & SISTERS:

I was arrested as a Spy & Tried & Sentenced to Be Hung to day at 3 o'clock. The time is fast approaching, but thank God I am Prepared to Die. I Exspect to meet you all in Heaven. I will Soon Be out of this World of Sorrow & Trouble. I would like to See you all Before I Die, but let God's will Be Done, not Ours. I Pray to God to give you Strength to Bear your Troubles while in this World. I Hope God will Receive you in Heaven. There I will meet you... Mother I Know it will Be Hard for you to give up your only Son But you must Remember that it is God's will.

Good Bye God will give you Strength to Bear your Troubles. I Pray that we may meet in Heaven.

Good Bye God Bless you all
Your Son & Brother

David O. Dodd

War Between the States

Test

1. What are the dates for the War Between the States?

2. What one person influenced the beginning of the war? How?

3. How did the North and South disagree about State government?

4. Who made up the Confederate States of America? Who was their president?

5. What were the northern soldiers referred to as?

   What were the southern soldiers referred to as?

6. What happened at Fort Sumter in April 1861?

7. How did the war end in April of 1865?

8. How did the majority of deaths occur during the War Between the States?

WAR BETWEEN THE STATES
Test

Review

1. What was unique about Andrew Jackson's presidential election?

2. What occurred at the Battle of the Alamo?

3. When was gold first discovered in California? By whom?

4. What was the reason that California became a state quickly?

5. List in chronological order all the events studied to date.

   Next to each list the appropriate dates.

The Battle of Gettysburg
Worksheet

1. In what year did the Battle of Gettysburg take place?

____

____

2. How many days did the Battle of Gettysburg last?

____

____

3. The Battle of Gettysburg was the _________Confederate invasion of the ____________.

4. Why did General Lee invade Pennsylvania?

____

____

____

5 The meeting of the Union and Confederate soldiers at Gettysburg was _______________.

The ___________ moved in and made camp on the neighboring ____________ around the town.

7. What did the Confederates do on the second day?

____

____

____

8. How did General Lee attack?

____

____

____

____

____

____

THE BATTLE OF GETTYSBURG
Worksheet, Page 2

9. Who won the Battle of Gettysburg? How many men did each side lose?

____

____

____

____

10. After Gettysburg, with depleted ____________ and ________ men, the South was easily subdued by the ______________.

THE BATTLE OF GETTYSBURG
Project

BATTLE OF GETTYSBURG (JULY 1-3)

FIRST DAY.—The Confederate advance unexpectedly met the Union cavalry just westward from Gettysburg, on the Chambersburg road. Reinforcements came up on both sides; but the Federal troops were finally forced back, and, becoming entangled in the streets of the village, lost many prisoners. All that night, the troops kept arriving and taking their positions by moonlight, to be ready for the contest which they saw was now close at hand.

SECOND DAY.—In the afternoon, Longstreet led the first grand charge against the Union's left, in order to secure Little Round Top. General Sickles, by mistake, had here taken a position in front of Meade's intended line of battle. The Confederates, far out-flanking, swung around him; but, as they reached the top of the hill, they met a brigade which Warren had sent just in time to defeat this attempt. Sickles was, however, driven back to Cemetery Ridge, where he stood firm. Ewell, in an attack on the Federal right, succeeded in getting a position on Culp's Hill.

THIRD DAY.—At one o'clock P.M. Lee suddenly opened on Cemetery Ridge with one hundred and fifty guns. For two hours, the air was alive with shells. Then the cannonade lulled, and out of the woods swept the Confederate double battle-line, over a mile long, and preceded by a cloud of skirmishers. A thrill of admiration ran along the Union ranks, as, silently and with disciplined steadiness, that magnificent column of eighteen thousand men moved up the slope of Cemetery Ridge. A hundred guns tore great gaps in their front. Infantry volleys smote their ranks. The line was broken, yet they pushed forward. They planted their battle-flags on the breastworks. They bayoneted the cannoneers at their guns. They fought hand to hand so close that the exploding powder scorched their clothes. Upon this struggling mass, the Federals converged from every side. No human endurance could stand the storm. Out of that terrible fire, whole companies rushed as prisoners into the Union lines, while the rest fled panic-stricken from the field.

The Federal loss in the three-days fight was twenty-three thousand; the Confederate was not officially reported, but probably much exceeded that number. Meade slowly followed Lee, who recrossed the Potomac, and took position back of the Rapidan.

The effect of this battle was to put an end to the idea of the South invading the North. Lee's veterans who went down in the awful charges of Gettysburg could never be replaced.

After reading the above summary of the three day Battle of Gettysburg, discuss the event with your teacher.

THE BATTLE OF GETTYSBURG
Project 2

Four score and seven years ago

There are five known "original" copies of the Gettysburg Address. President Lincoln gave two of the original manuscripts to his private secretaries John Nicolay and John Hay. It is unclear and under great debate as to which of these, if any he read in the actual Address. The other three known copies were written for charitable purposes by Lincoln well after November the nineteenth. The Bliss copy which is in the Lincoln room in the White House is one that has been published many times over. We will never know exactly what was said, but we chose to show you one of the original two copies still in existence.

Have your students read the Gettysburg Address out loud and then discuss it.

TRANSCRIPT OF THE HAY COPY OF THE GETTYSBURG ADDRESS—

Four score and seven years ago our fathers brought forth, upon this continent, a new nation, conceived in Liberty, and dedicated to the proposition that all men are created equal.

Now we are engaged in a great civil war, testing whether that nation, or any nation so conceived, and so dedicated, can long endure. We are met here on a great battlefield of that war. We have come to dedicate a portion of it as a final resting place for those who here gave their lives that that nation might live. It is altogether fitting and proper that we should do this.

But in a larger sense we can not dedicate we can not consecrate we can not hallow this ground. The brave men, living and dead, who struggled, here, have consecrated it far above our poor power to add or detract. The world will little note, nor long remember, what we say here, but can never forget what they did here. It is for us, the living, rather to be dedicated here to the unfinished work which they have, thus far, so nobly carried on. It is rather for us to be here dedicated to the great task remaining before us that from these honored dead we take increased devotion to that cause for which they here gave the last full measure of devotion that we here highly resolve that these dead shall not have died in vain; that this nation shall have a new birth of freedom; and that this government of the people, by the people, for the people, shall not perish from the earth.

The Battle of Gettysburg
Project 3

Reading and Reenactment

The Charge at Gettysburg

The battle of Chancellorsville marked the zenith of Confederate good fortune. Immediately afterward, In June 1863, Lee led the victorious army of Northern Virginia into Pennsylvania. The South was now the invader, not the invaded, and its heart beat proudly with hopes of success; but these hopes went down in bloody wreck on July 4, when word was sent to the world that the high valor of Virginia had failed at last on the field of Gettsyburg, and that in the far West Vicksburg had been taken by the army of the "silent soldier."

At Gettysburg Lee had under him some seventy thousand men, and his opponent, Meade, about ninety thousand. Both armies were composed mainly of seasoned veterans, trained to the highest point by campaign after campaign and battle after battle; and there was nothing to choose between them as to the fighting of the rank and file. The Union army was the larger, yet most of the time it stood on the defensive; for the difference between the generals, Lee and Meade, was greater than could be bridged by twenty thousand men. For three days the battle raged. No other battle of recent time has been so obstinate and so bloody. The victorious Union army lost a greater percentage in killed and wounded than the allied armies of England, Germany, and the Netherlands lost at Waterloo. Four of its seven corps suffered each a greater relative loss than befell the world-renowned British infantry on the day that saw the doom of the French emperor. The defeated Confederates at Gettysburg lost, relatively, as many men as the defeated French at Waterloo; but whereas the French army became a mere rabble, Lee withdrew his formidable soldiery with their courage unbroken, and their fighting power only diminished by their actual losses in the field.

The decisive moment of the battle, and perhaps of the whole war, was in the afternoon of the third day, when Lee sent forward his choicest troops in a last effort to break the middle of the Union line. The center of the attacking force was Pickett's division, the flower of the Virginia infantry; but many other brigades took part in the assault, and the column, all told, numbered over fifteen thousand men. At the same time, the Confederates

THE BATTLE OF GETTYSBURG
Project 3, Page 2

attacked the Union left to create a diversion. The attack was preceded by a terrific cannonade, Lee gathering one hundred and fifteen guns, and opening a fire on the center of the Union line. In response, Hunt, the Union chief of artillery, and Tyler, of the artillery reserves, gathered eighty guns on the crest of the gently sloping hill, where attack was threatened. For two hours, from one till three, the cannonade lasted, and the batteries on both sides suffered severely. In both the Union and Confederate lines caissons were blown up by the fire, riderless horses dashed hither and thither, the dead lay in heaps, and throngs of wounded streamed to the rear. Every man lay down and sought what cover he could. It was evident that the Confederate cannonade was but a prelude to a great infantry attack, and at three o'clock Hunt ordered the fire to stop, that the guns might cool, to be ready for the coming assault. The confederates thought that they had silenced the hostile artillery, and for a few minutes their firing continued; then, suddenly, it ceased, and there was a lull.

The men on the Union side who were not at the point directly menaced peered anxiously across the space between the lines to watch the next move, while the men in the divisions which it was certain were about to be assaulted, lay hugging the ground and gripping their muskets, excited, but confident and resolute. They saw the smoke clouds rise slowly from the opposite crest, where the Confederate army lay, and the sunlight glinted again on the long line of brass and iron guns which had been hidden from view during the cannonade. In another moment, out of the lifting smoke there appeared, beautiful and terrible, the picked thousands of the Southern army coming on to the assault. They advanced in three lines, each over a mile long, and in perfect order. Pickett's Virginians held the center, with on their left the North Carolinians of Pender and Pettigrew, and on their right the Alabama regiments of Wilcox; and there were also Georgian and Tennessee regiments in the attacking force. Pickett's division, however, was the only one able to press its charge home. After leaving the woods where they started, the Confederates had nearly a mile and a half to go in their charge. As the Virginians moved, they bent slightly to the left, so as to leave a gap between them and the Alabamians on the right.

The Confederate lines came on magnificently. As they crossed the Emmetsburg Pike the eighty guns on the Union crest, now cool and in good shape, opened upon them, first with shot and then with shell. Great gaps were made every second in the ranks, but the gray-clad soldiers closed up to the center, and the color-bearers leaped to the front, shaking and waving the flags. The Union infantry reserved their fire until the Confederates were within easy range, when the musketry crashed out with a roar, and the big guns began to

THE BATTLE OF GETTYSBURG

Project 3, Page 3

fire grape and canister. On came the Confederates, the men falling by hundreds, the colors fluttering in front like a forest; for as fast as a colorbearer was shot some one else seized the flag from his hand before it fell. The North Carolinians were more exposed to the fire than any other portion of the attacking force, and they were broken before they reached the line. There was a gap between the Virginians and the Alabama troops, and this was taken advantage of by Stannard's Vermont brigade and a demibrigade under Gates, of the 20th New York, who were thrust forward into it. Stannard charged front with his regiments and fell on Pickett's forces in flank, and Gates continued the attack. When thus struck in the flank, the Virginians could not defend themselves, and they crowded off toward the center to avoid the pressure. Many of them were killed or captured; many were driven back; but two of the brigades, headed by General Armistead, forced their way forward to the stone wall on the crest, where the Pennsylvania regiments were posted under Gibbon and Webb.

The Union guns fired at the last moment, until of the two batteries immediately in front of the charging Virginians every officer but one had been struck. One of the mortally wounded officers was young Cushing, a brother of the hero of the Albemarle fight. He was almost cut in two, but holding his body together with one hand, with the other he fired his last gun, and fell dead, just as Armistead, pressing foward at the head of his men, leaped the wall, waving his hat on his sword. Immediately afterward the battle-flags of the foremost Confederate regiments crowned the crest; but their strength was spent. The Union troops moved forward with the bayonet, and the remnant of Pickett's division, attacked on all sides, either surender or retreated down the hill again. Armistead fell, dying, by the body of the dead Cushing. Both Gibbon and Webb were wounded. Of Pickett's command two thirds were killed, wounded or captured, and every brigade commander and every field officer, save one, fell.

The above reading was written by Theodore Roosevelt. After reading this discuss it with your teacher and then do the following reenactment.

The Battle of Gettysburg
Project 3, Page 4

The Battle of Gettysburg
Project 3, Page 5

Reenacting the Battle of Gettysburg

I. Cut out cardboard props to represent the key landmarks at Gettysburg and lay them out as follows: (Note: it is up to the teacher's discression to decide just how precise and artistic these props should be. Keep in mind, however, that their primary purpose is to serve as

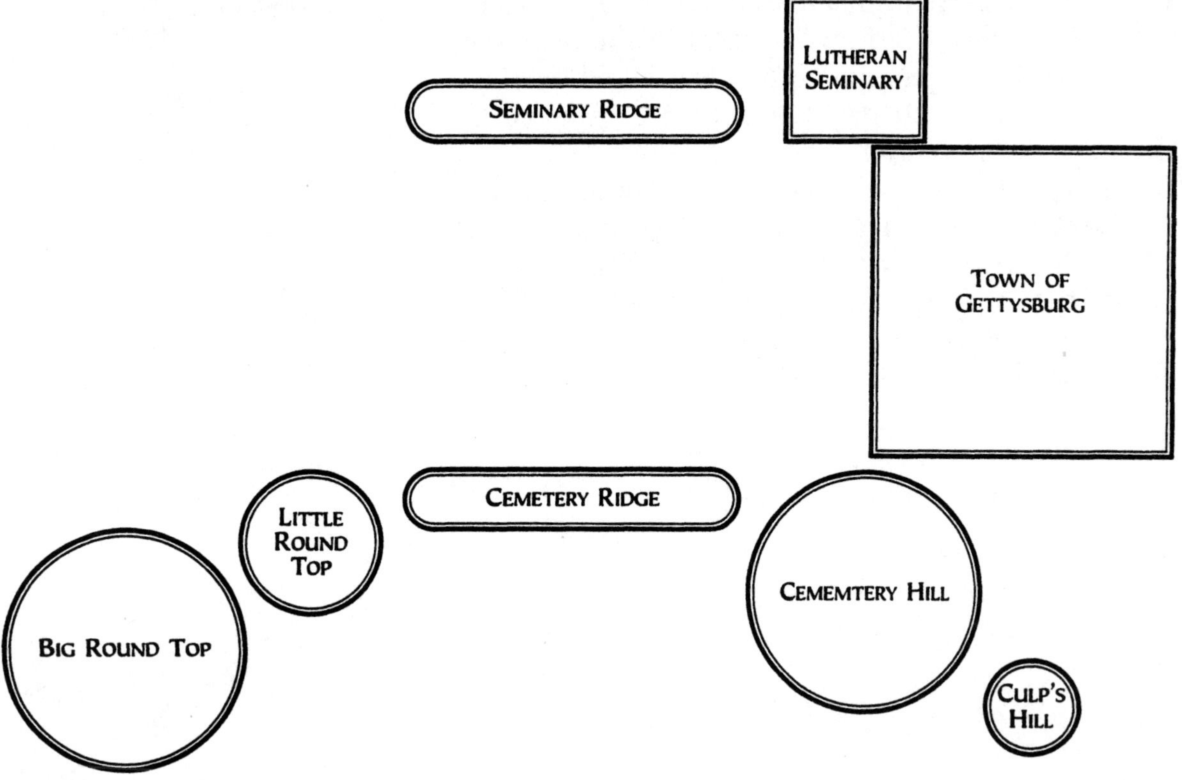

guides for the children by standing on them.)
II. Read the children the narrative for the Battle of Gettysburg.

III. Have them act out the Battle using the 3 days as the basic stages. If possible have the union "forces" slightly outnumber the confederate "forces" (a ratio of 3/2 or 4/3).

THE BATTLE OF GETTYSBURG
Project 4

Making Union and Confederate Flags

Color the flags on the following page or design a flag for your family, school, or state if you were going to secede from the United States of America. Flags were carried into battle by both the North and the South and were symbols of pride for both.

Shown from top to bottom: U.S. National flag at the time of the Civil War; the flag displayed in the Secession Convention at Charleston. The design was based on the State flag of South Carolina; "Stars and Bars" adopted by the Montgomery Convention; "Southern Cross" unofficially adopted by the armies of the Confederacy because "Stars and Bars" had been mistaken in battle for the "Stars and Stripes"; Official flag of the Confederacy adopted in 1863—subsequently a red stripe was added perpendicularly along the outer edge because the flag appeared all white when hanging idle.

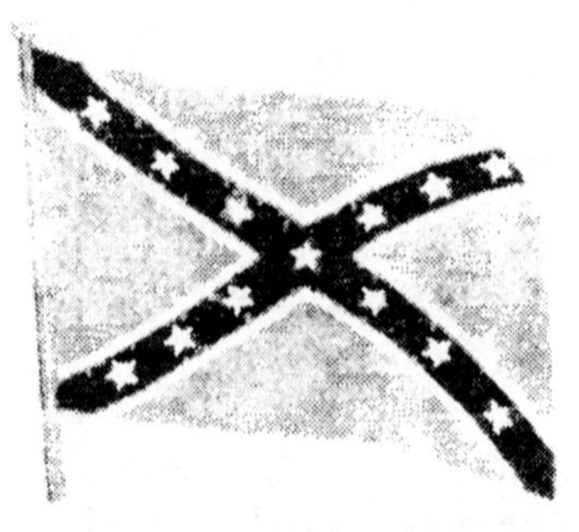

THE BATTLE OF GETTYSBURG
Project 4, Page 2

The Battle of Gettysburg
Project 4, Page 3

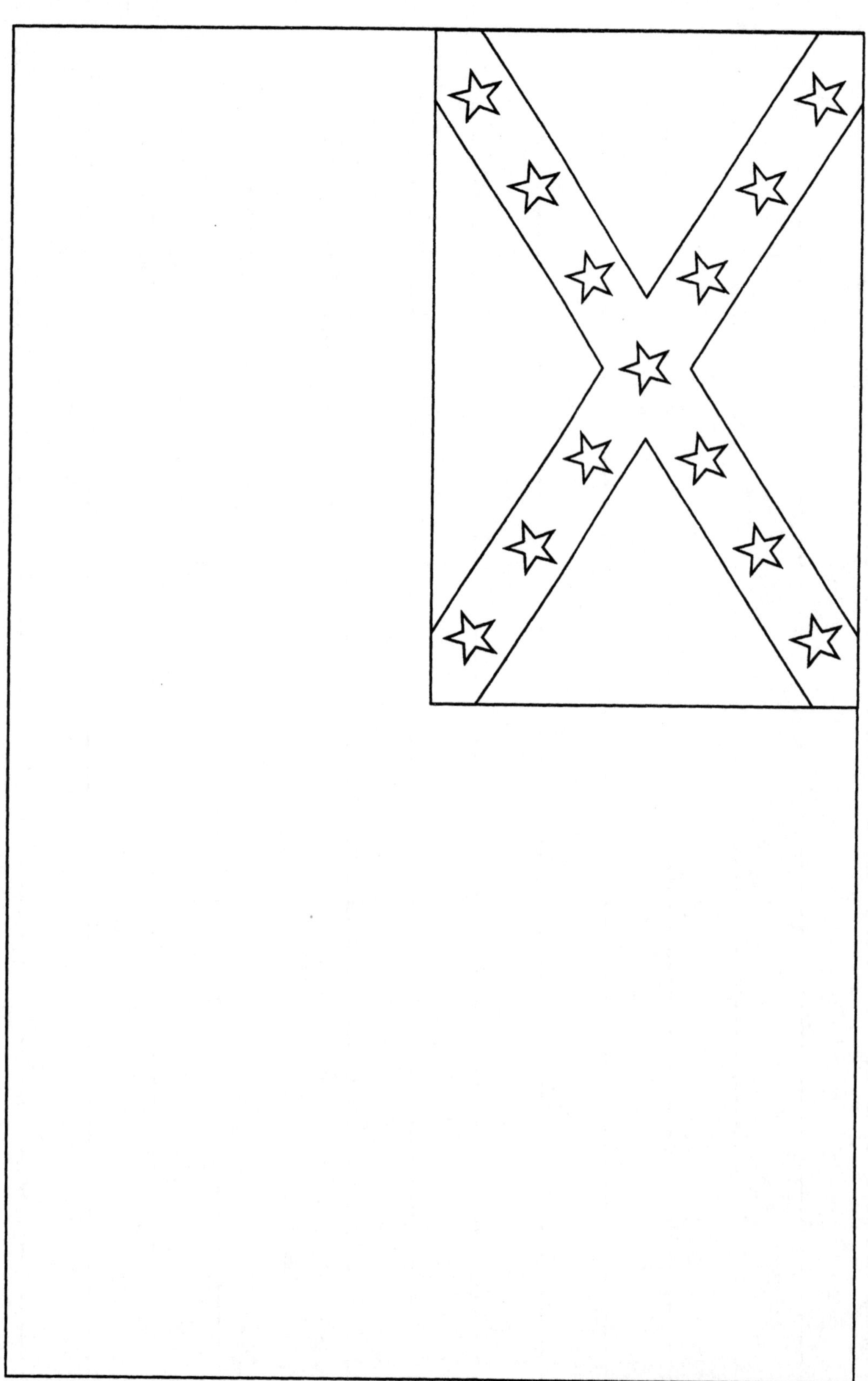

THE BATTLE OF GETTYSBURG
Test

1. In what year was the Battle of Gettysburg?

____

____

2. How long did the Battle of Gettysburg last?

____

____

3. The Battle of Gettysburg was the last ____________ invasion of the __________.
4. What was General Lee's purpose in invading Pennsylvania?

____

____

5. The meeting of the Union and Confederate soldiers was unintentional. How did it occur?

____

____

6. Explain what happened on the second day of the battle.

____

____

____

____

7. What were Generals Lee, Pickett and Pettigrew's involvements in the battle?

____

____

____

____

____

____

THE BATTLE OF GETTYSBURG
Test, Page 2

8. Who won the battle of Gettysburg?

____

____

____

9. About how many men did each side lose?

   Which side was the loss more difficult for and why?

____

____

____

____

____

10. After Gettysburg, with depleted ________ and ________ men, the ____________ was easily subdued by the Union.

Review

1. What did the Monroe Doctrine State?

____

____

____

____

2. Where was Andrew Jackson educated?

____

____

3. Why was the invention of the cotton gin so important?

4. What occurred at the Battle of the Alamo?

5. List in chronological order all the events studied to date.

Great Generals of the War Between the States

Worksheet

1. On which side of the war between the states did Robert E. Lee fight?

____

____

2. What was Lee's home state?

____

____

3. What were Lee's religious beliefs?

____

____

4. To what did Lee urge the country to be loyal after the war?

____

____

5. On which side of the war between the states did Stonewall Jackson serve?

____

____

Lee

Jackson

Grant

Great Generals of the War Between the States

Worksheet, Page 2

6. Who was Lee's right hand man?

7. What were Jackson's religious beliefs?

8. How did Jackson die?

9. On which side of the war did Ulysses S. Grant fight?

10. When Jackson realized he could not win the battle what plan of attack did he take?

11. Which of the above three men became President of the United States?

Great Generals of the War Between the States
Project

On the following pages you will find pictures of Lee and Grant to color. Read the text on the page in order to find out how to color them accurately.

Following each picture you will find a letter written by each of the above men. Read them out loud as a class and discuss them.

'Lee Surrenders at Appomatt

Great Generals of the War Between the States

Project, Page 2

Robert E. Lee

General Robert E. Lee, C.S. Army, 1863. Lee, Commander of the Army of Northern Virginia, is shown in the uniform he normally wore in the field. Lee is wearing a gray felt hat with light brown hatband, instead of the gold-laced kepi. His double-breasted frock coat and trousers are cadet gray. (General officers were supposed to wear dark blue trousers with gold stripes at the sides.) As insignia of rank Lee is wearing three gold stars on his collar rather than the regulation three stars within a gold wreath. Neither is he wearing the prescribed sleeve braid or the buff facings to his coat. His sash and gauntlets are the general officer's regulation buff. His belt is gold with a gold buckle. The binocular case and strap are of brown leather. His sword has a gold hilt and brass scabbard fittings. His scabbard and shoes are made of black leather. The General's shirt is white, his tie black and his vest is gray and his buttons are brass.

Great Generals of the War Between the States
Project, Page 3

Below is a transcription of a letter General Lee wrote to his two daughters.

Savannah 22 Nov 1861

My darling daughters

I have rec[eive]d your joint letter of the 24th Oct: from Clydale. It was very cheering to me & the affection & sympathy you expressed were very grateful to my feelings. I wish indeed I could see you, be with you & never again part from you. God only can give me that happiness. I pray for it night & day. But my prayers I know are not worthy to be heard. I rec[eive]d your former letter in Western Virginia but had no opportunity to reply to it. I enjoyed it nevertheless. I am glad you do not wait to hear from me, as that would deprive me of the pleasure of hearing from you often. I am so pressed with business. I am much pleased at your description of Stratford & your visit. It is endeared to me by many recollections & it has always been a great desire of my life to be able to purchase it. Now that we have no other home, & the one we so loved has been so foully polluted, the desire is stronger with me than ever. The horse chestnut you mention in the garden was planted by my mother. I am sorry the vault is so dilapidated. You did not mention the spring, one of the objects of my earliest recollections.

I am very glad my precious Agnes that you have become so early a riser. It is a good habit, & in these times for mighty works advantage should be taken of every hour.

I regretted much at being obliged to come from Richmond without seeing your poor mother. I hope she is well & happy with her gr[an]dchild. Fitzhugh you may have heard has come in to see his little wife.

This is my second visit to Savannah. I have been down the Coast as far as Amelia Is[lan]d t examine the defenses. They are poor indeed & I have laid off work enough to employ our people a month. I hope our enemy will be polite enough to wait for us. It is difficult to ge our people to realize their position.

I have seen good old Mrs MacKay, now 83, & her daughters Mrs. Joseph Stiles (the mother your friends) & Mrs. Elliott. Mrs Wm H Stiles is in Cass with her gr[an]dchildren. Henry & Robt Stiles are here. You may have heard that Mr. Lowe has been captured on his way fr England & that Mrs Lowe is with the Glens in Baltimore. She I presume will soon be her but he will be detained by our Yankee enemies. Give much love to all with you. Lucien Innes is here,

Your affectionate
R E Lee

Great Generals of the War Between the States

Project, Page 4

Below find a transcript of the Farewell Address of General Robert E. Lee to the Army of Northern Virginia.

Hd Qtrs Army Northern Virginia
10th April 1865

General Order
No 9

After four years of arduous service, marked by unsurpassed courage and fortitude, the Army of Northern Virginia has been compelled to yield to overwhelming numbers and resources.

I need not tell the brave survivors of so many hard fought battles who have remained steadfast to the last, that I have consented to this result from no distrust of them, But feeling that valor and devotion could accomplish nothing that could compensate for the loss that would have attended the continuance of the contest, I determined to avoid the useless sacrifice of those whose past services have endeared them to their countrymen.

By the terms of the agreement, Officers and men can return to their homes and remain until exchanged. You will take with you the satisfaction that proceeds from the consciousness of duty faithfully performed and I earnestly pray that a merciful God will extend to you His blessing and protection.
With an unceasing admiration of your constancy and devotion to your country, and a grateful remembrance of your kind and generous consideration of myself, I bid you all an affectionate farewell.

R E Lee
Genl

Great Generals of the War Between the States
Project, Page 5

Ulysses S. Grant

Major General Ulysses S. Grant, Commander of the Army of the Potomac, U.S. Army, 1865. Grant is wearing a field variation of the regulation general officer's uniform. A black tie and felt hat contrast his white shirt. His dark blue frock coat features black collar and cuffs finished with brass buttons. White stars and gold edging trim his shoulder straps of dark blue. While his vest and trousers are also dark blue. Grant isn't wearing the authorized badge ("U.S." in silver, within a gold wreath) on his hat, the general officer's sash, a sword or sword belt. His shoes are made of black leather.

Great Generals of the War Between the States
Project, Page 6

Lee's Surrender

The great Civil War which was begun on April 12th, 1861, when the first Confederate shot was fired against Fort Sumter, was now drawing rapidly to a close. The backbone of the Confederacy was broken. Lee, the greatest Confederate general still living, with his large army, was yet to be conquered. Lee had defeated the Union soldiers so many times that he began to think his own army was equal to anything. And well he might, for he had defeated at different times four of the greatest generals which the Union army had. His retreat, after being driven from Richmond, was conducted with wonderful skill, and the experience which he had had in the past encouraged him to hope for the best. In starting out he was in excellent spirits, expecting to receive plenty of rations on his journey. He had started out with only provisions enough to last a single day, and you can imagine his surprise, to say nothing of the disappointment, to find that these had been cut off. His men were famishing, and it was impossible to proceed until supplies were obtained from the surrounding country. This delay robbed Lee of the advantages he had gained in the start, and proved the ruin of all his plans.

On the other side, the Union armies were strong and cheerful. The Government had plenty of money to meet all necessity. The combined forces and location of Grant, Sheridan and Meade's armies enabled Grant to take in the situation at once. "Lee is caught," he said, "it will be hard work for him to get away. "Lee was not only cut off from his main line of retreat, but was overtaken by vastly superior numbers of the enemy. Lee's entire force of dispirited and hungry men did not exceed 20,000, while Sheridan alone had an excellent force of 18,000 men. Both Lee's men and horses were sinking from sheer exhaustion. Thousands had let their muskets fall from pure inability to carry them. There are few battles where the horrors of the march could possibly equal these, so when Grant wrote asking Lee on what terms he would surrender, we quote here his reply:

April 7th, 1865.

General: I have received your note of this date. Though not entertaining the opinion you express of the hopelessness of further resistance on the part of the Army of Northern Virginia, I reciprocate your desire to avoid useless effusion of blood, and, therefore, before considering your proposition, ask the terms you will offer on condition of its surrender.
R. E. LEE, General.

GREAT GENERALS OF THE WAR BETWEEN THE STATES
Project, Page 7

Two other letters passed between them and finally April 9th, General Grant wrote the, following letter:

April 9th, 1865.

General: Your note of yesterday is just received. As I have no authority to treat on the subject of peace, the meeting proposed for 10 A. M. to-day could lead to no good. I will state, however, General, that I am equally anxious for peace with yourself; and the whole North entertain the same feeling. The terms upon which peace can be had are well understood. By the South laying down their arms, they will hasten that most desirable event, save thousands of human lives, and hundreds of millions of property not yet destroyed. Sincerely hoping that all our difficulties may be settled without the loss of another life, I subscribe myself,
U. S. GRANT, Lieutenant-General.

After the terms of surrender were made and the papers signed, Lee remarked to Grant that he had forgotten one thing. It was this, many of the cavalry and artillery horses belonged to the men who had charge of them. "It is too late, however," he said, "to speak of that now." Grant replied, "I will instruct my officers that all the enlisted men of your cavalry and artillery who own horses are to retain them 'ust as the officers do theirs. They will need them for their spring plowing and other farm work." Lee seemed greatly pleased and said in reply, "There is nothing which you could have accomplished more for the good of the people, or of the Government." Grant's terms were liberal. He will not only live in iiistory as a great soldier, but he will be honored as a high-souled hero in the hour of victory. Lee then rode back to his soldiers and bade them farewell.. It is said that whole lines of battle rushed up to their beloved general, and with choking emotion wrung his hand. Hard as it was for the soldiers, and hard as it must have been for the whole Southern Confederacy, it is still a pleasure to know that their leading general possessed such tenderness, unselfishness and honor. With tears rolling down both his cheeks, General Lee replied to his soldiers, saying, "Men, we have fought through the war together. I have done the best I could for you."

The war was now practically over.

GREAT GENERALS OF THE WAR BETWEEN THE STATES
Project 2—Literature Unit

With Lee in Virginia—Comprehension Questions

CHAPTER 1

1. How old is Vincent when the story begins?

2. What is the name of Vincent's home?

3. Even though the Wingfield's owned slaves, what did Vincent's father say was "horrible and abominable" about slavery?

4. What was the name of the overseer at the Wingfield estate?

5. At the age of fourteen, what did Vincent do every morning after breakfast?

6. What was the agreement between Vincent and his mother about the flogging of slaves?

Great Generals of the War Between the States

Project 2, Page 2—Literature Unit

Chapter 2

1. What did the slave states threaten to do if a Republican president was elected?

2. Whom did Vincent fight over the whipping of a slave?

3. What did Vincent ask Dan to do?

4. What did Vincent want to happen for the slaves?

5. Summarize Mrs. Wingfield's response to Mr. Jackson's letter.

6. What was Vincent's plan in order to amend for his interference with the flogging of Jackson's slave?

Great Generals of the War Between the States
Project 2, Page 3–Literature Unit

Chapter 3

1. What signal was given to Dinah that she could secretly meet with her husband, Tony?

2. How were runaway slaves able to survive in the woods?

3. Summarize Vincent's plan to help Tony and reunite him with Dinah.

4. Why did Vincent decide to walk to the boathouse instead of ride?

5. What signal did the captain give so that Vincent would recognize the right ship?

6. In which city did Vincent recommend for Tony to settle?

Great Generals of the War Between the States
Project 2, 4–Literature Unit

Chapter 4

1. How much money did the captain charge for Tony's fare?

2. What happened to Dan as the boat sailed back to shore?

3. What prevented Vincent and Dan from reaching shore sooner?

4. What two things was Vincent able to use to find his way back to shore?

5. How long were Vincent and Dan gone on the boat?

6. From whom did Andrew Jackson learn about Vincent's sailing expedition?

Great Generals of the War Between the States
Project 2, Page 5—Literature Unit

Chapter 5

1. In addition to a large population, what gave the North an "immense advantage" `over the South?

____

____

____

2. What act led to Virginia's secession?

____

____

3. Which corps did Mrs. Wingfield want Vincent to join?

____

____

4. Why did Maj. Ashby think Vincent was a first-rate rider?

____

____

____

5. What helpful aide was Vincent able to take along with him to war?

____

____

6. What was the main objective of the Confederate soldiers at Harper's Ferry?

____

____

____

Great Generals of the War Between the States

Project 2, Page 6—Literature Unit

Chapter 6

1. What special duty was given to Vincent because of his fine horsemanship?

2. How far did Vincent ride to take the dispatch to Gen. Johnston? How long did it take?

3. What amazing feat did Col. Stuart accomplish by himself?

4. What strategy did Gen. Johnston employ to detain Gen. Patterson's troops?

5. How did "Stonewall" Jackson receive his nickname?

6. What prevented Vincent from seeing much action at Bull Run?

Great Generals of the War Between the States
Project 2, Page 7–Literature Unit

Chapter 7

1. How did the Confederate victory at Bull Run become a disadvantage for the South?

2. What was different about the Southern balls during the time of war?

3. For what did Gen. Magruder ask Mrs. Wingfield? Why?

4. What was Vincent's new commission after he recovered from his injury?

5. What was the Merrimac? Who controlled it?

6. What federal "surprise" awaited the Merrimac on the second day of battle?

Great Generals of the War Between the States
Project 2, Page 8—Literature Unit

Chapter 8

1. What "delay" saved Richmond?

2. What "evidence" did Vincent say could refute the accusations of cruelty to slaves?

3. Who was responsible for the victory at Cedar Run?

4. What characterized the young men of the 7th Virginia Cavalry before the campaign began?

5. What was Vincent's greatest fear about the outcome of the war?

6. What two "luxuries" did Dan prepare for the soldiers?

Great Generals of the War Between the States
Project 2, Page 9–Literature Unit

Chapter 9

1. What "good news" did Vincent receive from the captain?

2. According to Vincent, what is the only way to ride in the dark?

3. What invaluable item was captured during the raid on Gen. Pope's headquarters?

4. What weapon did soldiers use when their ammunition failed?

5. Why did Vincent remain a prisoner of the North after he had been offered his freedom?

6. Whom did Vincent meet in the prison camp at Elmira?

Great Generals of the War Between the States

Project 2, Page 10–Literature Unit

Chapter 10

1. What did Dan give Vincent the first time he saw him at the prison camp?

2. What did Vincent request from Dan to aid in his escape from prison?

3. What kind of disguise did Dan provide for Vincent?

4. To which city did Vincent go after his escape?

5. What led to the altercation in Vincent's hotel lobby?

6. What "shocking news" did Vincent read in the morning newspaper?

Great Generals of the War Between the States

Project 2, Page 11—Literature Unit

Chapter 11

1. What happened to Vincent on the train to Nashville?

2. Why did Vincent decide not to press charges against his assailant?

3. Why did Vincent leave Nashville earlier than planned?

4. What sight "roused Vincent's indignation"?

5. Why did Vincent go to the small farm house?

6. What did Miss Kingston give Vincent as he was about to leave the house?

Great Generals of the War Between the States
Project 2, Page 12—Literature Unit

Chapter 12

1. Whom did Vincent suspect had told the authorities about his disguise and companion?

2. What was Dan to do if he heard a pistol shot?

3. What happened when Mullens counted, "Two!"?

4. What happened to Miss Kingston when she heard the pistol shot?

5. What gave the impression that a large band of bush-whackers had surrounded the house?

6. How did Vincent plan to protect Miss Kingston?

Great Generals of the War Between the States
Project 2, Page 13—Literature Unit

Chapter 13

1. Why did Vincent's group stop near Mt. Pleasant?

2. What did the newspaper report about the incident at Lucy's house?

3. Who was "Mr. James of Baltimore"? Who attacked him?

4. What "medicines" were required for Vincent's full recovery?

5. How much money did the doctor charge for his services?

6. What other "service" did the doctor provide for Vincent?

Chapter 14

1. What did Vincent carry in the cart? Why?

2. Who escorted the group along their journey?

3. Why did Lucy give a "start of surprise" and flush?

4. What question did Mrs. Wingfield have about Vincent's journey?

5. Who guessed that Vincent was engaged to be married?

6. What disturbing news did Vincent receive upon his arrival at home?

Chapter 15

1. Where did Vincent go with Harry Furniss after he reported for duty?

2. What did Vincent plan to do with his three month leave?

3. What threat did Vincent use to try to get Mr. Jackson to admit he stole Dinah?

4. What did the Union use to cross the river at Fredericksburg?

5. Why did the Federal army not succeed in reaching the Confederate front at Fredericksburg?

6. What did Vincent receive in the mail when he returned home after the battle of Fredericksburg?

Chapter 16

1. Why did Mrs. Wingfield dismiss Pearson?

2. Write a description of Jonas Pearson.

3. What reasons did Dan give for Pearson's involvement in the plot to steal Dinah?

4. According to his lawyer, what was absolutely necessary for Vincent to proceed with his hunt for Dinah?

5. What did the railway man say Vincent should do when he found Pearson?

6. Where did Vincent find Dinah?

Chapter 17

1. What did Mr. Jackson do when he learned of the incident at the Matheson place?

2. What did Vincent do after he returned from rescuing Dinah?

3. According to the author, what was responsible for the death of Gen. Jackson?

4. What mistake resulted in Gen. Jackson being wounded?

5. What was the battle cry of the Confederate army as they attacked Chancellorsville?

6. What was Grant's two-point plan against the Confederate army?

Chapter 18

1. What had been a "heavy blow" to Vincent?

2. For what "dangerous service" did Vincent volunteer?

3. Why did Vincent want some eggs and chickens?

4. What role did Vincent assume when he encountered Gen. Sheridan?

5. Whom did Vincent meet and kill during his spying adventure?

6. Who was the sergeant in charge of watching Vincent?

Chapter 19

1. What was to happen to Vincent because he had been found out as a spy?

2. What was the only plan Tony had thought up to free Vincent?

3. What drug did Tony use to knock-out the sentries?

4. How did Vincent show his gratitude to Mrs. Grossmith?

5. Why did Tony join the Northern army?

6. Why did Vincent decide to row across the river during daylight?

Chapter 20

1. What type of boat began to chase Vincent and Tony?

2. What two things would prevent the soldiers from diligently searching for Vincent and Tony in the swamps?

3. Why was Tony anxious to push on?

4. Where did Vincent decide to go instead of Richmond?

5. What commission did Vincent receive for his brave service?

6. What was Vincent's plan to soften the blow from the abolition of slavery?

Answers

Chapter 1

1. sixteen
2. Orangery
3. selling slaves and breaking up families
4. Jonas Pearson
5. he rode six miles to Richmond to attend school
6. Jonas would appeal to Vincent before flogging a slave

Chapter 2

1. the South would secede
2. Andrew Jackson
3. find out what was going on at the Jackson plantation
4. laws passed to protect against ill-treatment
5. - Vincent acted properly
   - Vincent could defend himself in court and pay any necessary fine
   - people in Virginia looked down upon brutality to slaves
6. buy the slave's wife, Dinah

Chapter 3

1. a nod by Dan
2. friends from plantations left food at appointed spots
3. - get Tony on a boat to England
   - Tony should sail to Canada
   - Tony would contact Vincent once settled in Canada
   - Vincent would give Dinah her papers of freedom and send her to Tony
4. he did not want to attract attention to his extended absence
5. a red flag with a white ball on it
6. Montreal, Canada

Chapter 4

1. none; Tony's work on board would cover the fare
2. he became seasick
3. a gale came up
4. a compass and the sun
5. five days
6. Jonas Pearson

Chapter 5

1. control of the Federal navy
2. Pres. Lincoln called for troops to fight against the Southern states
3. the mounted corps (cavalry)
4. he was able to tame Wildfire
5. his servant, Dan
6. protect the flank of the main Confederate army

Chapter 6

1. carry dispatches between Maj. Ashby and Col. Stuart
2. 50 miles in 5 hours
3. captured 44 Federal infantry men
4. skirmish and retreat
5. his brigade stood like a "stonewall" in battle
6. he was hit by shrapnel from a Federal canon

Chapter 7

1. they became over confident and underrated the North
2. men dressed in uniforms and women wore cheap fabrics
3. the use of slaves to build a "chain of works" between the York and James Rivers
4. aide-de-camp for Gen. Magruder

5. a steamer which the Confederates plated with railroad iron
6. the Monitor

Chapter 8
1. Gen. McClellan overestimated the strength of the Confederate army and did not attack
2. the lack of slave trouble on the plantations while the men were away at war
3. Gen. Jackson and the Stonewall Brigade
4. they had never done half an hour's hard work in their life
5. the Confederates would get used up before the North tired of fighting
6. turkey and rum

Chapter 9
1. his troop was being called up for duty
2. trust the horse
3. a box of official papers
4. piles of stones
5. he refused to go home and not fight any more
6. Andrew Jackson

Chapter 10
1. a watermelon with a note in it
2. 20 yds strong string, 20 yds rope, turn-screw, a disguise
3. a clergy's suit
4. St. Louis, MO
5. a disagreement between the Unionists and the Confederates
6. a description of his disguise and companion

Chapter 11
1. he was attacked by a ruffian
2. he feared being found out as a fugitive
3. the story of his fight on the train was in the newspaper
4. ruined farms and burnt houses
5. to get directions and food
6. two pistols and ammunition

Chapter 12
1. Andrew Jackson
2. stampede the horses
3. he fell back with a bullet in his forehead
4. she fainted
5. the stampeding horses
6. he would escort her to her relatives in Georgia

Chapter 13
1. to tend to Vincent's broken shoulder
2. Mullen's gang had been attacked by Confederate plunderers
3. Andrew Jackson; Tony
4. quiet and patience
5. none; he only wanted a letter indicating Vincent's safe return home
6. he loaned him $100 along with a horse and cart

Chapter 14
1. apples, pumpkins, and other vegetables; to appear as farmers
2. the host from each night's stay
3. Vincent told her he loved her
4. why did he go 70-80 miles out of his way
5. his sister, Annie
6. Dinah was missing

Chapter 15
1. to the Jackson plantation
2. search for Dinah
3. to charge is son, Andrew, with an act of treachery
4. two pontoon bridges
5. they had to cross an open field
6. a letter and photograph from Lucy

Chapter 16
1. he was robbing her
2. tall, thin, short hair, gray goatee, looked like a Yankee
3. -it would vex the Wingfield's
-Jackson paid him
-the slave would bring $1000
4. to be armed with legal powers and backed by the force of the law
5. shoot him on sight
6. in the kitchen at the Matheson house

Chapter 17
1. he put his estate up for sale and left quickly
2. he went to Georgia to get Lucy
3. he caught a cold which resulted in pneumonia
4. his troops mistook him for the enemy and fired upon him
5. "Remember Jackson"
6. -use the greatest number of troops against the main army
-continue hammering until there was nothing left but submission

Chapter 18
1. the death of Gen. Stuart
2. go behind enemy lines and acquire information about their position
3. to sell in the Federal camps
4. he pretended to be a half-wit
5. Andrew Jackson
6. Tony

Chapter 19
1. he was to be shot
2. shoot the sentry and fight the soldiers
3. laudanum
4. gave her $200
5. he heard they were going to Richmond and he thought he could get his wife and child
6. it would be less conspicuous

Chapter 20
1. a steam launch
2. -no reward money
-they might get mud on their shoes and uniforms
3. he would finally see his wife and child
4. to the Orangery
5. Major
6. -give the slaves their freedom
-give the slaves a plot of land to work
-hire the slaves to work the land

1. List four significant facts about Robert E. Lee.

2. List four significant facts about "Stonewall" Jackson.

3. List four significant facts about Ulysses S. Grant.

Review

1. Who was elected President shortly before the War between the States began?

2. Who was Marcus Whitman?

3. Who first discovered gold in California?

4. What was the Cherokee Trail of Tears?

5. List in chronological order the events studied to date.

   Next to each place the appropriate date.

Completion of the Transcontinental Railroad
Worksheet

1. What is the date of the completion of the Transcontinental Railroad?

2. Where did the completion of the transcontinental railroad occur?

3. What did the transcontinental railroad make possible?

4. What were the two companies which did the work on the transcontinental railroad?

5. Who subsidized the work?

6. From what country did 7,000 people come to work on the railroad?

7. What was the background of many of the Union Pacific workers?

8. Why did the Transcontinental Railroad seem to make the nation smaller?

Completion of the Transcontinental Railroad
Project

Do you know why large numbers of Chinese were brought to our country during the Civil War? This story will tell you.

Binding the West to the East

While the overland stage and the pony express were carrying news between the East and the West, the first telegraph reached the Pacific coast. Seven years later the railway followed it.

The Uniting of Railway Lines in the East

Meanwhile, in the East, there were so many short railroads owned by different men and using different widths of track, that the shipping of goods was still slow and costly. Cars on one line had to be unloaded. and their contents carried over to another line. Going from New York to Chicago, freight had to change from one line to another nineteen times.

An old ship captain became interested in this problem. He believed that it would be a good thing to buy a number of these short railroads and unite them into one main line, or trunk line. This man's name was Cornelius Vanderbilt. His friends told him that he would lose all his money, but he did not. His railroads prospered. They became the great New York Central Line, and his family became one of the wealthiest families in America. The Vanderbilts had the help of the great banker J. P. Morgan.

At the same time the railways in Pennsylvania were uniting to form the Pennsylvania Railroad. This line became prosperous largely because of the iron and coal trade around Pittsburgh. It was generally among the first to use new improvements.

These lines and a few others owned many railroads running between the Atlantic seaboard and the Mississippi River. Already they were beginning to use dining-cars and sleeping-cars. They also used double tracks, steel rails instead of iron rails, and were beginning to use larger locomotives, as well as to build iron bridges.

Need of a Transcontinental Railway

When the people of the West learned of the improvements in railway service in the East, they more than ever wanted a railroad. They needed it to take their grain, lumber, cattle, and mules to St. Louis and Chicago. The Mississippi River was no longer a satisfactory route for carrying the trade of the West.

During the second year of the Civil War it was decided that a transcontinental railroad (clear across the continent) would have to be built to California in order to hold that state in the Union. So Congress passed a bill permitting the building of the Union Pacific Railroad.

Railroad Train of the 1830's

COMPLETION OF THE TRANSCONTINENTAL RAILROAD
Project, Page 2

The Building of the Union Pacific

That part of the road which was to be built from California eastward was the harder part. It had to cross high mountains; many tunnels had. to be dug and many snowsheds built. Then it had to cross the deserts. All the iron used had to be brought in ships from the East around Cape Horn, but in the mountains there was plenty of stone and lumber. To build this railroad thousands of Chinese were brought from Asia.

The part of the road which was to be built from Missouri westward was over flat country, but all the supplies, even the wood, had to be brought from farther east. Most of the workers on this railroad were Irishmen who had just come to America.

Surveyors were sent ahead to survey the route; then came men to grade it, so that the roadbed would be smooth, and then men to lay the tracks. As the road was built, locomotives ran over the completed section to bring up the supplies. They had to bring sleeping and eating tents for the workers, supplies for building, and guards to protect them all against the Indians. There was much fighting, and hundreds of workmen were killed. But they laid about two miles of track each day.

At last, four years after the close of the Civil War, the lines coming from the East met those coming from the West. The last tie was laid and the rails were joined. One state gave a silver spike, and another a gold one to use in fastening the rails to the last tie. As these spikes were driven into the wood, the telegraph spread the news over all the country. At last the Atlantic and the Pacific had been joined. The West was firmly united with the East. Columbus's dream had come true after all these years. A short way had been found to trade with the Far East.

Best Friend—*the first passenger train built and used in the U.S., South Carolina, 1833.*

Completion of the Transcontinental Railroad
Project, Page 3

James J. Hill and the Great Northern

The railroad had gone far beyond the settlements. There were no people living in the Rocky Mountain region, and many years passed before a thin line of villages grew up along the tracks. The early transcontinental railways made no money neither the Union Pacific, nor the Northern Pacific, nor the Southern Pacific, which soon followed.

But back in Minnesota a man who kept a little store liked to dream of doing great things. He wanted to build a railroad to the coast, and to build it where the mountains were lowest and where long and heavy trains could therefore be pulled. His name was James J. Hill. In time he got help from some men in Canada.

First these men bought a short line. Then they began to build it steadily through to the coast. At last they succeeded, without having had any help from the government either in money or in land. And from the first their Great Northern Railroad made a profit.

They tried very hard to persuade settlers to move to the new lands along their line, offering them very low rates, and even giving cattle to help them to get started. Soon settlers came in such great numbers that Hill was called "the Empire Builder."

Few great north-and-south railway lines were built until much later.

Thus transcontinental railroads made it possible for the products of the West to reach the East, and the manufactured goods of the East to reach the West. They opened up the Western lands to farmers, they carried away the products of the mines and the farms, and they tied all parts of the Union firmly together as one nation.

Completion of the Transcontinental Railroad

Project, Page 4

A Matching Game

I. Answering these questions will help you to play the game below.
1. What great improvement was made in the short railway lines in the East?
2. When was the Union Pacific Railroad completed?
3. Why did the building of the railroad take a long time?
4. What were some of the results of the building of the transcontinental railroads ?

II. In the blanks below put the corresponding number from the numbered list below. Put a figure 1 before those words which describe Cornlius Vanderbilt, a figure 2 before those words which describe the Union Pacific Railroad, and so on.

_____ the line owned by the Vanderbilts

_____ "the Empire Builder"

_____ a main line that has many branches

_____ a trunk line which first used many improvements

_____ across a continent

_____ the man who was the first to make trunk lines

_____ James J. Hill's railroad

_____ the first of the transcontinental railroads

_____ the banker who helped the Vanderbilts

1. Cornelius Vanderbilt
2. Union Pacific Railroad
3. James J. Hill
4. New York Central Line
5. Great Northern Railroad
6. Pennsylvania Railroad
7. Trunk line
8. J. P. Morgan
9. Transcontinental

Completion of the Transcontinental Railroad

Project 2

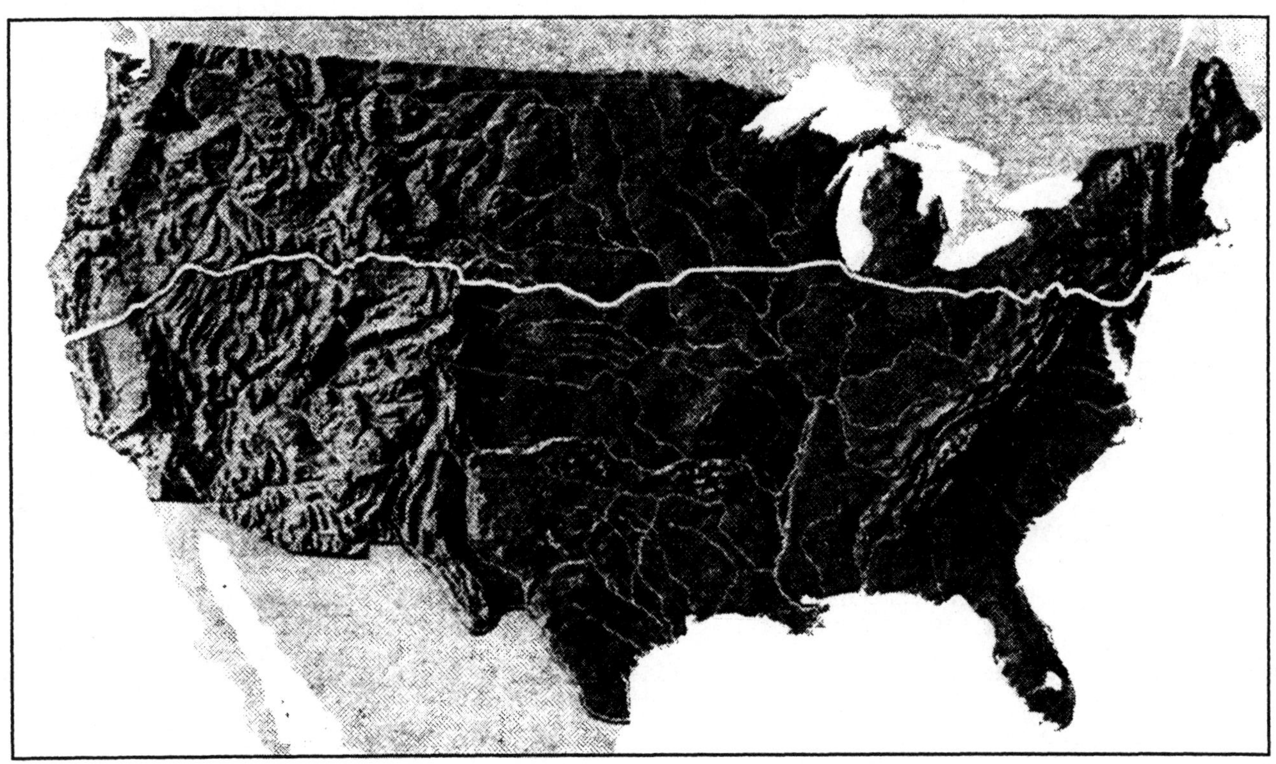

Take a look at the above map and discuss where the transcontinental railroad went across the country.

COMPLETION OF THE TRANSCONTINENTAL RAILROAD
Test

1. When and where did the completion of the transcontinental railroad occur?

____

____

3. With the transcontinental railroad completed how many days did it take to travel from New York to California?

____

____

4. What were the names of the two railroad companies which did the work on the transcontinental railroad? Also include which direction they worked (from east or west) and what the people were like that worked on each line.

____

____

____

5. Who subsidized the work on the transcontinental railroad?

____

____

6. Railroad work was hazardous. Name some of the problems the men faced.

____

____

7. Why did the transcontinental railroad seem to make the nation smaller?

____

____

____

____

Completion of the Transcontinental Railroad

Test, Page 2

Review

1. What is another name for the War Between the States?

2. Who was the sixteenth president of the United States?

3. What was the cause of the War with Mexico?

4. What was the "Underground Railroad?"

5. List in chronological order all the events studied to date.

   Next to each one list the appropriate date.

Reconstructing the South
Worksheet

1. When was "Reconstruction?"

2. Where was Lincoln assassinated?

3. Who succeeded Lincoln as president? Did he support "Reconstruction?"

4. What was the 13th amendment to the Constitution?

5. What was the 14th amendment to the Constitution?

6. What was the 15th amendment to the Constitution?

7. Was "Reconstruction" successful? Why or why not?

Ford's Theatre in Washington, D.C.

Reconstructing the South
Project

The Tailor Who Became President

There are many things which have had to do with making men Presidents of the United States, but it was not until April, 1865, that murder was one of those things. In that fair month, just after the Civil War came to its end, and peace and happiness seemed ready again to settle down upon the land, the foul hand of a murderer took from us one of the best Presidents we had ever known, the revered Abraham Lincoln. Then, according to law, Andrew Johnson, the Vice-President, became President.

He and Abraham Lincoln, who were, elected together to these two great offices, both began life as very poor boys. Johnson began, in one way, lower than Lincoln, for he did not even know how to read and write until after he was sixteen years old, and by that age Lincoln had read many books and was getting to be what the people called learned.

Andrew Johnson was born in the city of Raleigh, North Carolina, on the 29th of September, 1808. Like Lincoln, he was born in a small log-cabin. His parents belonged to that class known as "poor white trash," whom even the slaves of the South looked down on and despised. But his father must have been a good and brave man, for he was drowned in trying to save a friend who had fallen overboard.

Little Andrew was then only four years old. His mother had to work hard to keep both of them alive, and he had to help all he could, so he had no chance to go to school. He was only ten years old when he was made a tailor's apprentice, and he worked hard for five years before he ever heard a man read. In those days there was not much education for the poor, and hardly any at all in the South.

When the ignorant prentice boy heard a man read to the tailors he thought it was wonderful. It seemed to him almost like magic. A strong wish came to him to do this wonderful thing himself, and he got some of the men in the shop to teach him his letters. He was quick to learn them, for he had a very good mind.

But Andrew Johnson did not get what we may call an education until he was eighteen years old, and then he owed it to a good woman whom he made his wife. His mother and he had moved to Greenville, a small town in the mountain part of Tennessee, and here he did the best thing in his life, for he met and married a bright young girl who was well educated and had read a great many books.

The young couple were poor enough, but they both wanted to get on in life, and the young wife, who was a very attractive and ambitious girl, set herself to teaching her husband. She read to him while he worked at his trade, and in the evenings she became an earnest teacher and he became an eager pupil. In that way he soon got something of an education. He had a very good memory and held on to all that was read to him or that he read himself, and few boys ever got along more rapidly than the poor young tailor under the careful teaching of his wife.

The little house in Greenville where Andrew Johnson worked at his trade, is still standing; and on it hangs his old sign, "A. Johnson, Tailor."

Reconstructing the South
Project, Page 2

Young Johnson soon began to take part in affairs in his town. From the first he was on the side of the poor. He was one of them, and knew all they had to bear. And he soon showed that he was a born orator. He could speak in a sharp and fiery manner that took with all who heard it, and the people who lived near gathered in numbers to hear him. When he was only twenty they elected him for one of their aldermen, and when he was twenty-two he was made mayor of Greenville. That was getting along very fast for the boy who had first begun to read six years before.

And now we come to the story of the rapid way the tailor's apprentice climbed upward. When he was twenty-seven his friends, the common people, sent him to the Tennessee Legislature, first to the House and afterward to the Senate. That was not honor enough for their favorite, and he was sent to Congress in 1843 and kept there for ten years. In 1853 came another great lift, for he was elected Governor of Tennessee. When his term was up he was elected again. The tailor of Greenville was getting along famously, was he not?

In fact, there was then no more popular man in the State of Tennessee than Andrew Johnson. He kept doing things that amazed and interested the people. He was not ashamed of his early business, and here is one of the odd things he did when he was Governor of Tennessee. He made with his own hands a very handsome suit of clothes and sent it as a present to the Governor of Kentucky, one of his old friends. But the Kentucky Governor had been a blacksmith in his young days, and was not ashamed of it either, so he forged on the anvil a shovel and tongs and sent them to Governor Johnson, saying that he "hoped they would keep alive the flame of their old friendship."

When Johnson's second term as Governor had ended he was as great a favorite as ever, and was elected to a still higher office, that of Senator of the United States. This was in 1857 when politics in Congress were red-hot. He was a Democrat and a Southerner, and might be expected to be a strong advocate for the cause of the slave-holders, but he was not. Nearly all the States of the South voted to leave the Union, and to form what they named "The Confederate States of America," of which Jefferson Davis of Mississippi was the first and only President. But Andrew Johnson worked with all his strength to save Tennessee, and keep it in the old Union.

President Lincoln made Andrew Johnson Military Governor of Tennessee. He went South determined to hold, by the hand of authority, what had been gained by the hand of war. He did not mince words with his enemies, but threatened to send them to prison or to hang them. When the mayor and council of Nashville refused to take the oath of obedience to the government he locked them up in the city jail.

Some time after that the Confederate armies marched back into the State. Their coming filled many people with alarm, but it did not frighten the bold Governor. This is what he said: "I am no military man, but any one who talks of surrendering I will shoot." You may be sure that all this made Governor Johnson very popular in the North, and that, in 1864, it brought him the nomination for the Vice-Presidency.

The greatest day and most famous speech of Andrew Johnson came in October, 1864. Then, in the streets of Nashville, a great assembly of colored men gathered to hear him speak. Never did he show more fire and spirit. The vast audience went wild with enthusiasm. When he reached the climax of his speech, and said that he would be the

Reconstructing the South
Project, Page 3

Moses to lead them from bondage into liberty and peace, his hearers broke into sobs of feeling and shouts of joy. That speech went like wildfire through the North. It won him a host of votes. A week or two after that he was elected Vice-President of the United States. Inauguration day came on the 4th of March, 1865, and six weeks later the murder of Abraham Lincoln lifted Andrew Johnson to the highest place in his country, that of President of the United States. Never had the country known anything like the progress of these two men, Lincoln from the lowly position of wood-chopper, and Johnson's from the bench of the tailor's apprentice, to preside over one of the greatest nations of the earth and make the White House at Washington their palatial home.

The war was at an end. The South, which had fought with all its strength, lay conquered and prostrate before the Government at Washington. To the astonishment of everybody the new President did not treat the South with severity. Instead of seeking to punish the rebels severely, he wished to let them off without any punishment at all. He did not wait for Congress to act, but at once invited them back into the Union, without asking of them any security against future troubles.

The whole country stood amazed. The members of Congress were made angry by his hasty action which almost everybody in the North thought unwise, and even dangerous. When they came together in December they hastened to undo all that the President had done, and made it plain that the South would not be brought back into the Union until the powers of secession were tied hand and foot.

Then there came a war of a different kind from that in the field. It was between the President and Congress. He went so far at length that they declared he had broken the Constitution and must be impeached that is, put on trial for what were called "high crimes and misdemeanors."

Never before had such a charge been brought against a President of the United States. It is to be hoped it never will be again. The Senate of the United States was formed into a great court, before which the President was tried as a breaker of the law and a traitor to his oath. He was not convicted; it took a two-thirds vote to do that; but he escaped by only a single vote. Soon after that his term of office came to an end and he was succeeded by a very different man, Ulysses S. Grant, the great war general. But President Johnson had many friends in the South, for his course as President had pleased the Southern people

highly, and six years after his term as President had ended he was sent back to the Senate by Tennessee. But his term was very short, for in July, 1875, soon after he had returned to Tennessee from his first session in Congress, he suddenly died.

No other President ever had so stormy a career as Andrew Johnson. Yet he was a man of kindly nature and had qualities which endeared him to his friends. He always had women of fine character about him. His wife, who had done so much to start him in his career, was too feeble in health to take on herself the duties of mistress of the White House, but her daughter, Mrs. Martha Patterson, took her place, and performed the social duties of the position with suitable grace and dignity. He was surrounded to the last by those who loved and believed in him, and died in the full assurance that he had done his best for the country's welfare, and had been very badly treated by Congress.

After reading about Andrew Johnson, use the next page to build a web about his life. Fill in each of the circles with the information listed below the circle. You do not need to use complete sentences.

RECONSTRUCTING THE SOUTH

Project, Page 5

Marriage

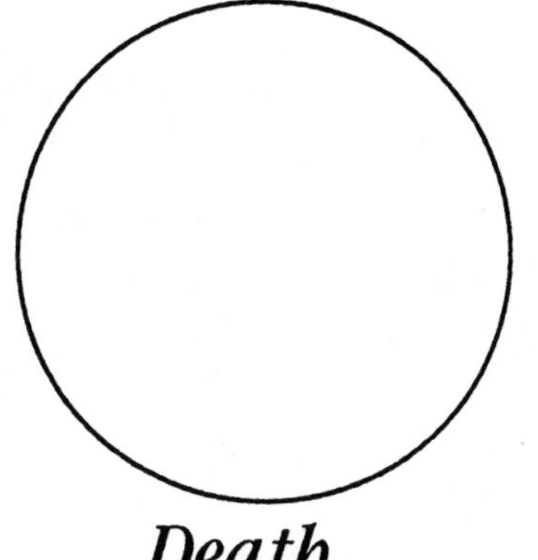

Death

Childhood

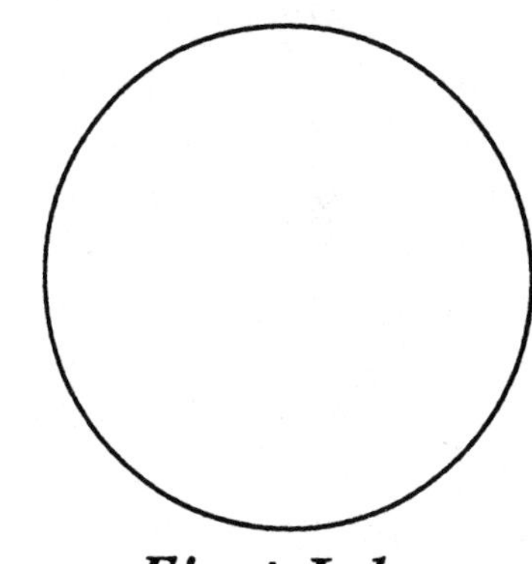

First Job

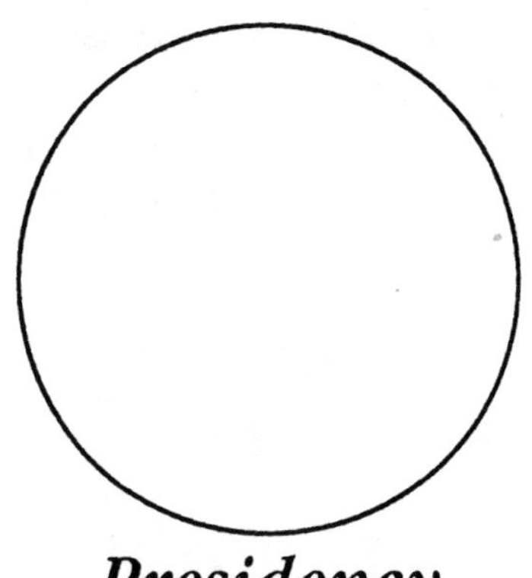

Presidency

ANDREW JOHNSON

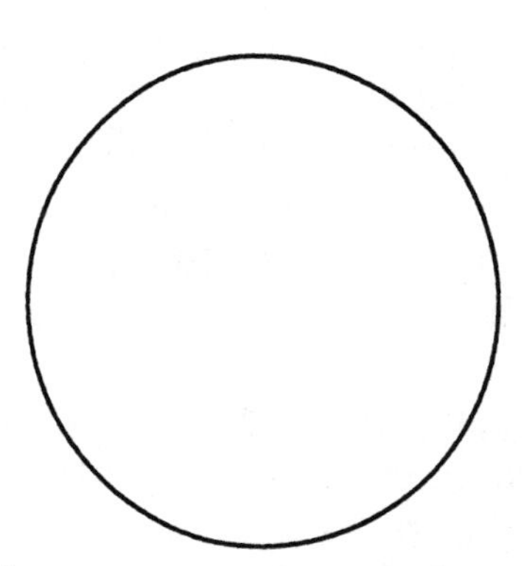

Tennessee Legislature

Vice-presidency

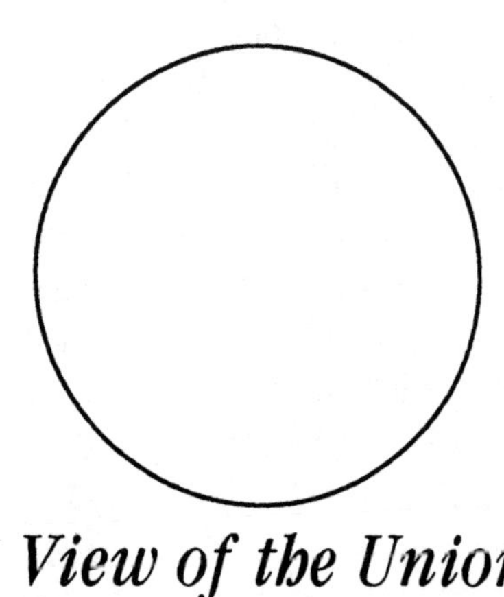

View of the Union

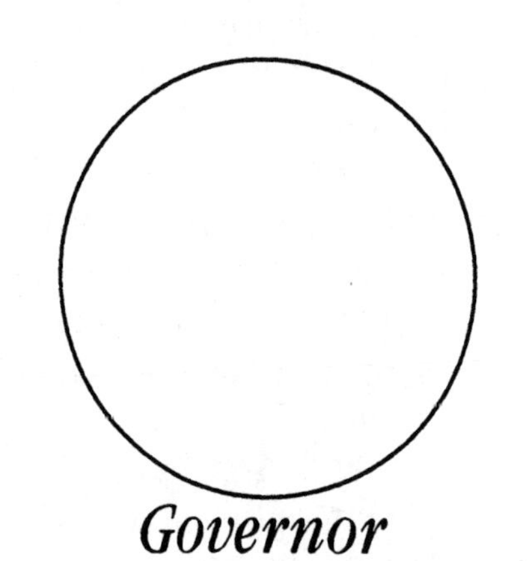

Governor

RECONSTRUCTING THE SOUTH
Project 2

Report of the Joint Committee on Reconstruction, June 20, 1866

A claim for the immediate admission of senators and representatives from the so-called Confederate States has been urged, which seems to your committee not to be founded either in reason or in law, and which cannot be passed without comment. Stated in a few words, it amounts to this: That inasmuch as the lately insurgent States had no legal right to separate themselves from the Union, they still retain their positions as States, and consequently the people thereof have a right to immediate representation in Congress without the imposition of any conditions whatever. . . . It has even been contended that until such admission all legislation affecting their interests is, if not unconstitutional, at least unjustifiable and oppressive.

It is believed by your Committee that these propositions are not only wholly untenable, but, if admitted would tend to the destruction of the government.

It must not be forgotten that the people of these States, without justification or excuse, rose in insurrection against the United States. They deliberately abolished their State governments so far as the same connected them politically with the Union. . . . They opened hostilities and levied war against the government. They continued this war for four years with the most determined and malignant spirit. . . . Whether legally and constitutionally or not, they did, in fact, withdraw from the Union and made themselves subjects of another government of their own creation. And they only yielded when they were compelled by utter exhaustion to lay down their arms . . . expressing no regret, except that they had no longer the power to continue the desperate struggle

It cannot, we think, be denied by any one, having tolerable acquaintance with public law, that the war thus waged was a civil war of the greatest magnitude. The people waging it were necessarily subject to all the rule which, by the law of nations, control a contest of that character, and to all the legitimate consequences following it. One of those consequences was that, within the limits prescribed by humanity, the conquered rebels were at the mercy of the conquerors. That a government thus outraged had a most perfect right to exact indemnity for the injuries done, and security against the recurrence of such outrages in the future, would seem too clear for dispute. .

Your committee came to the consideration of the subject referred to them with the most anxious desire ascertain what was the condition of the people of the States recently in insurrection, and what, if anything, was necessary to be done before restoring them to the full enjoyment of all their original privileges. It was undeniable that the war into which they had plunged the country had materially changed their relations to the people of the loyal States. Slavery had been abolished by constitutional amendment. A large proportion of the population had become, instead of mere chattels, free men and citizens. Through all the past struggle these had remained true and loyal, and had, in large numbers, fought on the side of the Union. It was impossible to abandon them, without securing them their rights as free men and citizens. . . . Hence it became important to inquire what could be done to secure their rights, civil and political. It was evident to your committee that adequate security could only be found in appropriate constitutional provisions. By an original provision of the Constitution, representation is based on the whole number of free persons in each State, and three-fifths of all other persons. When all become free, representation for all necessarily follows. As a consequence the inevitable effect of the rebellion would be to increase the political power of the insurrectionary States, whenever they should be allowed to resume their position as States of the Union.... It did not seem just or proper that all the political advantages derived from their becoming free should be confined to their former masters, who had fought against the Union, and withheld from themselves, who had always been loyal.... Doubts were entertained whether Congress had power, even under the amended Constitution, to prescribe the qualifications of voters in a State, or could act directly on the subject. It was doubtful... whether the States would consent to surrender a power they had always exercised, and to which they were attached. As the best if not the only method of surmounting the difficulty, and as eminently just and proper in itself, your committee came to the conclusion that political power should be possessed in all the States exactly in proportion as the right of suffrage should be granted, without distinction of color or race. This it was thought would leave the whole question with the people of each State, holding out to all the advantage of increased political power as an inducement to allow all to participate in its exercise. Such a provision would be in its nature gentle and persuasive, and would lead, it was hoped, at no distant day, to an equal participation of all, without distinction, in all the rights and privileges of citizenship, thus affording a full and adequate protection to all classes of citizens, since all would have, through the ballot-box, the power of self-protection...

With such evidence before them, it is the opinion of your committed

I. That the States lately in rebellion were, at the close of the war, disorganized communities, without civil government, and without constitutions or other forms, by virtue of which political relations could legally exist between them and the federal government.

II. That Congress cannot be expected to recognize as valid the election of representatives from disorganized communities, which, from the very nature of the case, were unable to present their claim to representation under those established and recognized rules, the observance of which has been hitherto required.

III. That Congress would not be justified in admitting such communities to a participation in the government of the country without first providing such constitutional or other guarantees as will tend to secure the civil rights of all citizens of the republic; a just equality of representation; protection against claims founded in rebellion and crime; a temporary restoration of the right of suffrage to those who had not actively participated in the efforts to destroy the Union and overthrow the government, and the exclusion from positions of public trust of, at least, a portion of those whose crimes have proved them to be enemies to the Union, and unworthy of public confidence.

Reconstructing the South
Project 3

An address to the Loyal Citizens and Congress of the United States of America adopted by a convention of Negroes held in Alexandria, Virginia, from August 2 to 5, 1865.

We , the undersigned members of a Convention of colored citizens of the State of Virginia, would respectfully represent that, although we have been held as slaves, and denied all recognition as a constituent of your nationality for almost the entire period of the duration of your Government, and that by your permission we have been denied either home or country, and deprived of the dearest rights of human nature: yet when you and our immediate oppressors met in deadly conflict upon the field of battle —the one to destroy and the other to save your Government and nationality, we, with scarce an exception, in our inmost souls espoused your cause, and watched, and prayed, and waited, and labored for your success.

When the contest waxed long, and the result hung doubtfully, you appealed to us for help, and how well we answered is written in the rosters of the two hundred thousand colored troops now enrolled in your service; and as to our undying devotion to your cause, let the uniform acclamation of escaped prisoners, "whenever we saw a black face we felt sure of a friend," answer.

Well, the war is over, the rebellion is "put down," and we are declared free! Four fifths of our enemies are paroled or amnestied, and the other fifth are being pardoned, and the President has, in his efforts at the reconstruction of the civil government of the States, late in rebellion, left us entirely at the mercy of these subjugated but unconverted rebels, in everything save the privilege of bringing us, our wives and little ones, to the auction block. . . . We know these men-know them well-and we assure you that, with the majority of them, loyalty is only "lip deep," and that their professions of loyalty are used as a cover to the cherished design of getting restored to their former relations with the Federal Government, and then, by all sorts of "unfriendly legislation," to render the freedom you have given us more intolerable than the slavery they intended for us.

We warn you in time that our only safety is in keep ing them under Governors of the military persuasion until you have so amended the Federal Constitution that it will prohibit the States from making any distinction between citizens on account of race or color. In one word, the only salvation for us besides the power of the Government, is in the possession of the ballot. Give us this, and we will protect ourselves. . . . But, _ is said we are ignorant. Admit it. Yet who denies we know a traitor from a loyal man, a gentleman from a rowdy, a friend from an enemy? The twelve thousand colored votes of the State of New York sent Governor Seymour home and

Reuben E. Fenton to Albany. Did not they know who to vote for? . . . All we ask is an equal chance with the white traitors varnished and japanned with the oath of amnesty. Can you deny us this and still keep faith with us?

We are "sheep in the midst of wolves," and nothing but the military arm of the Government prevents us and all the truly loyal white men from being driven from the land of our birth. Do not then, we beseech you, give to one of these "wayward sisters" the rights they abandoned and forfeited when they rebelled until you have secured our rights by the aforementioned amendment to the Constitution. .

Trusting that you will not be deaf to the appeal herein made, nor unmindful of the warnings which the malignity of the rebels are constantly giving you, and that you will rise to the height of being just for the sake of justice, we remain yours for our flag, our country and humanity.

Reconstructing the South
Test

1. What are the dates for the Reconstruction of the South?

2. Describe what is meant by the term "Reconstruction?"

3. How did Abraham Lincoln die?

4. Who was Andrew Johnson?

5. What was the 13th amendment to the Constitution?

6. What was the 14th amendment to the Constitution?

7. What was the 15th amendment to the Constitution?

8. Describe why "Reconstruction" was not successful?"

Reconstructing the South
Test, Page 2

Review

1. Write a paragraph of at least seven sentences about the most interesting event that you have studied to date. Be sure to include important dates, places and names.

2. List in chronological order all the events studied to date. Next to each place the appropriate date.

Black Leadership Emerges in the South

Worksheet

1. What is the approximate date when Black Leadership emerged in the south?

2. In 1870 the Constitution was amended. What right was given to black men? What happened as a result of this?

3. For what was Booker T. Washington known?

4. From what school did Booker T. Washington graduate?

5. What was the Tuskegee Institute? Who ran it?

6. What is George Washington Carver best known for inventing?

7. Where did Carver teach? What did he urge farmers to do?

Black Leadership Emerges in the South
Worksheet, Page 2

8. What did Carver learn about cotton?

____

____

____

____

____

____

9. From what plants did Carver invent hundreds of products?

____

____

____

____

____

Black Leadership Emerges in the South
Project

How to Grow a Peanut Plant

The peanut plant first came from South America. Shortly after Columbus discovered America, Spanish explorers in Mexico took the peanut back to Spain. From there explorers and traders introduced the peanut to Asia and Africa.

The Africans referred to the peanut as a goober. The peanut may look like a nut, but it is really a pea. They were used as a cheap source of food and brought over on the ships to North America with slaves to be sold.

When the boll weevil, a bug, began to eat crops in the south a scientist named George Washington Carver came to the rescue. He urged farmers to burn what was left of their infested fields and plant peanuts instead. Carver invented over 300 uses for the peanut, including soap, cosmetics, synthetic marble, bleach, shoe polish and peanut butter.

This is what you will need to grow a peanut plant.

Materials
1. Large, deep pot
2. Soil
3. Raw peanuts without their shell that have been soaked in water overnight.
4. Small spade

Instructions
1. Place the soil in the pot, filling it to about one inch below the rim and loosen it with the spade.
2. Dig a small hole and plant the seeds (peanuts) about two inches deep and cover with the loose soil.
3. Water the seeds, but too much water will drown the plants.
4. The peanut plant needs direct sunlight and should not be any colder than 65 degrees Fahrenheit.

Black Leadership Emerges in the South

Project 2

Peanut Butter Recipe

You may want to try your hand at making homemade peanut butter.

Ingredients

2 cups shelled fresh roasted peanuts
2 tblsp. salad oil
1 blender

Instructions

Place the shelled peanuts into a blender. Add oil. Turn on the blender from low to high speed. Blend the mixture until chunky or smooth.

Black Leadership Emerges in the South
Project 3

The Religious Life of the Negro. by Booker T. Washington
—North American Review 181 (July 1905): 20-23.

In everything that I have been able to read about the religious life of the Negro, it has seemed to me that writers have been too much disposed to treat of it as something fixed and unchanging. They have not sufficiently emphasized the fact that the Negro people, in respect to their religious life, have been, almost since they landed in America, in a process of change and growth.

The Negro came to America with the pagan idea of his African ancestors; he acquired under slavery a number of Christian ideas, and at the present time he is slowly learning what those ideas mean in practical life. He is learning, not merely what Christians believe, but what they must do to be Christians.

The religious ideas which the Negroes brought with them to America from Africa were the fragments of a system of thought and custom, which, in its general features, is common to most barbarous people. What we call "fetichism" is, I suppose, merely the childish way of looking at and explaining the world, which did not, in the case of the people of West Africa, preclude a belief in the one true God, although He was regarded by them as far away and not interested in the little affairs of men.

But the peculiarity of their primitive religion, as I have learned from a very interesting book written by one who has been many years a missionary in Africa, consists in this, that it sought for its adherents a purely "physical salvation."

In the religion of the native African there was, generally speaking, no place of future reward or punishment, no heaven and no hell, as we are accustomed to conceive them. For this reason, the Negro had little sense of sin. He was not tortured by doubts and fears, which are so common and, we sometimes feel, so necessary a part of the religious experiences of Christians. The evils he knew were present and physical.

During the period of servitude in the New World, the Negro race did not wholly forget the traditions and habits of thought that it brought from Africa. But it added to its ancestral stock certain new ideas.

Slavery, with all its disadvantages, gave the Negro race, by way of recompense, one great consolation, namely, the Christian religion and the hope and belief in a future life. The slave, to whom on this side of the grave the door of hope seemed closed, learned from Christianity to lift his face from earth to heaven, and that made his burden lighter. In the end, the hope and aspiration of the race in slavery fixed themselves on the vision of the resurrection, with its "long white robes and golden slippers."

This hope and this aspiration, which are the theme of so many of the old Negro hymns, found expression in the one institution that slavery permitted to the Negro people – the Negro Church. It was natural and inevitable that the Negro Church, coming into existence as it did under slavery, should permit the religious life of the Negro to express itself in ways almost wholly detached from morality. There was little in slavery to encourage the sense of personal responsibility.

The attitude of some Negro communities in this respect is very clearly illustrated in the story of the slave who was a "professor" of religion, in the current phrase of the time, but made his master so much trouble by his persistence in certain immoral practices that it was finally necessary to call in a clergyman to try to reform him. The clergyman made the attempt, and sought to bring the terrors of the law to bear upon the slave's conscience.

"Look yeah, Massa," said the culprit, "don't de Scripture say, Dem who b'lieves an' is baptize' shall be saved?"

"Certainly," was the reply, and the clergyman went on to explain the passage to him, but the slave interrupted him again.

"Jus' you tell me now, Massa, don't de good book say dese words: 'Dem as b'lieve and is baptize' shall be saved?'"

"Yes, but — "

"Dat's all I want to know, sar. Now, wat's de use of talkin' to me. You ain't ago'n to make me believe wat de blessed Lord say ain't so, not if you tries forever."

This illustrates one of the difficulties that we have to contend with today. In our Tuskegee Negro Conference, we have constantly to insist that the people draw moral distinctions within the limits of their own communities, that they get rid of immoral ministers and school-teachers, and refuse to associate with people whom they know to be guilty of immoral practices.

It has been said that the trouble with the Negro Church is that it is too emotional. It seems to me that what the Negro Church needs is a more definite connection with the social and moral life of the Negro people. Could this connection be effected in a large degree, it would give to the movement for the upbuilding of the race the force and inspiration of a religious motive. It would give to the Negro religion more of that missionary spirit, the spirit of service, that it needs to purge it of some of the worst elements that still cling to it.

The struggle to attain a higher level of living, to get land, to build a home, to give their children an education, just because it demands more earnestness and steadfastness of purpose, gives a steadiness and a moral significance to the religious life, which is the thing the Negro people need at present.

A large element of the Negro Church must be recalled from its apocalyptic vision back to the earth; the members of the Negro race must be taught that mere religious emotion that is guided by no definite idea and is devoted to no purpose is vain.

It is encouraging to notice that the leaders of the different denominations of the Negro Church are beginning to recognize the force of the criticism made against it, and that, under their leadership, conditions are changing. In one of these denominations, the A. M. E. Zion Church alone, $2,000,000 was raised, from 1900 to 1904, for the general educational, moral and material improvement of the race. Of this sum, $1,000,000 was contributed for educational purposes alone. The A. M. E. Church and the Baptists did proportionally as well.

The mere fact that this amount of money has been raised for general educational purposes, in addition to the sum expended in each local community for teachers, for building schoolhouses and supplementing the State appropriations for schools, shows that the colored people have spent less money in saloons and dispensaries; that less has been squandered on toys and gimcracks that are of no use. It shows that there has been more saving, more thought for the future, more appreciation of the real value of life.

Black Leadership Emerges in the South
Project 3, Page 3

In this connection, it is well to have in mind that the industrial schools have performed a great and useful service, in so far as they have impressed upon the young men who go out from these schools as preachers the importance of learning a trade, something of agriculture, so that they can give the members of their congregations an example of industrial thrift.

At Tuskegee Institute, we insist upon the importance of service. Every student in this department is expected to do, in connection with his other work either as a teacher or preacher, some part of the social and religious work that is carried on under the direction of the Bible Training School in the surrounding country. We are seeking to imbue these young men who are going forth as leaders of their people with the feeling that the great task of uplifting the race, though it may be for others merely a work of humanity, for them, and every other member of the Negro race, is a work of religion.

In this great modern world, where every individual has so many interests and life is so complicated there is a tendency to let religion and life drift apart. I meet men every day who, honest and upright though they be, have lost in their daily lives this connection with religion, and are striving vainly to regain it. There is no one great dominating motive in their lives which enters into every task and gives it significance and zest.

It is one of the compensations which hardships bring, that the race problem is a thing so real and so present to the Negro people that it enters, as a motive, into everything they do. It is this that makes it possible for them to realize that the acts of every individual have an importance far beyond the measure in which they make or mar his or her personal fortunes.

So soon as a man, white or black, really learns to comprehend that fact, he will cease to whine and complain, and he will be content to do his best, humble though it be, to improve his own condition, and to help his less fortunate fellows.

Slowly but surely, and in ever larger numbers, the members of my race are learning that lesson; they are realizing that God has assigned to their race a man's part in the task of civilization; they are learning to understand their duty, and to face uncomplainingly and with confidence the destiny that awaits them.

Black Leadership Emerges in the South

Test

1. In 1870 the constitution was amended. What right was given to black men?

2. Write a short paragraph about Booker T. Washington.

   Be sure to include where he went to school and what his vocation was.

3. Write a short paragraph about George Washington Carver.

   Be sure to include his vocation and inventions.

Black Leadership Emerges in the South

Test, Page 2

Review

1. Why was Abraham Lincoln referred to as the "Log Cabin President?"

2. Who won the Battle of Gettysburg? What impact did this have on the war?

3. What did Eli Whitney invent? Why was this important?

4. Who was Harriet Tubman?

5. In chronological order list all the events studied to date.

   Next to each place the approximate date.

THE AGE OF INDUSTRY
Worksheet

1. What are the approximate dates for the Age of Industry?

___

___

2. What did the completion of the Transcontinental Railroad allow?

___

___

___

3. What did the factories built during the War between the States now produce?

___

___

___

4. New products were created that used __________ and ___________.
5. List some items that caused people to move from the farm to the city.

___

___

___

6. What did huge companies make available to people?

___

___

___

7. List four large company owners and what they produced.

___

___

___

___

THE AGE OF INDUSTRY
Project

Story Telling

Using the resourses listed on the card and others you may find, tell the story of one of the famous industrialists of the time. (Carnegie, Rockefeller, Vanderbilt, etc.)

The Age of Industry
Test

1. What are the dates for the Age of Industry?

2. In what year was the transcontinental railroad completed? What did this allow?

3. Why were most people now wearing machine made clothes?

4. Why was life easier for people to live now?

5. Why were people moving to the cities?

6. Why did huge companies develop?

7. Name two powerful industrialists of the day and tell what their company made.

The Age of Industry
Test, Page 2

1. What state did the Erie Canal cross?

2. Who was the first President from a state not of the original thirteen?

3. When was slave trade first outlawed?

4. Who was Santa Anna?

5. List in chronological order all the events studied to date.

   Next to each place the appropriate date.

The Battle of Little Big Horn

Worksheet

1. What is the date for the Battle of Little Big Horn?

____

____

2. Who fought in the Battle of Little Big Horn? Who won the battle?

____

____

3. Why were the government treaties with the Indians broken?

____

____

4. Why did people flock to the Black Hills of South Dakota in 1875?

____

____

5. What were the names of two Indian leaders who led the Sioux from the Dakotas to Montana?

____

____

6. Many Indian tribes came together to wage a grand battle. Describe what occurred in this battle.

____

____

7. When did Crazy Horse and Sitting Bull die?

____

____

____

____

THE BATTLE OF LITTLE BIG HORN

Project

Below you will find some quotes from Tatanka Iyotake better known to us as Sitting Bull. These should help you to better understand how the Chief of the Sioux viewed the "white man." Information on Custer is not included as it is more readily available in the resources listed on the card. Using this and the references on the card discuss how Custer and Sitting Bull each believed they were right for what they were fighting.

Sitting Bull joined in the attack on Fort Phil Kearny and in the subsequent hostilities, but he accepted in good faith the treaty of 1868, and soon after it was signed he visited Washington with Red Cloud and Spotted Tail, on which occasion the three distinguished chiefs attracted much attention and were entertained at dinner by President Grant and other notables. He considered that the life of the white man as he saw it was no life for his people, but hoped by close adherence to the terms of this treaty to preserve the Big Horn and Black Hills country for a permanent hunting ground. When gold was discovered and the irrepressible gold seekers made their historic dash across the plains into this forbidden paradise, then his faith in the white man's honor was gone forever, and he took his final and most persistent stand in defense of his nation and home. His bitter, and at the same time well-grounded and philosophical dislike of the conquering race, is well expressed in a speech made before the purely Indian council before referred to, upon the Powder River.

Red Cloud

"Behold, my friends, the spring is come; the earth has gladly received the embraces of the sun, and we shall soon see the results of their love! Every seed is awakened, and all animal life. It is through this mysterious power that we too have our being, and we therefore yield to our neighbors, even to our animal neighbors, the same right as ourselves to inhabit this vast land. Yet hear me, friends! We have now to deal with another people, small and feeble when our forefathers first met with them, but now great and overbearing. Strangely enough, they have a mind to till the soil, and the love of possessions is a disease in them. These people have made many rules that the rich may break, but the poor may not! They have a religion in which the poor worship, but the rich will not! They even take tithes of the poor and weak to support the rich and those who rule. They claim this mother of ours, the Earth, for their own use, and fence their neighbors away from her, and deface her with their buildings and their refuse. They compel her to produce out of season, and when sterile she is made to take medicine in order to produce again. All this is sacrilege.

THE BATTLE OF LITTLE BIG HORN

Project 2, Page 2

Other Quotes by Sitting Bull

"In my early days, I was eager to learn and to do things, and therefore I learned quickly. Each man is good in the sight of the Great Spirit."

"What white man can say I ever stole his land or a penny of his money? Yet they say that I am a thief. What white woman, however lonely, was ever captive or insulted by me? Yet they say I am a bad Indian.

"What white man has ever seen me drunk? Who has ever come to me hungry and left me unfed? Who has seen me beat my wives or abuse my children? What law have I broken?

"Is it wrong for me to love my own? Is it wicked for me because my skin is red? Because I am Sioux? Because I was born where my father lived? Because I would die for my people and my country? God made me an Indian."

The Battle of Little Big Horn

Test

Write an essay describing the Battle of Little Big Horn. Be sure to include dates, places, names and details.

The Battle of Little Big Horn
Test, Page 2

Review

1. What was the Monroe Doctrine?

2. What was "Reconstruction" of the south?

3. Describe one of the famous generals of the War beteen the states.

4. What was the Pony Express?

5. In chronological order list all the events studied to date.

   Next to each place the approximate date.

COWBOYS AND THE WEST
Worksheet

1. What is the date for the Cowboys and the West?

____

____

2. For what was the cowboy first needed?

____

____

3. Why were cows put on the trains?

____

____

____

4. What was The Chisholm Trail?

____

____

____

____

5. What did cowboys wear out on the range?

____

____

6. When did the cowboy trail period end?

____

____

7. Lots of ________, __________, and __________ have been made about the cowboy, settling the west, outlaws, and sheriffs.

COWBOYS AND THE WEST

Project

The Marks of a Cowboy

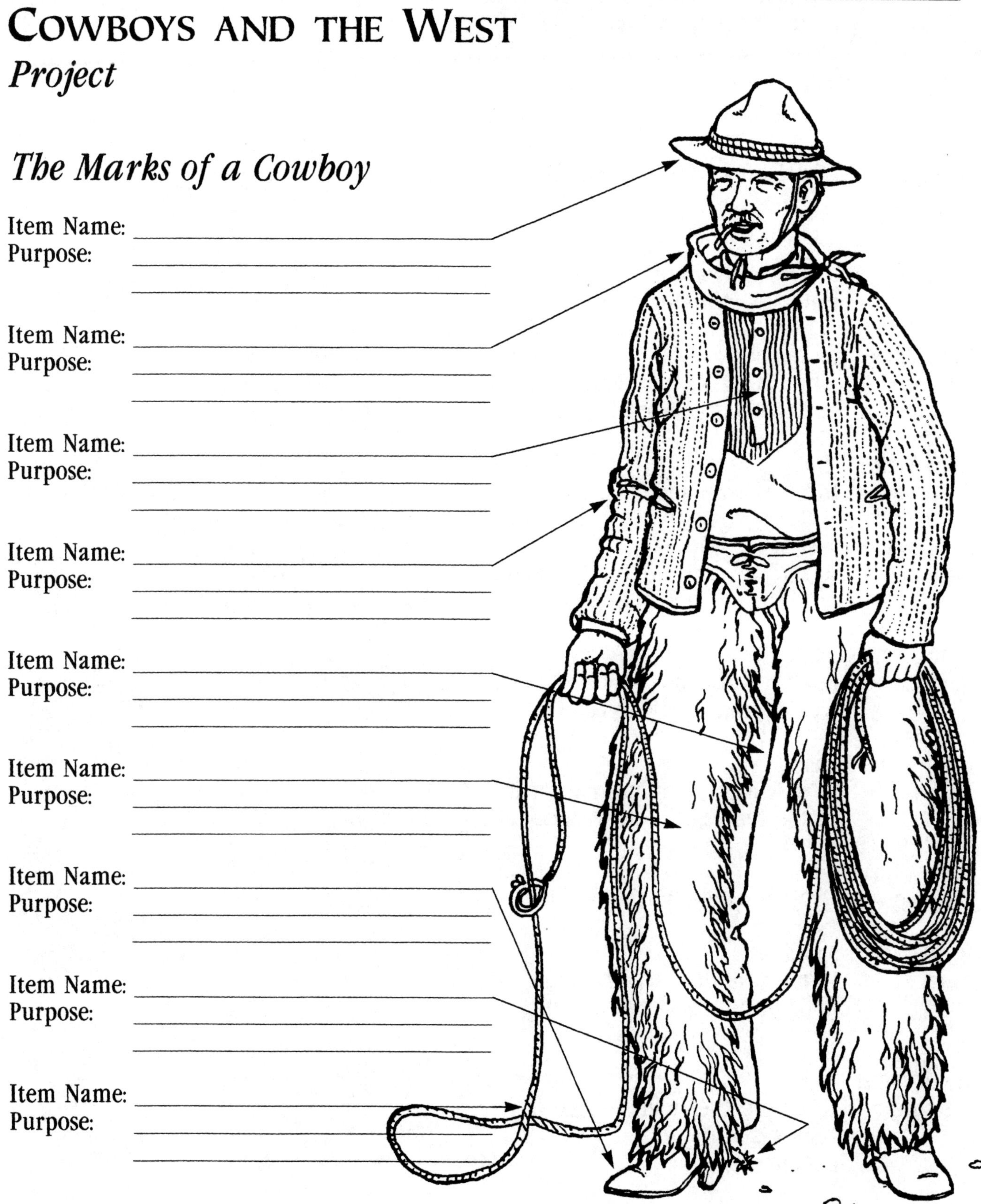

Item Name: ____________________
Purpose: ____________________
____

Item Name: ____________________
Purpose: ____________________
____

Item Name: ____________________
Purpose: ____________________
____

Item Name: ____________________
Purpose: ____________________
____

Item Name: ____________________
Purpose: ____________________
____

Item Name: ____________________
Purpose: ____________________
____

Item Name: ____________________
Purpose: ____________________
____

Item Name: ____________________
Purpose: ____________________
____

Item Name: ____________________
Purpose: ____________________
____

Using the resources listed on the card (particularly Cowboy, An Album*) fill in the information about the items and purposes of a cowboy's attire.*

Cowboys and the West

Project, Page 2

The Marks of a Cowboy –Answers

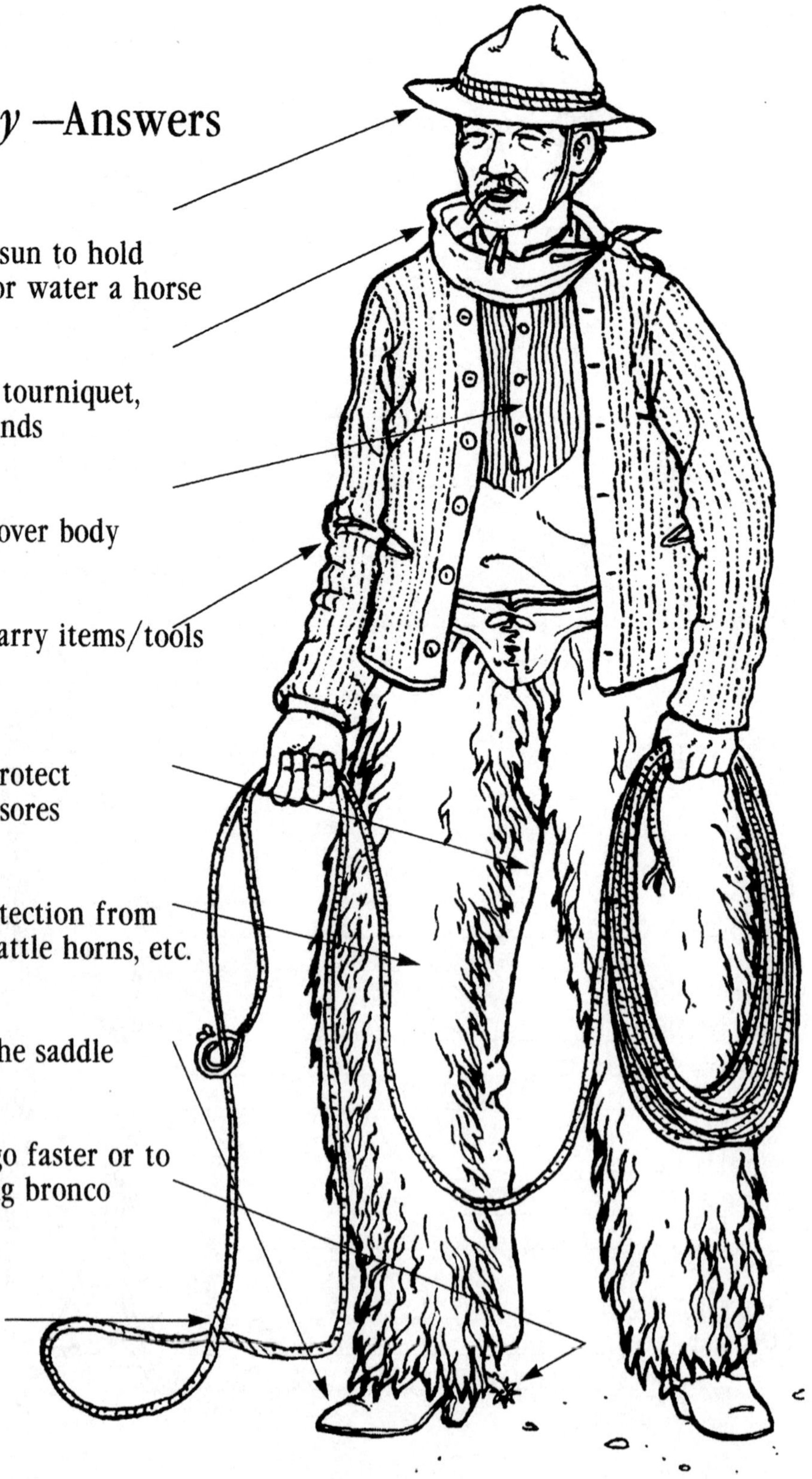

Item Name: hat
Purpose: to protect from the sun to hold water for drinking or water a horse

Item Name: neckerchief
Purpose: a breathing mask, a tourniquet, and to bandage wounds

Item Name: shirt
Purpose: to keep warm and cover body

Item Name: vest or jacket
Purpose: to keep warm and carry items/tools

Item Name: pants
Purpose: to keep warm and protect wearer from saddle sores

Item Name: chaps
Purpose: to provide extra protection from cactus, fences, and cattle horns, etc.

Item Name: boots
Purpose: to brace a rider in the saddle

Item Name: spurs
Purpose: to prick a horse to go faster or to hang on to a bucking bronco

Item Name: rope
Purpose: to lasso cattle, hold horses, and tie equipment

Cowboys and the West

Project 2

Camp Fire Meal

Cowboys worked hard during the day and reguired lots of food to keep going. Most ranchers wanted to keep their hands happy so they hired good cooks to run the chuck wagon. The chuck wagon was the cooks kitchen away from home. It was a wooden wagon built on iron axles so that it could be pulled across the rough trails. The cook traveled ahead of the hands so that the food would be ready at the end of the day. He would make a fire and hang a pot over it to cook what usually was beans and stew.

Below is a recipe to experience a camp fire meal. They may be made over an open fire, or for the less adventuresome, a stove will do.

Campfire Stew

2 pounds sweet Italian sausage (they might have used chicken, armadillo, or even rattlesnake)
2 ounds beef chuck, cut in 1 inch cubes
1 large onion, slice
2 medium coves garlic, minced
2 green peppers, seeded and cut in eights (used to disguise old beef)
1 pound of white beans cooked
1 teaspoon basil
1/2 teaspoon salt
1 teaspoon paprika
1/4 teaspoon pepper
2 beef bouillon cubes disolved in 1 cup boiling water

Cut up sausages and beef and brown in the bottom of the pot. Add onion and garlic. When onion is cooked add peppers then add the rest of the ingredients. Cook over the open fire or stove until the meat is tender.

And don't forget the biscuits and hot coffee!

COWBOYS AND THE WEST
Test

Write an essay to describe the life of cowboys. Be sure to include their purpose, what they wore and why their popularity diminished.

COWBOYS AND THE WEST

Test, Page 2

Review

1. Who was one of the first black leaders in the south?

2. What was the transcontinental railroad?

3. For what side did Ulysses S. Grant fight in the War Between the States?

4. Who was the sixteenth president of the United States?

5. In chronological order list all the events studied to date. Next to each place the approximate date.

THE SPANISH-AMERICAN WAR
Worksheet

1. What is the date of The Spanish American War?

2. What country had been cruelly controlling Cuba for many years in the late 1800's?

3. What is yellow journalism?

4. Why did many believe that the United States should help the Cubans?

5. Who was Frederic Remington?

6. What did President McKinley send to Cuba?

7. When did the United States declare war against Spain?

The Spanish-American War

Worksheet, Page 2

8. Who were the "Rough Riders?"

____

____

____

9. What was one of the main reasons that America lost 5,000 men during the Spanish-American War?

____

____

____

THE SPANISH-AMERICAN WAR
Project

THE CUBAN REBELLION, 1894-98

The Cubans laid down their arms in 1877 because they relied on the promises of better government made by the Spaniards. But these promises were never carried out. Year after year the Cuban people bore their oppression. At last, however, their patience was worn out. In 1894 they again rebelled. The Spaniards sent over an army to subdue them. Soon tales of cruelty on the part of the Spaniards reached the United States. Finally the Spanish governor, General Weyler, adopted the cruel measure of driving the old men, the women, and the children from the country villages and huddling them together in the seaboard towns. Without money, without food, with scant shelter, these poor people endured every hardship. They died by thousands. The American people sent relief, but little could be done to help them. The Cubans also fitted out expeditions in American ports to carry arms and supplies to rebels. The government did everything in its power to stop these expeditions, but the coast line of the United States is so long that it was impossible to stop them all, especially as large numbers of the American people heartily sympathized with the Cubans. Constant disputes with Spain over the Cuban question naturally came up and gave rise to irritation in the United States and in Spain.

THE DECLARATION OF WAR, 1898

On January 5, 1898, the American battleship Maine anchored in Havana harbor. On February 15 she was destroyed by an explosion and sank with two hundred and fifty-three of her crew. A most competent Court of Inquiry was appointed. It reported that the Maine had been blown up from the outside. The report of the Court of Inquiry was communicated to the Spanish government in the hope that some kind of apology and reparation might be made. But all the Spanish government did was to propose that the matter should be referred to arbitration. The condition of the Cubans was now dreadful. Several Senators and Representatives visited Cuba. They reported that the condition of the Cubans was shocking. The President laid the whole matter before Congress for its determination. On April 19, 1898, Congress reorganized the independence of the Cuban

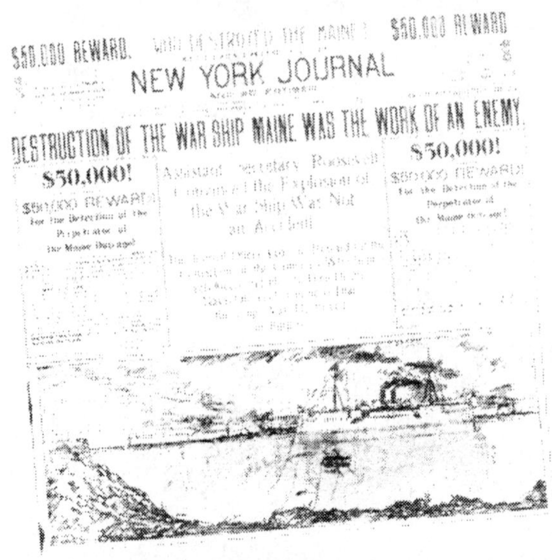

$50,000 REWARD.

$50,000 REWARD

NEW YORK JOURNAL

DESTRUCTION OF THE WAR SHIP MAINE WAS THE WORK OF AN ENEMY.

$50,000!

$50,000!

THE SPANISH-AMERICAN WAR

Project, Page 2

people and demanded the withdrawal of the Spaniards from the island. Congress also authorized the President to compell Spain's withdrawal and stated that the United States did not intend to annex Cuba, but to leave the government of the island to its inhabitants. Before these terms could be formally laid before the Spanish government, it ordered the American minister to leave Spain.

THE DESTRUCTION OF THE SPANISH PACIFIC FLEET

Admiral Dewey commanding the American squadron on the Asiatic station, had concentrated all his vessels at Hong Kong, in the belief that the war was at hand. Of course he could not stay at Hong Kong after the declaration of war. The only thing that he could do was to destroy the Spanish fleet and use Spanish ports as a naval base. The Spanish fleet was in Manila Bay. Thither sailed Dewey. In the darkness of the early morning of May 1, Dewey passed the Spanish forts at the entrance of the bay. The fleet was at anchor near the naval arsenal, a few miles from the city of Manilla. As soon as it was light Dewey opened fire on the Spaniards. Soon one ship caught fire, then another, and another. Dewey drew off out of range for a time while his men rested and ate breakfasts. He then steamed in again and completed the destruction of the enemy's fleet. Not an American ship was seriously injured. Not one American soldier was killed. This victory gave the Americans the control of the Pacific Ocean and the Asiatic waters, as far as Spain was concerned. It relieved the Pacific seacoast of the United States of all fear of attack. It made it possible to send soldiers and supplies to Manila, without fear of attack while on the way. And it was necessary to send soldiers because Dewey, while he was supreme on the water and could easily compel the surrender of Manilla, could not properly police the town after its capture.

THE ATLANTIC SEACOAST AND THE BLOCKADE

No sooner did war seem probable than the people on the Atlantic seacoast were seized with an unreasoning fear of the Spanish fleets. For the Spaniards had a few new fast ships. The mouths of the principal harbors were blocked with mines and torpedoes. The government bought merchant vessels of all kinds and established a patrol along the coast. It also blockaded the more important Cuban seaports. But the Cuban coast was so long that it was impossible to blockade it all. As it was, great suffering was inflicted on the principal Spanish armies in Cuba.

THE ATLANTIC FLEETS

Before long a Spanish fleet of four new, fast armored cruisers and three large sea-going torpedo-boat destroyers appeared in the West Indies. The Spanish admiral did not seem to know exactly where to go. After sailing around the Carribean Sea for a time, he anchored in Santiago harbor on the southern coast of Cuba. In the American navy there

The Spanish-American War
Project, Page 3

were only two fast armored cruisers, the New York and the Brooklyn. These with five battleships - the Oregon, Iowa, Indiana, Massachusetts, and Texas - and a number of smaller vessels were placed under the command of Admiral Sampson and sent to Santiago. Another fleet of sea-going monitors and unarmored cruisers maintained the Cuban blockade.

THE OREGON'S GREAT VOYAGE

When the Maine was destroyed, the Oregon was at Puget Sound on the northwest coast. She was at once ordered to sail to the Atlantic coast at her utmost speed. Steadily the great battleship sped southward along the Pacific coast of North America, Central America, and South America. She passed through Magellan Straits and made her way up to the eastern coast of South America. As she approached the West Indies, it was feared that she might meet the whole Spanish fleet, but she never sighted them. She reached Florida in splendid condition and at once joined Sampson's squadron.

THE BLOCKADE OF THE SPANISH FLEETS

Santiago harbor seemed to have been designed as a place of refuge for a hard-pressed fleet. Its narrow winding entrance was guarded by huge mountains strongly fortified. The channel between these mountains was filled with mines and torpedoes. The American fleet could not go in. The Spanish fleet must not be allowed to come out unseen. Lieutenant Hobson was ordered to take the collier Merrimac into the narrow entrance and sink her across the channel at the narrowest part. He made the most careful preparations. But the Merrimac was disabled and drifted by the narrowest part of the channel before she sank. The Spanish admiral was so impressed by the heroism of this attempt that he sent a boat off to the American squadron to assure them that Hobson and his six brave companions were safe.

DESTRUCTION OF THE SPANISH FLEET

As the American vessels could not enter Santiago harbor to sink the Spanish ships at their anchors, it became necessary to send an army to Santiago. But the Spaniards did not wait for the soldiers to capture the city. On Sunday morning, July 3, the Spanish fleet suddenly appeared steaming out of the harbor. The Massachusetts was away at the time, getting a supply of coal, and the New York was steaming away to take Admiral Sampson to a conference with General Shafter. But there were enough vessels left. On came the Spaniards. The American ships rushed toward them. The Spaniards turned westward and tried to escape along the coast. Soon one of them was set on fire by the American shells. She was run on shore to prevent her from sinking. Then another followed her, and then a third. The torpedo-boat destroyers were sunk off the entrance to the harbor. But one ship now remained afloat. Speedily, she, too, was overtaken and surrendered. In a few hours the whole Spanish fleet was destroyed; hundreds of Spanish seamen were killed, wounded, or drowned, and sixteen hundred Spanish sailors captured. The American loss was one man killed and two wounded. The American ships were ready to destroy another Spanish fleet had one been in reach. At Manila Bay and off Santiago the American fleets were superior to the enemy's fleets. But the astounding results of their actions were due mainly to the splendid manner in which the American ships had been cared for and, above all, to the magificent training and courage of the men behind the guns. Years of peace had not in any way dimmed the splendid qualities of the American sea-fighters.

THE AMERICAN ARMY

Meantime the American soldiers on shore at Santiago were doing their work under great discouragement, but with a valor and stubborness that will always compel admiration. While the navy was silently and efficiently increased to be a well-ordered force, the army was not so well managed at first. Soldiers there were in plenty. From all parts of the Union, from the South and from the North, from the West and from the East, from the cattle ranches of the plains and the classrooms of the great universities, patriots offered their lives at their country's call. But there was great lack of order in the management of the army. Sickness broke out among the soldiers. Volunteer regiments were supplied with old-fashioned rifles. It seemed to be difficult to move one regiment from one place to another without dire confusion. When the Spanish fleet was shut up in Santiago harbor, a force of fifteen thousand soldiers under General Shafter was sent to capture Santiago itself and make the harbor unsafe for the ships.

THE SANTIAGO EXPEDITION

On June 22 and 23 the expedition landed not far to the east of the entrance to Santiago harbor. Steep and high mountains guard this part of the coast; but no attempt was made to prevent the landing of the Americans. Dismounted cavalrymen of the regular army and Roosevelt's Rough Riders, also on foot, at once pushed on toward Santiago. At La Guasimas the Spaniards tried to stop them. But the regulars and the Rough Riders drove them away, and the army pushed on. By June 28 it had reached a point within a few miles of the city. The Spaniards occupied two very strong positions at San Juan (San Huan) and Caney. On July 1 they were driven from them. The regulars and the volunteers showed the greatest courage and heroism. They crossed long open spaces in the face of a terrible fire from the Spaniards, who were armed with modern rifles. The rains now set in, and the sufferings of the troops became terrible. On July 3 the Spanish fleet sailed out of the harbor to meet its doom from the guns of the American warships. Reenforcements were sent to Shafter, and heavy guns were dragged over the mountain roads and placed in positions commanding the enemy's lines. The Spaniards surrendered, and on July 17 the Americans entered the captured city.

THE PUERTO RICO CAMPAIGN

The only other important colony still remaining to Spain in America was Puerto Rico. General Nelson A. Miles led a strong force to its conquest. Instead of landing on the northern coast near San Juan, the only strongly fortified position on the seacoast, General Miles landed his men on the southern coast near Ponce. The inhabitants received the

THE SPANISH-AMERICAN WAR
Project, Page 5

Americans with the heartiest welcome. This was on Augusat 1. The American army then set out to cross the island. But before they had gone very far news came of the ending of the hostilities.

FALL OF MANILA

When the news of Dewey's victory reached the United States, soldiers were sent to his aid. But this took time, for it was a very long way from San Fransisco to the Philippines and vessels suitable for transports were not easily procured on the Pacific coast. General Wesley Merritt was given command of the land forces. Meantime, for months Dewey with his fleet blockaded Manila from the water side, while Philippine insurgents blockaded it from the land side. Foreign vessels, especially the German vessels, jealously watched the operations of the American fleet and severely taxed Dewey's patience. On August 17 Merrit felt strong enough to attack the city. It was at once surrendered to him.

END OF THE WAR

The destruction of the Spanish Atlantic fleet and the fall of Santiago convinced the Spaniards that further resistance was useless. So it was agreed that the fighting should be stopped. This was in July, 1898, but the actual treaty of peace was not made until the following December. The conditions were that Spain should abandon Cuba, should cede to the United States, Puerto Rico, the Philippines, and some smaller islands, and should receive from the United States twenty million dollars. For many years Americans missionaries, merchants, and planters had been interested in the Hawaiian Islands. The war showed the importance of these islands to the United States as a military and naval station, and they were annexed.

After reading the above, use the following questions for discussion, or have your students answer them on paper.

1. What promises had the Spaniards made to the Cubans and how had they kept them?
2. Give the immediate cause of the war.
3. Why could Admiral Dewey not remain at Hong Kong?
4. Describe the battle of Manila Bay. What were the results of this action?
5. Why were the American people on the Atlantic seacoast alarmed? How was the coast protected?
6. Compare the American and Spanish fleets. Why was the voyage of the Oregon important?
7. Describe the harbor of Santiago. What advantages did it have for the Spaniards?
8. How did Hobson try to prevent the escape of the Spanish fleet?
9. Describe the encounter of the two fleets.
10. To what was this great success due?
11. Describe the American army. Why was there so much confusion in it?
12. Describe the Santiago campaign and the suffering of the soldiers.
13. Describe the Puerto Rico expedition. Why did General Miles land on the southern coast?
14. Why were the soldiers needed after Dewey's victory?
15. Give the conditions of peace. Exactly what was the condition as to Cuba?
16. Why were the Hawaiian Islands important to the United States?

THE SPANISH-AMERICAN WAR
Test

1. What was the date of the Spanish American War?

2. How did most Americans first hear of the cruelty of Spanish over Cuba?

3. Who was Frederic Remington?

4. What happened to the U.S.S. Maine in Cuba?

5. Who were the "Rough Riders?" What did they do in Cuba?

6. Why did America lose 5,000 men in the Spanish American War?

THE SPANISH-AMERICAN WAR
Test, Page 2

Review

1. For what is George Washington Carver best known?

2. What was the 13th amendment to the Constitution?

3. What was the 15th amendment to the Constitution?

4. Why was the South easily subdued by the Union after Gettysburg?

5. In chronological order list all the events studied to date.

   Next to each place the approximate date.

A President Named Teddy
Worksheet

1. What are the dates for a President Named Teddy?

2. When and where was Theodore Roosevelt born?

3. Describe Teddy's childhood and family.

4. What did his sisters call him?

5. Where did Teddy Roosevelt go to college?

6. Who did Teddy Roosevelt marry?

7. What happened to Teddy's wife and mother?

A PRESIDENT NAMED TEDDY

Worksheet, Page 2

8. What was another nickname for Theodore Roosevelt other than Teddy?

____

____

9. Under what president was he vice-president?

____

____

10. How did he become president?

____

____

11. How many years was he president?

____

____

A President Named Teddy
Project

Theodore Roosevelt, the Boy Who Grew Strong

In 1644 one Claes van Roosevelt came from the Netherlands to the little town growing up at the foot of Manhattan Island. There his descendants continued to live and prosper as the town grew into the city of New York. One of them, Theodore, married Martha Bullock, of Georgia. One of their four children, also called Theodore, the future president, was born October 27, 1858, in the family home, 28 East Twentieth Street, which is now a memorial museum.

The boy was delicate almost from birth, and attended school very little, but his father's wealth provided the best of private tutors and the opportunity of travel in Europe. From boyhood the boy was interested in natural history, and seriously considered preparing himself to be a college professor. His father fitted up a gymnasium in the home, and the boy worked hard to strengthen his frail body. He improved so much that he was able to enter Harvard College in 1876, and graduated with honors four years later. While in college he continued to work at strengthening his body as well as his mind. He was always fond of hunting, horseback-riding and other outdoor sports.

Soon after leaving college he married Miss Alice Lee, of Boston. There was no need for him to work for a living, as his father had left him a comfortable fortune, but he could not be idle and began the study of law and also worked upon a History of the Naval War of 1812. He was offered the Republican nomination for member of the Assembly in 1881, was elected and served three years. While in Albany he attracted much attention by his courage and his independence.

At that time his mother and his wife both died. He determined to leave public life. In 1884 went to Northern Dakota, where he had an interest in two cattle ranches. For two years he remained at the Elkhorn Ranch at Medora, working, hunting and taking part in the primitive life of the region. While still on the ranch he was nominated for mayor of New York, but was defeated. After the election he went to Europe and married a London playmate of his childhood, Miss Edith Kermit Carrow. On his return to the United States he settled at his country place, Sagamore Hill, at Oyster Bay, Long Island, which was his real home until his death. For a time he gave himself to writing history, biography and his hunting experiences.

In 1889 President Harrison appointed him to the United States Civil Service Commission, in which he served six years. Then he was a police commissioner in New York City, and did much to expose and correct corruption in the police force in the city by methods which attracted much attention and made his name known all over the United States.

On the election of President McKinley he was appointed assistant secretary of the navy, and here his energy did much to prepare the navy for the war with Spain which he believed was coming. As it drew nearer he resigned from the Navy Department and became lieutenant-colonel of the First Volunteer Cavalry, soon nicknamed the "Rough Riders." This was made up of men who could ride and shoot - cowboys, ranchmen and hunters from the West, with a few college men from the east. His dear friend Dr. Leonard Wood, now General Wood, was colonel.

A President Named Teddy

Project, Page 2

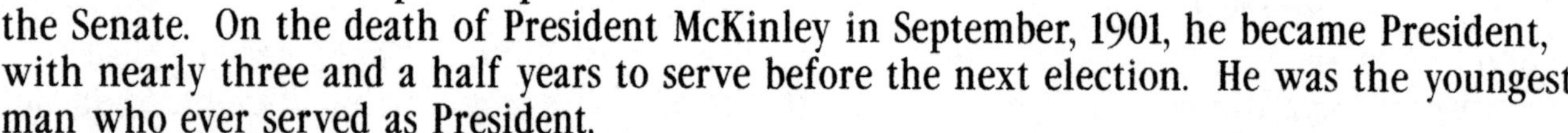

A whole book has been written about the Rough Riders. In Cuba the regiment saw some sharp fighting now under the command of Colonel Roosevelt after his friend Colonel Wood had been promoted. The reputation he won in Cuba led to his nomination for governor of New York in 1898, and he was elected, but soon quarreled with the party leaders in the state, who determined to nominate him for vice-president in 1900. He was too popular to drop, but in the vice-presidency he would be out of their way.

Rather against his will Governor Roosevelt became Vice-President Roosevelt, but was never called upon to preside over the Senate. On the death of President McKinley in September, 1901, he became President, with nearly three and a half years to serve before the next election. He was the youngest man who ever served as President.

No president has ever been busier during his service. The story of the seven and a half years—for he was elected for a full term in 1904—is too long to tell here. He started the Panama Canal, he made peace between Russia and Japan, he prosecuted the trusts, he settled the great coal strike, he urged the conservation of natural resourses, he took an active part in foreign affairs, and did dozens of other things. At the end of his term he and his son Kermit spent a year in Africa collecting big game for the Smithsonian Institution. On his return through Europe he was received with great honors, and made several important speeches which were read all ever the world.

President Taft had been nominated and elected largely through the influence of President Roosevelt. When the latter returned from Africa his friends informed him that Mr. Taft had not continued his policies, but had favored his opponents in the party. From every side came the demand that he should become a candidate in 1912. Finally he agreed, but so many of the delegates had already been chosen that his friends were at a great disadvantage. There were many contests in the convention, and it was soon plain that the result depended upon which of the contesting delegates were seated. The convention decided for the most part in favor of the Taft delegates, and many of Mr. Roosevelt's friends refused to remain in the convention.

Six weeks later a new convention met and organized the Progressive party. Mr. Roosevelt was nominated, of course, and began a hard campaign. While in Milwaukee he was shot, but not seriously injured, by a lunatic. With three candidates in the field, Woodrow Wilson was easily elected, through the popular vote of Taft and Roosevelt together was much greater.

Next Mr. Roosevelt and his son Kermit made an exploring trip to South America, visiting some parts not before seen by white men. While here he was attacked by fever and came

A President Named Teddy

Project, Page 3

near death. In fact, he never really recovered, and the trip shortened his life.

The last years of his life were busy. He wrote books, magazine articles and editorials for a newspaper, and continued to spend much time out of doors. He wished the United States to enter World War I almost as soon as it began, and was very impatient with President Wilson's conduct of affairs. When the United States did join in, he asked to be permitted to lead a volunteer force, but the request was denied. His four sons enlisted, and one was killed. Meanwhile he was far from well, and on the day of the armistice he went to the hospital and on January 6, 1919, he died in his sleep. He was buried in the cemetery at his beloved Oyster Bay, and every year thousands visit his grave.

After reading the above and the resources on the card and a History of U.S.: An Ages of Extremes, *pgs. 136-140, write a book about Theodore Roosevelt, using the pictures on the following page for illustrations. Be sure to include information on his childhood, the "Rough Riders", personal life, political life and his death. The blank panel is for your booklet's title.*

A President Named Teddy
Project, Page 4

Teddy's Birthplace

A President Named Teddy

Project, Page 5

Teddy the Cowboy

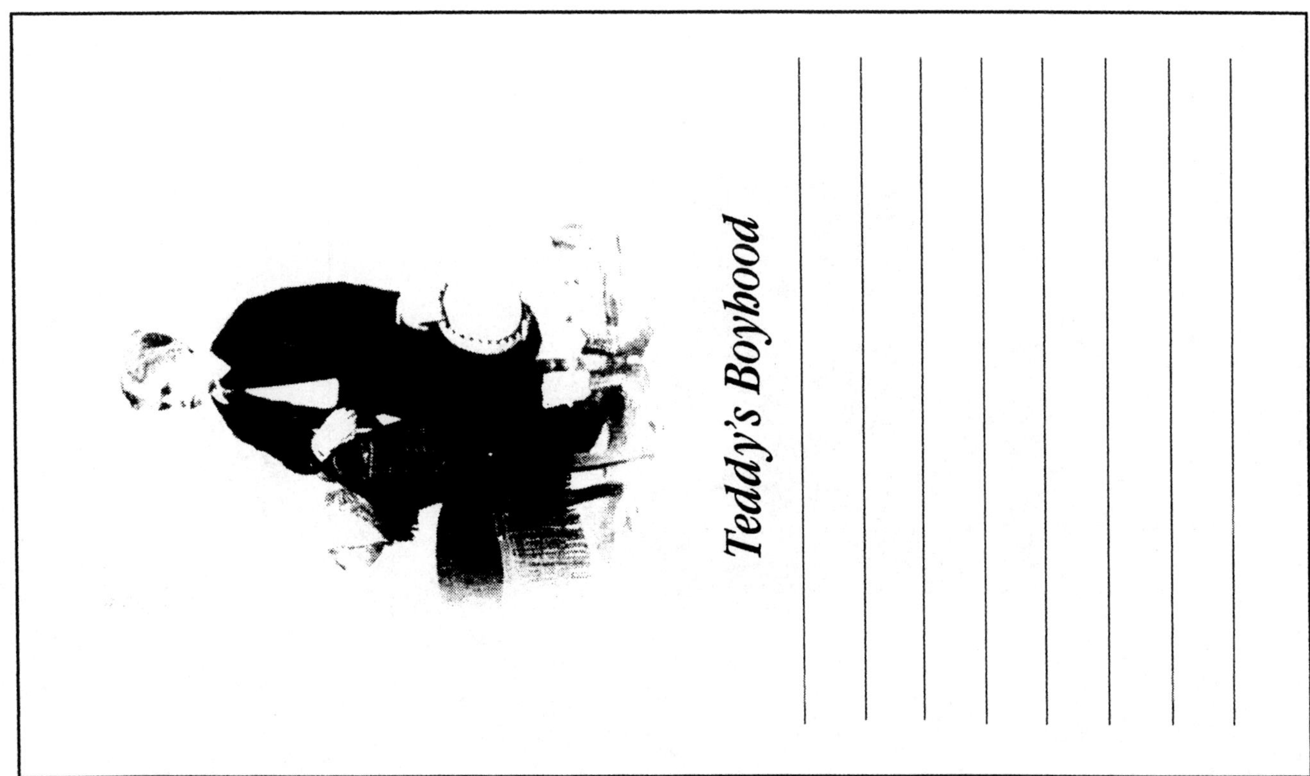

Teddy's Boyhood

A PRESIDENT NAMED TEDDY
Project, Page 6

Mr. President

Rough Rider

A President Named Teddy
Project 2–Literature Unit

Carry a Big Stick: The Uncommon Heroism of Theodore Roosevelt–Comprehension Questions

Introduction
1. The opening paragraph asserts Theodore Roosevelt was a remarkable man. List 5 of his political accomplishments and 3 of his nonpolitical accomplishments.
2. How many books a week did Roosevelt read?
3. How many books did he write? What topics did they cover?
4. Briefly describe what the times were like during the lifetime of Theodore Roosevelt.
5. What view did Roosevelt have concerning the times in which he lived?
6. According to the author, why does Roosevelt stand out as one of the greatest leaders in the history of the US?

Part I
A Bull Moose
1. What happened to Roosevelt the evening of October 14, 1912?
2. What did he still accomplish that evening?
3. How was this event characteristic of Theodore Roosevelt?

A Slow Start
1. When and where was Roosevelt born.
2. Name and briefly describe his father.
3. Name and briefly describe his mother.
4. Contrast the "two proud traditions" of his family.
5. What happens to disturb Teddy's early life? Just as the country was divided, describe how the Roosevelt family was divided (include the actions of his mother and father).
6. What was the second trial of his early life?
7. What did his father say to confront Teddy's problem?
8. How did Teddy respond to his father's words?

Precocious Youth
1. Theodore, Sr. took his family each spring and summer to Oyster Bay on Long Island. How does this influence Roosevelt?
2. Where did the Roosevelt family go in 1869? How does this influence Roosevelt, Jr.?
3. List 5 activities of Theodore, Sr.

The Harvard Dandy
1. What advice did Theodore Sr. give to Teddy when he went to college?
2. Although he had a full academic course load, list 5 other activities he involved himself in.
3. Where did the devotion lay which motivated his work?
4. What happened during his second year at Harvard?
5. Despite his grief, what was he determined to do?

Fairy Tale Love
1. Who was Edith Carrow?
2. Even though they were "perfect" for each other, what happened?
3. Who was Alice Lee?
4. What was his determination concerning Alice?
5. What project did he begin during his Senior year at Harvard?

A President Named Teddy

Project 2, Page 2—Literature Unit

6. What happened on January 25, 1880?
7. What "dark cloud" hung over him? How did he respond to the doctor's orders to live a quiet life?
8. What took place on October 26, 1880?

A Reformer's Zeal
1. After their honeymoon, where do Roosevelt and Alice settle?
2. Where did he go to school? What did he want to do?
3. On top of studying hard, what did he spend his time doing?
4. How old was Roosevelt when *The Naval War of 1812* was published? How was this book praised?
5. Describe his political philosophy.
6. Of what did he become the youngest member?
7. Why did he "symbolize the hope of reformers everywhere"?

Tragedy
1. What happy event happened 3 years after they married?
2. What did Roosevelt start having constructed? Where was it located?
3. What happened on February 12, 1884?
4. What two-fold tragedy took place in Roosevelt's home?

Go West Young Man
1. Why did Roosevelt leave NY? Where did he go?
2. Nathan Miller says "he so successfully identified himself with the __________ that for the remainder of his life, the public thought him a ____________ ___________ rather then a ____ _____ __________."
3. List three activities found within the pages of 49 and 50 which can describe Roosevelt's life in the West.
4. Roosevelt wrote 4 books during his years in the West. Name them. What did the books describe?

Destiny Fulfilled
1. How does he return to the city from the West?
2. Who does Roosevelt marry?
3. The NY Republicans urged him to accept the party's nomination for what?. Describe how Roosevelt involved himself in the race.
4. Did he win this race?

A Political Quest
1. What was the house at Oyster Bay named?
2. Thinking his political career was over, what did Roosevelt start doing?
3. Name the two books he worked on during this time period. How were the books received after they were published?
4. In 1888, when Benjamin Harris became President, what job was Roosevelt given?
5. Describe his role as reformer in this job.
6. What job did he take after his years in the civil service.
7. Describe his role as a reformer in this job.
8. What type of husband and father was Roosevelt?

Rough Rider
1. When President McKinley came into office, what job did Roosevelt want?
2. Why did he want this job?
3. What did he set to do when he got the job?
4. What was Roosevelt convinced would come? What did happen?
5. What did Roosevelt do which proved to be the decisive difference in the war?
6. Roosevelt resigned from his position to

A President Named Teddy
Project 2, Page 3—Literature Unit

do what? Why did he do this?
7. Who made up the Rough Riders?
8. Describe what they were involved in doing?
9. Describe what Roosevelt was like during this battle.

A Political Accident
1. What does he become after he commanded the Rough Riders?
2. What was his administration noted for?
3. For what did he continually appeal?
4. "It is absolutely ____________," Roosevelt declared, "for a Republic long ____ __________ if it becomes either ____________ or _____________."
5. In 1900 Vice President Garret Hobart died. What did President McKinley consent to?
6. Why did the ditty "Tis Teddy alone that's running, and ain't just running, he's galloping" sum up the campaign of 1900?
7. After winning, how did Roosevelt respond to being vice-president? What did he end up doing?
8. President McKinley was visiting the Pan America Exposition in New York. Describe what happened to the President. What was the final outcome on September 13?
9. At age 42, what did Roosevelt become?

TR:Rex
1. What did Roosevelt's "progressive innovation and reforms" stem from?
2. Roosevelt caused a scandal by inviting who to dinner?
3. List three things he did in office during his first term.
4. How was Roosevelt's "Big Stick" policy a success?
5. Why didn't Roosevelt want to run for a third term?
6. Who did he choose for his successor?
7. When did Roosevelt and his family leave the White House?

A Restless Heart
1. What did Roosevelt do after he left office?
2. Why did he keep such a long absence?
3. What was Taft like as a president?
4. What was Roosevelt's response to Taft?

1912
1. What did Roosevelt do in 1912?
2. Who was the Democratic nominee for president? What message did he bring during the elections?
3. How were Wilson and Roosevelt different in their messages (or philosophies)?
4. How did Taft respond to Roosevelt during the elections?
5. Who received the Republican nomination?
6. What did Roosevelt form to continue running in the race?
7. Who won the presidential race? Why did he win?

Years of Exile
1. What did Roosevelt do after the presidential race?
2. How many miles in the jungle and river did he and his crew map?
3. What was this trip like?
4. What was Roosevelt's message concerning the upcoming war?
5. How did the public respond to him?
6. Once war did happen, how was Roosevelt involved?

A President Named Teddy

Project 2, Page 4—Literature Unit

7. What did Roosevelt learn on July 16, 1918?
8. What was Roosevelt's physical response to his son's death?
9. What happened on January 5, 1919?

Vindication
1. How did the world respond to Roosevelt's death?
2. Where was Roosevelt's legacy given the greatest tribute?
3. Did Wilson prove a popular and effective leader?
4. What was Warren G. Harding's message as he ran for president?
5. Harding called himself a _______________ Republican.

Part 2
The Character of Theodore Roosevelt
Learn about Roosevelt by focusing on his own words and how he "practiced what he preached." Choose 15 character traits and answer the questions.

His Family

Theodore Roosevelt said the family was the source of his strength. "No other success in life...comes up to success of the man and woman who can feel that they have done their duty and that their children and grandchildren rise up to call them blessed." Give 3 examples found in the chapter which support this quote.

His Father

Roosevelt said of his father "All that I have ever done has been little more than an attempt to live up to and honor that legacy." Give 3 examples, as found in the chapter, why Roosevelt wanted to live up to his father.

The Strenuous Life

Roosevelt's philosophy of life can be summed up as "I wish to preach not the doctrine of ignoble ease but the doctrine of the strenuous life; the life of toil and effort; of labor and strife..." Give 3 examples from the chapter which show Roosevelt practiced what he preached.

The Great Outdoors

Roosevelt had a passion for the natural world and was great sportsman. "I love all the seasons" he once said. He was considered an expert in many fields, including the outdoor world and conservation. How was this true in his life? Give 3 examples as found in the chapter.

An Appetite for Learning

It was said that his range of reading was amazing. Roosevelt said of himself "When I read one [book] I want in the first place to enjoy myself, and in the second place to feel that I am a little better and not a little worse for having read it." How was this true of him? Give 3 examples, as found in the chapter, of his appetite for learning .

Story Teller

"I am always in the mood for a good story." Roosevelt loved stories and telling stories. Give 3 examples from the chapter which highlight this love of Roosevelt's.

Good Deeds

"We in America can attain our great destiny only by service; not by rhetoric...our service must be a service of deeds." How was Roosevelt's life a commitment to good deeds? Give 3 examples as found in the chapter.

A President Named Teddy
Project 2, Page 5—Literature Unit

Reformer
Roosevelt was most definitely a reformer throughout his political career. "I believe in waging war on rank growing evils of all kinds." Give 3 examples from the chapter which describe what he was like as a reformer. List 5 areas he worked on to reform.

Socialism
"We are steadily bent on preserving the institution of private property; we combat every tendency toward reducing the people to economic servitude." Give 3 examples, as found in the chapter, of Roosevelt's response to socialism.

The Bully Pulpit
"The White House is a bully pulpit." said Roosevelt. He also said, "I am far more interested in influence I might be able to wield speaking my heart and mind to the nation than I am in money and power." He was always very intent on speaking directly to the people. Give 3 examples, as found in the chapter, of why or how this was true.

The Common Man
Roosevelt "believed that it was a noble pursuit to remind people, especially to remind young people—of men and women of the past 'who showed that they knew how to live and how to die; who proved their truth by their endeavor.'" He also believed the best example were the "forgotten and obscure." Give 3 examples, as found in the chapter, of how Roosevelt championed the common man.

Humility
Roosevelt was quite a humble man. "The things I have done are all, with the possible exception of the Panama Canal, just such things any ordinary man could have done." Give 3 examples as found in the chapter of how he lived a humble man.

War and Peace
"A nation is not wholly admirable unless in times of stress it will go to war for a great ideal." Give 3 examples as found in the chapter of how Roosevelt responded or acted concerning war and peace.

Science
Roosevelt was very interested in science and scientific knowledge. He considered himself a "man of science". Give three examples as found in the chapter of how this was true of Roosevelt.

The South
"I can quite legitimately claim to be a proud son of the South." Give 3 examples as found in the chapter of how this was true of Roosevelt.

Humor
His friend Henry Cabot Lodge said of Roosevelt, "His ready smile and contagious laugh made countless friends and saved him from many an enmity." Give 3 examples as found in the chapter of Roosevelt's humorous side.

Courage
"My success so far has only been won by absolute indifference to my future career." Give 3 examples found in the chapter of how Roosevelt was a courageous man throughout his life.

A President Named Teddy

Project 2, Page 6–Literature Unit

Failure

"There is no disgrace in a failure, only in a failure to try." Give 3 examples as found in the chapter of how Roosevelt responded to his failures.

Friendship

"It may be true that he travels farthest who travels alone; but the goal thus reached is not worth reaching." Give 3 examples as found in the chapter of how he was a friend to others or how he interacted with others.

A Pro-life Stalwart

"Never will I sit motionless while directly or indirectly apology is made for the murder of the helpless." Give three examples as found in the chapter which highlight Roosevelt's stand against abortion or anything which threatened the American family.

Progressive

"A great democracy must be progressive or it will soon cease to be a democracy." Give three examples of reform which took place with Roosevelt's leadership of the progressive movement.

Prejudice

"The wise and honorable and Christian thing to do is to treat each black man and each white man on his merits as a man, giving him no more or no less than he shows he is worthy to have." As the author points out, Roosevelt found prejudice intolerable. He could not fathom how anyone, especially Christians, could condone racism. Give three examples as found in the chapter which shows he was not prejudice or how he believed racism wrong.

Heroes

"A nation needs heroes. It needs examples of valor so that it will know just how it ought to behave." Give five examples of Roosevelt's heroes. Give one reason why Roosevelt felt having heroes was important for "ordinary Americans."

Bull Feathers

"Why curse when there is such a magnificent language with which to discourse?" Roosevelt enjoyed the English language. Many of his sayings have become every day sayings for us. List three common quotes of Roosevelt's that we hear or use today.

Faith

"I am a Christian statesman." Roosevelt's faith and believe in truth was a total part of who he was and what he did. Give three examples, as found in the chapter, of Roosevelt's faith life.

The Bible

"A thorough knowledge of the Bible is worth more than a college education." Give three examples, as found in the chapter, which show the importance of the Bible in Roosevelt's life.

The Church

"A churchless society is most assuredly a society on the downgrade." Roosevelt also said, "After a week of wrestling with a perplexing problem, it does so rest my soul to come into the house of the Lord..." Give three examples, as found in the chapter, of Roosevelt as a churchgoer.

A PRESIDENT NAMED TEDDY

Project 2, Page 7—Literature Unit

TR and FDR

Franklin Roosevelt was Roosevelt's cousin. But as the author points out, what ever similarities they had were far out weighed by their differences. Give three examples, as found in the chapter, of how they were politically different.

Sagamore Hill

"I wonder if you will ever know how I love Sagamore Hill?" These were his last words to his wife Edith on the night he died. Give three examples, as found in the chapter, of how his home, overlooking Oyster Bay on Long Island, was important to him.

American Spirit
Part 3
The Legacy of Theodore Roosevelt

1. Write out the Micah Mandate.

Justice

1. "He believed...that any people that diligently __________ ____ ____ ______ - to do __________ - would inevitably pursue __________ as well.
2. According to Roosevelt, what two concepts were inseparably tied together?

Mercy

1. What did Roosevelt link mercy with?
2. Roosevelt said "The __________ men are those who willing ______ in the _______. The ______ and the _______ are the _______ and the __________.

Humility

1. Roosevelt "believed that a good man or women's life would be suffused with ..." what?
2. What did he believe the starting place of any fruitful endeavor was?

Our Need

1. At a memorial meeting for Theodore Roosevelt, Senator George Wharton Pepper spoke of him. As found in his speech, give three examples of why we need "the colonel."
2. Roosevelt said "But for this generation the task is clear: you who gird yourselves for this ________ _______ in the ______ - ________ ______ for the good of mankind, we _______ at Armageddon and we do battle for the __________.

The Lessons of Leadership

Read through the list and fill in the blanks:
"A leader will always prefer to be _______ than _________.

A President Named Teddy

Project 2, Page 8–Literature Unit

Answers

Introduction

1. See the first and second paragraph of the first page of the introduction.
2. At least 5 books every week
3. He wrote nearly 50 books. The topics covered history, biography, natural science and social criticism.
4. It was the sunset of one century and the dawning of another. The US had grown to 45 states by 1900 with a population of 76 million people. With the great many inventions, the US believed it would "meet and overcome all perils and prove to be the best that this steadily improving planet has ever seen."
5. He had a saner and more realistic view of his time- a view balanced by a Christian understanding of mankind. He understood his remarkable times and what things had to be done to sustain them.
6. He was willing to use his dynamic accomplishments and gifts for the good of all around him - regardless of political or career consequences.

Part 1

A Bull Moose

1. He was shot in the chest.
2. He still gave his campaign speech
3. He imposed the sheer force of his will upon a seemingly impossible situation.

A Slow Start

1. October 27, 1858 in New York City
2. Theodore Roosevelt, Sr. See page 28, first paragraph for a description.
3. Martha Bulloch Roosevelt. See page 28 first paragraph for a description.
4. Sturdy Dutch industrial mercantilism of the North (his father) and the Romantic Scottish agrarianism of the South (his mother).
5. The Civil War starts. See page 29 for how his family was divided.
6. He was sick with congenital asthma.
7. "Theodore, you have the mind, but you have not the body. And without the body the mind cannot go as far as it should. You must make your body. It is hard drudgery to make one's body, but I know you will do it."
8. "I'll make my body. By heaven, I will."

Precocious Youth

1. He learned to appreciate and study the joys of nature.
2. They went on a grand tour of Europe. He "revels" in art, architecture, history, pageantry, chivalry and the natural beauty of Europe.
3. See pages 33 and 34.

The Harvard Dandy

1. "Take care of your morals first, your health next and finally your studies."
2. See third paragraph on page 36.
3. Devotion to his family and determination to maintain their esteem.
4. His father died.
5. To uphold the honor of his father's name.

Fairy Tale Love

1. His childhood friend and sweetheart.
2. They quarreled and broke off their relationship.
3. The 17 year old daughter of a prominent Boston family. See bottom of page 38 and top of page 39.
4. He was determined to marry her.
5. Writing project on the naval history of the War of 1812.
6. She consented to marry him.
7. The doctors detected an erratic heartbeat and warned him to choose a

A President Named Teddy

Project 2, Page 9—Literature Unit

sedentary occupation. He said he was going to all the things the doctor told him not to do.

8. He married Alice.

A Reformer's Zeal

1. In New York
2. He went to Columbia University of Law School to study law.
3. He researched and wrote *The Naval War of 1812.*
4. He was 23 years old. "A formidable literary achievement" - it remains a standard work on the subject of this war.
5. A strong Republican on state matters but an independent on municipal matters.
6. The NY Assembly
7. See bottom of page 45 and top of page 46.

Tragedy

1. Alice was expecting their first child.
2. A new home on Oyster Bay
3. A daughter was born.
4. His wife and mother died on the same day.

Go West Young Man

1. The shock of his loss and political problems; he went west to the Dakota Territory.
2. "He so successfully identified himself with the West that for the remainder of his life, the public thought him a rough riding cowboy rather than a New York dude.
3. See pages 49 and 50
4. Hunting Trips of a Ranch Man, Ranch Life and the Hunting Trail, The Wilderness Hunter and Thomas Hart Benton; these books brought the world of the rancher to life with vivid descriptions of land, people and wild life.

Destiny Fulfilled

1. Rugged, bronzed and in the prime of health.
2. Edith Carrow, his childhood sweetheart
3. For mayor; with his usual enthusiasm. He worked 18 hour days, appeared 4 or 5 rallies every night, made it a real race.
4. No

A Political Quest

1. Sagamore Hill
2. Write books
3. Gouverneur Morris and The Winning of the West; with rave reviews
4. A position in the Civil Service Commission.
5. See page 55, fourth and fifth paragraphs and page 56, first and second paragraphs.
6. NYC Police Commissioner
7. He was to rid the police department of corruption and inefficiency. See bottom half of 56 and top of page 57.
8. He was "an ideal father and devoted husband."

Rough Rider

1. Undersecretary of the Navy
2. He wanted to be where the action was.
3. Expand and modernize the US Navy
4. A war with one of the great powers, especially Spain; he was right, a war with Spain started.
5. Roosevelt's mobilization plans
6. To command a volunteer group of troopers on the front lines of battle. He felt he would fail to practice what he preached when it came to do battle with Spain.
7. Eastern dandies, Western cowboys, a handful of experienced solders.
8. They were involved in several fierce fire-fights with the Spanish defenders.
9. "He seemed everywhere - securing essential provisions, opening direct

A President Named Teddy
Project 2, Page 10—Literature Unit

communications for officers back home, coordinating the inefficient quartermastering and maintaining high moral among the enlisted men..."

A Political Accident

1. Governor of New York
2. It's efforts to bring about bureaucratic efficiency, managerial economy, tax reform, meritorial advancement in civil service.
3. He appealed to "practical morality and manly virtue in the civic arena."
4. "It is absolutely impossible," Roosevelt declared, "for a Republic long to endure if it becomes either corrupt or cowardly."
5. To be put on the Republican ticket as Vice-President.
6. See page 65, third paragraph.
7. "The Vice President is really a fifth wheel to the coach." Living a Sagamore Hill and enjoying life.
8. President McKinley was greeting well-wishers when someone shot him at point-blank range. He died.
9. The President of the United States.

TR:Rex

1. His conservative Christian principles
2. The famous black educator Booker T. Washington
3. See page 68, second paragraph
4. He avoided war with other countries (see page 69, third paragraph).
5. He grew restless during the last part of his second term; he was very popular but did not have a lot of legislative success.
6. William Howard Taft
7. March 4, 1909

A Restless Heart

1. A year-long safari then a grand tour of Europe
2. So he could "get where no one could accuse me of running, nor do Taft the injustice of accusing him of permitting me to run the job."
3. See page 73, first paragraph
4. He was concerned that Taft might undo all the good he had done during his years as president.

1912

1. He entered the presidential race.
2. Woodrow Wilson; change (see page 75, third paragraph).
3. Wilson said Americans should reinvent the world by "interpreting the Constitution according to the Darwinian principles." Roosevelt said the nation should be ruled by the Ten Commandments, not by the Darwinian presumptions.
4. Taft led a negative campaign against Roosevelt (see page 76, paragraph 3).
5. Taft received the nomination.
6. Roosevelt led a third party
7. Wilson won the presidential race. Roosevelt was shot and unable to continue campaigning. There was not a large turnout of voters.

Years of Exile

1. Roosevelt launched a dangerous wilderness expedition to map the River of Doubt which flowed through the Amazon Rain Forest.
2. The trip was very dangerous. They fought off fierce fire ants, giant wasps, piranhas and reptiles. Two men died. Roosevelt contracted dysentery and malaria.
3. They mapped the 1500 mile-long river
4. Roosevelt's message was that Americans would be drawn into the war and should prepare themselves for it.
5. Americans did not listen to him. They thought being prepared would draw them

into the war.
6. His sons volunteered. Roosevelt tried to volunteer, but Wilson turned him down. He led a war effort "at home" - helped the sale of bonds, made speeches to raise moral, lobbied for better provisions.
7. His youngest son had been killed in an aerial dogfight over German lines.
8. Roosevelt faced a serious physical decline - nagging effects of malaria and bouts of rheumatism and gout.
9. Roosevelt died.

Vindication
1. Thousands of memorial services were held across America. Messages of grief and sorrow poured in from around the globe.
2. In the political arena.
3. No, he did not prove to be an effective or popular leader.
4. A return to normalcy.
5. Roosevelt

Part 2
The Character of Theodore Roosevelt
Answers

His Family
See page 92, paragraphs 2, 3 and 4; and page 93, paragraphs 1, 2, 3, and 4.

His Father
See page 96, paragraph 1, 3; and page 97.

The Strenuous Life
See page 98, paragraph 3 ;and page 99, paragraphs 1, 2, and 3.

The Great Outdoors
See page 101, paragraph 2; and page 102

An Appetite for Learning
See page 104, paragraph 2; page 105; and page 106, paragraph 1.

Story Teller
See page 107, paragraph 2; page 108, paragraphs 1, 2, and 3; and page 109, paragraph 1.

Good Deeds
See page 110, paragraph 2; page 111 paragraph 2; and page 112, paragraphs 1 and 2.

Reformer
(1) See page 114, paragraphs 1 and 2; and page 115, paragraph 1. (2) See page 114, paragraph 2.

Socialism
See page 116, paragraphs 2 and 3; page 117, paragraphs 1, 2, and 3; and page 118 paragraph 1.

The Bully Pulpit
See page 119, paragraph 2; page 120, paragraphs 1 and 2; and page 121, paragraph 1.

The Common Man
See page 123, paragraph 2; and page 124, paragraphs 1, 2, and 3.

Humility
See page 126, paragraphs 1, 2, 3, and 4; and page 127, paragraph 2.

War and Peace
See page 129, paragraph 2; page 130, paragraphs 1, 2, and 3; and page 131, paragraphs 1, 2, and 3.

Science
See page 133, paragraphs 1 and 2; page 134, paragraphs 1, 2, and 3.

A President Named Teddy

Project 2, Page 12—Literature Unit

The South
See page 136, paragraph 2 and 3; page 137; and page 138, paragraph 1.

Humor
See page 139, paragraph 3 and 4; page 140, paragraphs 1, 2, and 3; and page 141.

Courage
See page 142, paragraphs 2 and 3; page 143, paragraphs 1, 2, and 3.

Failure
See page 145, paragraphs 2 and 3; and page 146, paragraphs 1 and 2.

Friendship
See page 148, paragraphs 1 and 2; and page 149, paragraphs 1, 2, 3, and 4.

A Pro-Life Stalwart
See page 151, paragraphs 1 and 2; page 152, paragraphs 1, 4 and 5; and page 153, paragraph 1.

Progressive
See page 157, paragraph 1.

Prejudice
See page 160, paragraphs 1, 2, and 3; page 161, paragraphs 1 and 2; and page 162, paragraph 1.

Heroes
(1) See page 163, paragraph 2; page 164, paragraphs 1 and 2; and page 165, paragraph 2. (2) See page 164, paragraphs 3 and 4; and page 165, paragraph 1.

Bull Feathers
See page 166, paragraph 1; and page 167, paragraph 3.

Faith
See page 169, paragraphs 1 and 2; page 170, paragraph 2; and page 171, paragraph 1.

The Bible
See page 173, paragraphs 3 and 4; page 174, paragraphs 1 and 2; and page 175, paragraph 1.

The Church
See page 176, paragraph 3; and page 178, paragraphs 1, 2, and 3.

TR and FDR
See page 180, paragraphs 1, 2, 3, and 4.

Sagamore Hill
See page 183, paragraphs 2, 3, 4, 5, and 6; and page 184, paragraph 1.

PART 3
The Legacy of Theodore Roosevelt
Answers

1. He has shown you, O man, what is good and what the LORD requires of you: but to do justice, and to love mercy, and to walk humbly with your God. (Micah 6:8)

Justice
1. He believed...that any people that diligently sought to do right - to do righteousness - would inevitably pursue justice as well.
2. Seeking to do right (righteousness) and justice were linked together.

A President Named Teddy

Project 2, Page 13—Literature Unit

Mercy

1. He linked mercy with the exercise of authority.
2. Roosevelt said, "The greatest men are those who willingly serve in the shadows. The least and the last are the first and the foremost.

Humility

1. ...a holy fear and a reverence of God.
2. The fear of God was the starting place of any fruitful endeavor.

Our Need

1. See page 201, paragraph 1 and page 202, paragraph 2.
2. Roosevelt said, "But for this generation the task is clear: you who gird yourselves for this great fight in the never-ending warfare for the good of mankind, we stand at Armageddon and we do battle for the Lord.

The Lessons of Leadership

"A Leader will always prefer to be faithful than famous."

A PRESIDENT NAMED TEDDY
Test

1. What are the dates for a President Named Teddy?

2. When and where was Theodore Roosevelt born?

3. What did his sisters call him?

4. Who did Teddy Roosevelt marry?

5. What happened to Teddy's wife and mother?

6. How did he become president?

7. How many years was he president?

A President Named Teddy

Test, Page 2

Review

1. For what is George Washington Carver best known?

2. Why was the South easily subdued by the Union after Gettysburg?

3. Who first discovered gold in California?

4. What was the Cherokee Trail of Tears?

5. In chronological order list all the events studied to date.

   Next to each place the approximate date.

Immigration to America
Worksheet

1. What is the approximate date for Immigration to America?

2. List a number of reasons why immigrants came to America.

3. In the 50 years after the war between the states how many immigrants came to the United States?

4. From where did most of the above immigrants come?

5. What was the initial reception center?

6. After 1892 where were immigrants received?

7. What were immigrants checked for at these reception centers?

Immigration to America
Worksheet, Page 2

8. What were tenaments?

____

____

9. Why did people generally move to the specific city that they did?

____

____

10. What did Americans think about the newcomers?

____

____

____

Immigration to America

Project

Family Tree

Fill in the family tree provided. This is a good way to begin a study of genealogy. You should begin your study by asking your parents or grandparents for any information they may have on your families background. Look for family Bibles, diaries, marriage certificates and other old resources. If you really get interested in this you can receive further information from: *Ancestry,* P.O. Box 476, Salt Lake City, Utah 84110. You might consider having older children trace their roots back to immigrating to America.

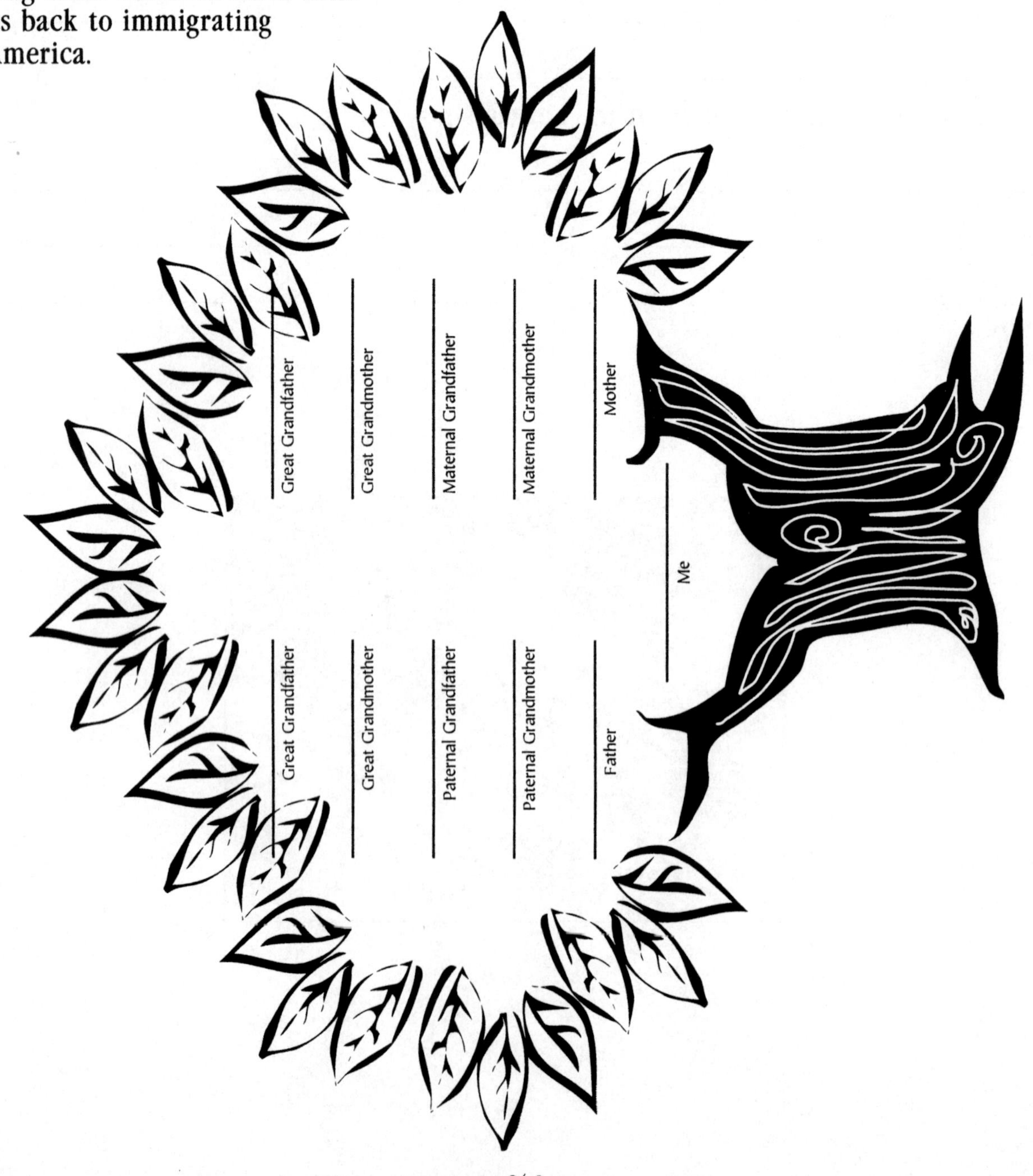

IMMIGRATION TO AMERICA

Project 2

Fiesta of the World

Using the resources on the cards and any others you might come up with make a list of all the places in the world that people emigrated from in the early 1900's. (Some other books worth looking at are *A Gift to America* by Jane Mylum Gardner, *Immigrant Kids* by Russell Freedman, *An Ellis Island Christmas* by Maxine Rhea Leighton, *Watch the Stars Come Out* by Riki Levinson, *When Jessie Came Across the Sea* by Amy Hest illustrated by P. J. Lynch and *The Statue of Liberty* by Thelma Nason.) After doing this put up a world map on the wall. Using colored push pins make all the places that you come up with.

Have each child chose a particular country and research what life was like for people in their country before they emigrated. Discuss some of the things that we see in the United States today that actually were ideas brought from other countries. For example our operas were greatly influenced by those of Italy.

After doing this, plan a party that will feature foods from many of the places that people emigrated from (on the next two pages you will find some sample recipes). Have the children make flags for each of the counties using the flag template on the bottom of this page.

Have fun and enjoy the party!!!

IMMIGRATION TO AMERICA
Project 2, Page 2

Hungarian Delight

Large cabbage
1/2 plound ground beef
1/2 pound ground turkey
1 cup cooked rices
1/2 teaspoon kosher salt
1/8 teaspoon pepper
1 onion sliced
15 ounce can tomato sauce
15 ounces of water
10 3/4 ounce can tomato soup
3/4 cup brown sugar
1/4 cup sugar
16 ounce can sauerkraut

Cook cabbage in pan of boiling water. Cool cabbage and remove the leaves from the stem. Combine ground beef, turkey, rice, salt and pepper in a bowl, mixing well. Place 1 tablespoon of mixture on a leaf and roll this up. Tuck in the ends and secure with a toothpick. Cut up leftover cabbage and place in a dutch oven. Mix the rest of the ingredients and pour over cabbage. Place cabbage rolls on top of this and bake for 1 1/2 to 2 hours at 300 degrees.

Greek Spinach Casserole

2 pks frozen chopped spinach, drained and thawed
2/3 cups chopped onion
1 tablespoon butter
4 eggs
1 1/3 cups cottage cheese
2/3 cups feta chees, crumbled
1 teaspoon salt
1 teaspoon pepper

Saute onion in butter and simmer. Add spinach and simmer for 5 minutes. Add mixture of eggs, cheese, salt, and pepper. Place in greased 8 x 8 inch pan. Bake at 350 degrees for 25 minutes or until fork comes out clean.

Greek Stew

2 pounds stew meat cubed
1 pound fresh mushrooms
2 tablespoons olive oil
1 teaspoon salt
1 teaspoomn pepper
1 pound frozen pearl onions peeled
3 ounces tomato paste
1/3 cup red wine
2 tablespoons red wine vinegar
3 tablespoons brown sugar
1 clove garlic, minced
1 bay leaf
2 tablespoons raisins
10 whole cloves
3/4 cups water
¨ teaspoon cumin
1 cinnamon stick

Season meat with salt and pepper. Saute the meat in the olive olive till browned. Add onions, mushrooms, tomato paste and the rest of the ingredients.

You may want to wrap the cinnamon stick, and cloves in gauze before placing them in the pot. Bring to a boil and simmer for 2 hours or until meat is tender. Remove cinnamon and cloves.

German Cabbage and Bratwurst

1/2 cup butter
2 medium cooking apples peeled and cored
1 medium onion sliced
1 head medium red cabbage, shredded
1 cup water
1 cup red wine vinegar
1 cup sugar
11 teaspoons salt
dash of pepper
1 bay leaf

In saucepan melt butter, add apples and onions, cook till tender. Add cabbage and rest of ingredients, heat until boiling. Reduce heat and simmer until tender. Remove bay leaf before serving.

Serve with Bratwurst. You may want to buy these and cook them or if really adventurous, try the recipe below.

10 pounds pork butt
2 tablespoons coarse pepper
4 cups water
2 ounces salt
1 teaspoon nutmeg
hog casings

Debone pork, removing fat and grind coarsely. Mix all ingredients and put through stuffer attached to meat grinder, with cutters, and into casings that are knotted at the end. Then knot both ends, twisting links about every 8 inches. Either grill or cook in pan until well done.
Serve the cabbage and bratwurst together.

Spaghetti

Another good dish would be to use your favorite spaghetti recipe.

Irish Soda Bread

4 cups all-purpose flour
1 tsp salt
1 tsp baking soda
4 tsp baking powder
3/4 cup granulated sugar
8 ounces raisins
2 cups buttermilk

Heat oven 400 degrees about 15 minutes before putting in the bread then, cook at this temperature for 15 minutes - turn down oven to 375 and bake 30 to 45 minutes.
Mix all well, bake in skillet that is well-greased and floured.
Butter entire surface while it is hot.

IMMIGRATION TO AMERICA
Test

1. What is the approximate date of Immigration to America?

   ____

   ____

2. Why did immigrants come to America?

   ____

   ____

   ____

3. How many immigrants came to the United States in the 50 years in the War Between the States?

   ____

   ____

4. What was Ellis Island?

   ____

   ____

5. Where did newcomers usually move?

   ____

   ____

6. Why did people become prejudiced?

   ____

   ____

7. What laws were passed that kept people from immigrating to the United States?

   ____

   ____

   ____

Immigration to America

Test, Page 2

Review

1. What was the California gold rush?

2. Why did the Mormons form the Mormon Trail to Utah?

3. Who won the Spanish-American War?

4. Who won the Battle of Little Big Horn?

5. In chronological order list all the events studied to date.
   Next to each place the approximate date.

WRIGHT BROTHERS AND OTHER INVENTORS
Worksheet

1. What was the date for the Wright Brothers and Other Inventors?

____

____

2. The late _________ and the early __________ saw Americans inventing wonderful things we take for granted today.

3. Who is known as American's most famous inventor? Name at least two things he invented.

____

____

____

4. Who flew the first manned airplane? Where was it flown?

____

____

5. When did the airplane gain popularity?

____

____

6. What was the first mass produced affordable car? By whom was it built?

____

____

____

7. Who invented the first telephone? When was it invented?

____

____

____

Wright Brothers and Other Inventors
Project

The Airplane

The airplane is heavier than air. So is a bird and so is a kite. What supports a kite or a bird as it soars? Every boy knows that the strings of a kite must be attached so that the kite is inclined and catches the wind underneath. Then the wind lifts the kite. In still air the kite will not fly unless the boy who holds the string runs very fast and so causes an artificial breeze to blow against the kite. In much the same way a hovering bird is held aloft by the wind. In a dead calm the bird must flap its wings to keep afloat. If the kite string is cut the kite tips over and drops to the earth because it has lost its balance. The lifting power of the wind is well shown in the man-lifting kites which were used in the British army service. In a high wind a large kite was used in place of a captive balloon. It is a box-kite made of bamboo and carried a passenger in a car; the car ran on the cable which attached the kite to the ground. Now suppose a kite with a motor and propeller in place of a string and a boy to run with it, and that the kite is able to balance itself, then it will sail against a wind of its own making and you have a flying-machine heavier than air.

The first airplane that would fly under perfect control of the operator was built by the Wright brothers at Dayton, Ohio. When they were boys, Bishop Wright gave his two sons, Orville and Wilbur, a toy flyer. From that time on the thought of flying through the air was in their minds. A few years later the death of Lilienthal, who was killed by a fall from his glider in Germany, stirred them, and they took up the problem in earnest. They read all the writings of Lilienthal and became acquainted with Mr. Octave Chanute, an engineer of Chicago who had made a successful glider. They soon built a glider of their own, and experimented with it each summer on the huge sand-dunes of the North Carolina coast.

A glider is an airplane without a propeller. With it one can cast off into the air from a great height and sail slowly to the ground. Before attempting to use a motor and propeller, the Wrights learned to control the glider perfectly. They had to learn how to prevent its being tipped over by the wind and how to steer in any direction. This took years of patient work. But the problem was conquered at last, and they attached a motor and propeller to the glider, and had an air-ship under perfect control and with the speed of an express train. Their flyer of 1905, which made a flight of twenty-four miles at a speed of more than thirty-eight miles an hour, carried a twenty-five horse power gasoline motor, and weighed, with its load, 925 pounds.

How the Wright Airplane Is Kept Aloft

The Wright airplane is balanced by a warping or twisting of planes 1 and 2, which form the supporting surfaces (fig. 1). If left to itself the machine would tip over like a kite when the string is cut and drop edgewise to the ground. Suppose the side R starts to fall. The corners a and e are raised by the operator while b and f are lowered, thus twisting the planes, as shown in the dotted lines of the figure. The side R then catches more wind than the side L. The wind exerts a greater lifting force on R than on L, and the balance is restored. The twist is then taken out of the machine by the operator. A ship when sailing on an even keel presents true unwarped planes to the wind.

The twisting is brought about by a pull on the rope 3, which is attached at d and c, and passes through pulleys at g and h. When the rope is pulled toward the left the right end is tightened and slack is paid out at the left. This pulls down the corner d, and raises e. The corner a is raised by the post which connects a and e. The rope 4, passing from a to b through pulleys at m and n, is thus drawn toward a and pulls down the corner b. Thus a is raised and b is lowered. At the same time rope 4 turns the rear rudder to the left, as shown by the dotted lines, thus forcing the side R against the wind. Of course, if the left side of the machine starts to fall, the rope 3 is pulled toward the right, and all the movements take place in the opposite direction. The ropes are connected to a lever, by which the operator controls the warping of the planes. These movements are possible because the joints are all universal, permitting movement in any direction. In whatever position the planes may be set, they are held perfectly rigid by the two ropes, together with others not shown in the figure. The machine is guided up or down by the front horizontal rudder.

When the airplane swings round a curve the outer wing is raised because it moves faster than the inner wing, and therefore has greater lifting force. Thus the airplane banks its own curves.

The Wright flying-machine is called a biplane because it has two principal planes, one above the other. A number of successful flying-machines have been built with only one plane, and these are called monoplanes. A monoplane that early became famous is that of Bleriot. The Bleriot monoplane was the first flying-machine to cross the English Channel. This machine is controlled by a single lever mounted with a ball-and-socket coupling, so that it can move in any direction. When on the ground it is supported by three wheels like bicycle wheels, so that it does not require a track for starting, but can start anywhere from level ground. The Wright and the Bleriot represent the two leading types of early successful flying-machines.

After reading the above make the model gliders on the following page.

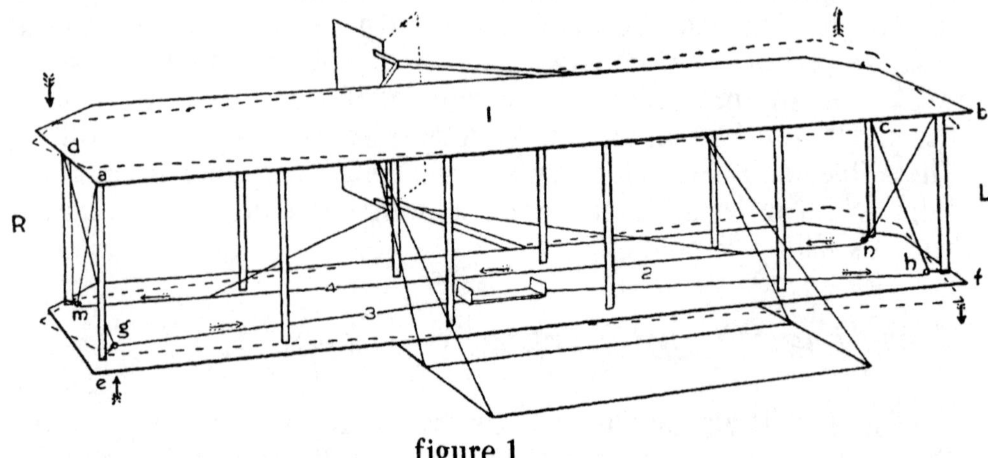

figure 1

Wright Brothers and Other Inventors

Project, Page 3

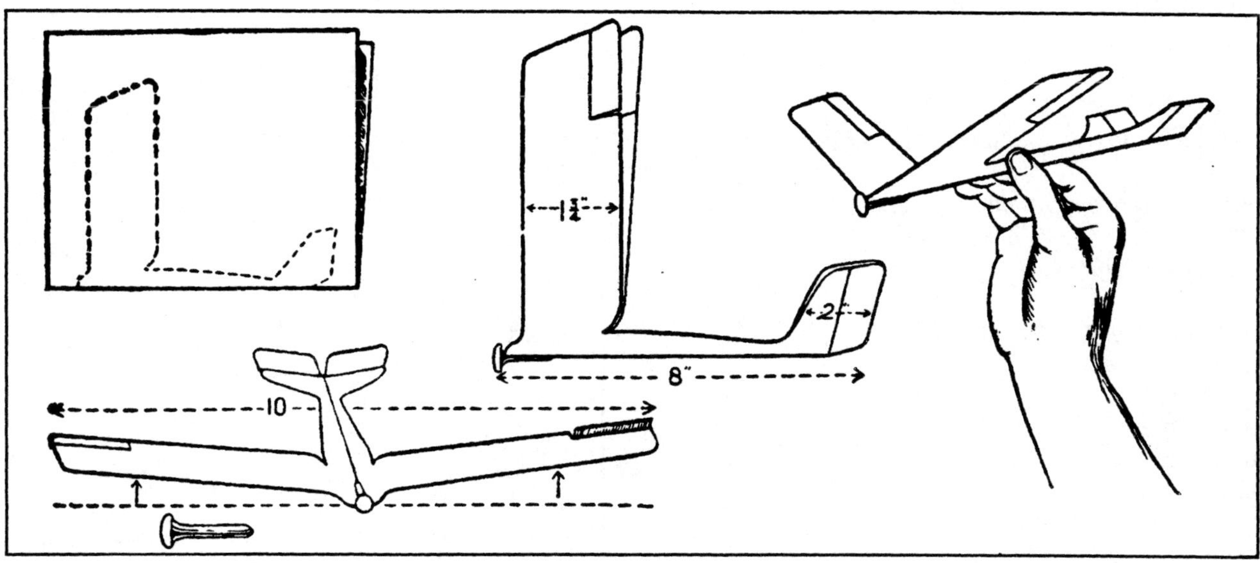

GLIDER 1

Take a piece of thin cardboard, or stiff paper, about 1 foot long and nine inches wide, and fold it across the middle. Then draw the outline of half the glider, as indicated by the dotted line, and, keeping the card folded, cut out the shape. Make cuts for the ailerons, and fix a paper-fastener to the nose as a weight.

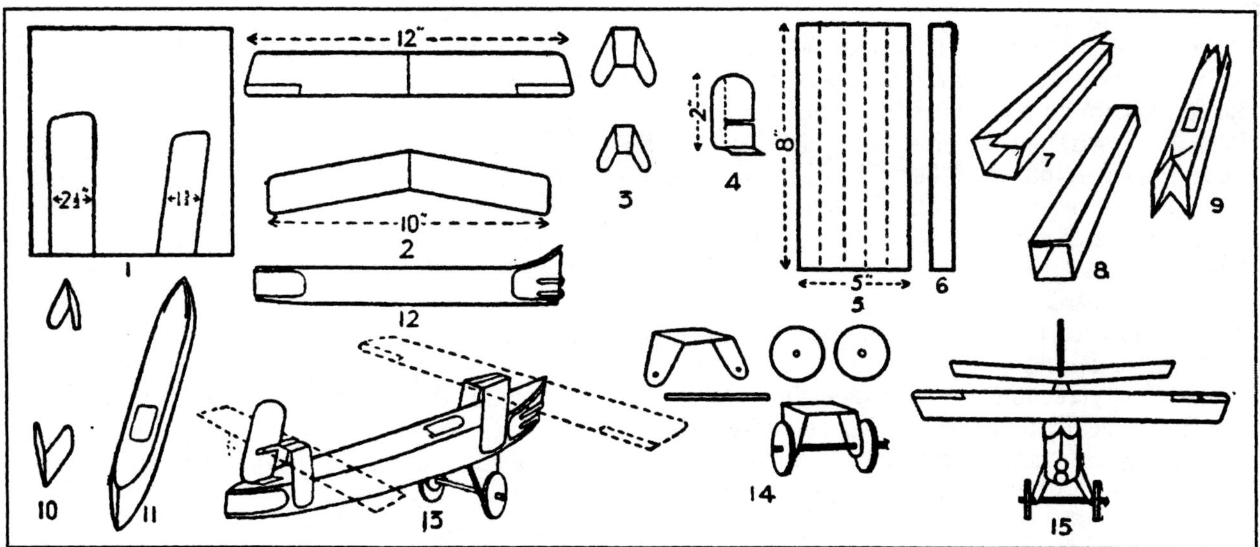

GLIDER 2

This is a more advanced type of glider. 1. The cardboard folded double and the measurements of the two planes. 2. The planes opened out. 3. Plane supports. 4. Rudder, with flap for gluing to fuselage. 5. Cardboard for the fuselage. The dotted lines show shallow cuts for folding. 6. Cardboard, when folded. 7. Ready for gluing. 8. After gluing. 9. The ends and cockpit. 10. Paper for ends. 11 and 12. The fuselage. 13. Supports and rudder in position. 14. Chassis with match for axle. 15. Glider with paper fasteners as weights.

WRIGHT BROTHERS AND OTHER INVENTORS

Project 2

Making a Telephone

Electro-Board Supplies

1 piece of soft wood, 16 cm x 7.5 cm x 2 cm
5 short screws (#6 x 3/8 self tapping)
4 Fahnestock clips
1 battery holder
1 snap connector for battery holder
an LED
1 33 ohm resistor
2 AA batteries
1 paper card 2 cm x 8 cm
20 gauge wire
a wire stripper/cutter
tape
a screwdriver
a straight pin
a black magic marker

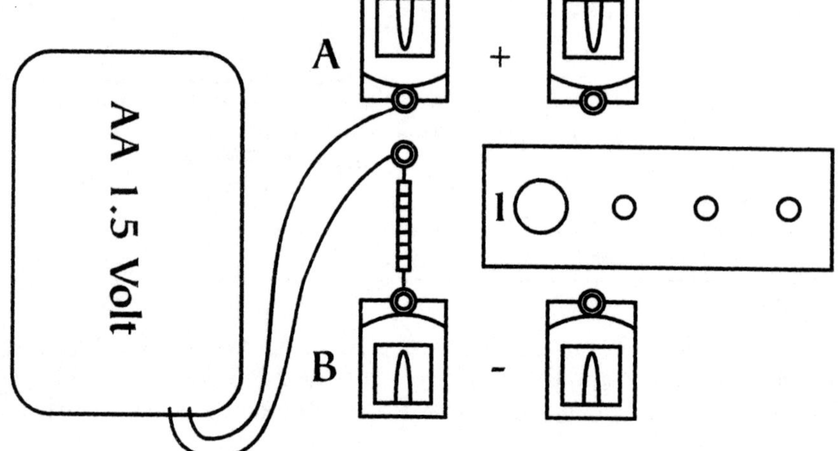

Instructions

1. Make 4 pairs of evenly spaced pinholes down the centre of the card. Mount the LED by pushing its wires through the first pin hole. These wires must not be touching. Use the marker to label the LED 1.
2. Place the card on the right end of the board
3. Bend the + wire out one side. Put a big + sign on the board above the card.
4. Bend the - wire out the other side. Put a big - sign on the board below the card.
5. Place one Fahnestock clip on each side.
6. Slide the end of a wire under each clip and use screws to attach them to the board.
7. Snap batteries into the holder and attach the snap connector. Tape the holder down on the end of the board.
8. Attach the wire at one end of the resistor and the bare end of the black wire both to the board with the same screw.
9. Use another screw and a Fahnestock clip to fasten the other end of the resistor down. Put them on the same side of the board as the - LED wire. Label this clip with a B.
10. Now, use a screw and Fahnestock clip to attach the bare end of the red wire to the + side of the board. Label this clip A.

Finally, test it. Experimenters and scientists always check out their equipment.

11. Cut two short wires and bare the ends. Attach one end of each to these Fahnestock clips. That connects them to the battery.
12. Now, place the free end of each wire into the two clips for the LED to check your circuit. It should glow as you complete its circuit. If not, make sure that the batteries are sitting properly in the holder, that everything is connected and that the LED is in the right way.

WRIGHT BROTHERS AND OTHER INVENTORS

Project 2, Page 2

Telephone Supplies

electro-board
3 pieces of wire
a light bulb
a bulb holder
a transmitter disc from
an old telephone

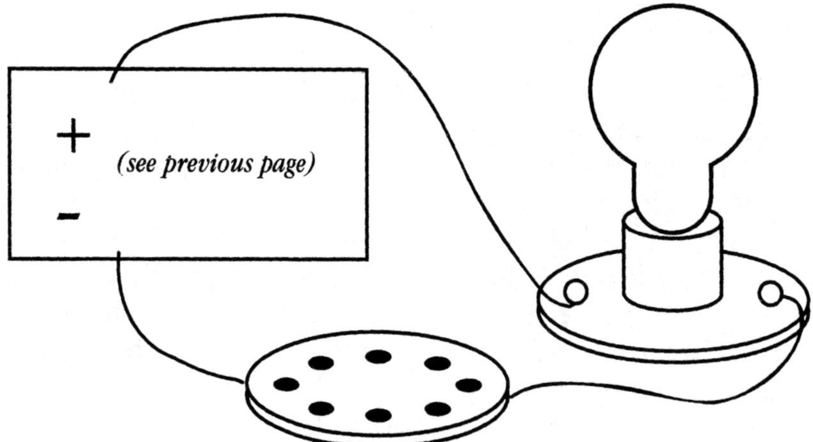

Instructions

1. Place the bulb in the holder.
   Wire it into the circuit.
2. Connect the transmitter disc to the circuit.
3. Speak into the disc.

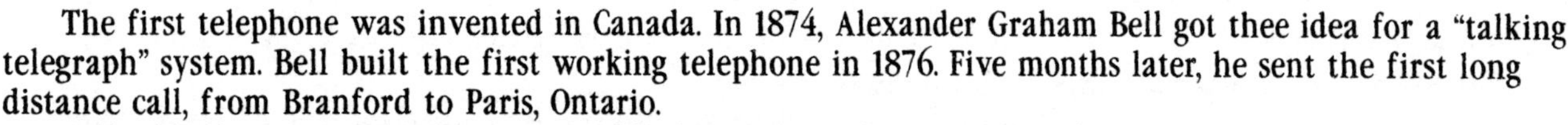

The first telephone was invented in Canada. In 1874, Alexander Graham Bell got thee idea for a "talking telegraph" system. Bell built the first working telephone in 1876. Five months later, he sent the first long distance call, from Branford to Paris, Ontario.

Bell's telephone contained a tiny cup filled with bits of carbon. This cup was the first transmitter disc. By controlling electric current, it helped to make voices clear over the telephone.

The first Canadian to install a telephone was Prime Minister Alexander Mackenzie. Bell had a phone in his laboratory, too. Whenever he arrived, he used to cover it with a towel so that its ringing would not disturb him!

Canada's first telephone exchange opened in Hamilton in 1878, with seven lines and fifty customers. Now, Canadians use telephones more than anyone else in the world. Obviously, not all Canadians feel the way Bell did.

A modern telephone has a different way of changing the current in a telephone wire. When you speak into a telephone, your voice waves hit a metal plate called a diaphragm. The diaphragm is attached to a magnet. A coil of wire is wrapped around the magnet, but not touching it. When your voice moves the diaphragm, it moves the magnet inside the coil to create a small electric current. So in this way, the sound waves are changed into electric current.

Different sound waves cause different amounts of current. A loud voice moves the diaphragm more, which moves the magnet more, which makes a stronger current. As your voice changes, different amounts of current are sent along the telephone wire as electric signals.

When the signals arrive at another telephone, it all happens in reverse. The changing current travels through the coil and its magnetism moves the magnet inside. The magnet vibrates the diaphragm which makes sound waves. The electric signals have been changed back into sound waves and someone hears your voice.

Not only telephones, but all of modern communications depends on electric signals. Sound and pictures are changed into signals and sent along wires. At the other end of the wires, the signals are received and changed back into sound and pictures. Sending signals along wires works fine if you don't have to send them too far.

When wires cannot be used, the signals are sent through the air by electromagnetic waves. These waves travel in straight lines from a sending antenna to a receiving antenna. If the distance is far enough that the waves have to travel over the curve of the earth, a series of antenna towers pass the signal along. However, satellites are often used to send long distance signals. Canada was the first country to use satellites to pass along communication signals.

Wright Brothers and Other Inventors

Project 3

Thomas Alva Edison

We live in a time where it would be hard to imagine not having lights to see by and appliances galor, that require electricity to run. But it has not always been this way. Our lives are much different from those of our great grandparents when they were young. We are going to learn about the man to whom we owe much of our modern convienences.

Thomas Alva Edison worked out his inventions by known laws of science. He had studied these laws, so that he was able to apply them to make real the visions of his imagination. Yet he had few advantages and little help, and his story if one of those that inspire us to great effort to cultivate the talents that have been given to each one of us by our heavenly Father.

He was born in February, 1847, in the little village of Milan, in Ohio. His parents were poor because his father did not keep to a settled occupation. Mr. Edison, senior, had the same kind of mind as his wonder-working son—the kind of mind that is called versatile, that can easily turn form one thing to another. He had not learned, however, that it is wise for a man with a versatile mind to find out how to do one thing thoroughly before he turns to another, and so he was not successful.

Thomas Alva Edison was a quiet, thoughtful little boy, but very inquisitive and always wanting to know how things were done. He was not very strong, however, and was not sent to school until he was quite a big child. When he did go, his teacher, who does not seem to have been very wise, thought him stupid because he asked so many questions. So his mother, who had herself been a teacher, took him away from school at the end of two months and taught him at home. With so kind and loving a teacher he made rapid progress; and above all, he learned to think. His mother had some good books, which he learned to enjoy; and when he was ten years old he read Gibbon's Decline and Fall of the Roman Empire and Hume's History of England. About that time he began to study an encyclopedia. It was probably from the encyclopedia that he first learned to take an interest in chemistry.

By this time his parents, who had moved with him to Port Huron, Michigan, were able to indulge him in his love for making experiments. He bought some books, made a little laboratory in the cellar of his home, and there laid the foundation of his knowledge of chemistry.

When he was twelve years old he decided to start out in life for himeself, and he became a newsboy on the train which ran from Port Huron to Detroit. Such a newsboy had never been seen before. He was given a corner in the baggage car in which to keep his stocks of newspapers, magazines and candy. To this corner he moved his little laboratory and library of chemical books, and when he was not engaged in business, went on with his experiments. Still time hung heavy on his hands, and to fill it up he bought a printing-press and type and published on the train a weekly newspaper filled with local news, stories of things that happened on the railway and notes of the markets.

All went well for two or three years. But when he was in his sixteenth year, one day a phosphorus bottle was jarred off one of his shelves and broke on the floor. It set fire to the baggage car, and in his anger at the danger to his train the conductor not only put the boy off the train, but soundly boxed his ears. That was the most unfortunate part of the accident, for as a result of the boxing Edison gradually lost his hearing and became almost totally deaf. His stock was lost, but an act of bravery on his part brought to his aid a new resourse and opened up a new field for him to work in.

He was standing one day on the platform of the station at Clemons, Michigan, watching a train come in, when he saw the station agent's little boy on the track right in front of the oncoming engine. Another moment and the child would have been crushed, but Edison sprang to the track, seized the little one in his arms, and rolled with him to one side, just in time to escape the wheels. To show his gratitude the baby's father offered to teach Edison telegraphy. The offer was gratefully accepted, and now that his career as a train newsboy was closed, he turned to his new accomplishemnt as a means of making a living.

He worked at telegraphy for some years, first in Port Huron, Michigan, then at Stratford, Canada, and a little later in the western states, and finally in Boston. At the same time he spent all his spare moments studying chemistry and electricity and experimenting on improved telegraph apparatus. It was during these years that he first turned his attention to duplex telegraphy, but through no fault of his own he was unable to sell his invention, and the matter dropped for a time.

In 1869, when he was in his twenty-second year, he went to New York. He arrived penniless in the city; but he was a good telegraph-operator, and was fearless of the future. And now a strange thing happened. He applied to the Gold and Stock Telegraph Company for work, and while he was waiting for a reply part of the apparatus broke down. No one knew what was the matter, and everything was in confusion until Edison said he could set the machine at work again. Permission was given him to try, and at the end of two hours, work in the offfice was going on as if nothing had happened. Edison was asked if he would accept a position at a salary of three hundred dollars a month and he accepted.

His new position gave him money and leisure for new inventions. In a little over a year he sold his telegraph inventions for a large sum of money. This enabled him once more to set up in business for himself. He built a factory in Newark, New Jersey, for the manufacture of telegraph apparatus, and since then his chief business has been that of making inventions.

The first great invention was the quadruplex system of telegraphy. About the same time Edison made an improvement in the transmitter of the telephone which made it easier for the voice-waves to travel, and improved the usefulness of the telephone very much.

It was at about the same time that he invented the phonograph. The idea of an instrument which would "write sound" and reproduce it had been thought of before by scientists, though it is doubtful if Edison knew of their efforts to make such an instrument. At any rate, he was the first to make an instrument which would work, and even he did not know that it would work until he heard it repeat the words that he had shouted into it. He says himself that when he put the reproducer in place and the instrument shouted back to him the words "Mary had a little lamb," he was never so taken aback in his life.

Edison patented his invention, which from the first excited the wonder of the world. Of course, like all first things, it was crude, and the sounds that it gave back were harsh.

Wright Brothers and Other Inventors

Project 3, Page 3

For the time he had to lay it aside, for other work pressed, but others took it up, and from his parent idea the phonograph, dictaphone and other instruments were invented. Later on, when he had more leisure, he commenced work on it again, and worked out an instrument which gives back every beautiful vibration from voice or instrument. The dictaphone, as you know, is a little instrument into which busy men and women dictate letters or documents or directions for work. The dictaphone operator causes the instrument to send the stored-up sound-waves into her ear, and from its dictation the letters on instructions can be written. Today computers have caused these to be used less and less.

When electricity was first used for illumination only large arc-lights were used. The lamps sputtered and scattered sparks, and the light was so harsh that it could be used only for street-lighting and large buildings, such as factories, drill halls and the like. Such a things as incandescent lights, which make possible the use of soflty shaded lamps, or indirect lighting in our homes, or the brilliant illumination of churches, concert halls and theatres, was not even thought of. This was the work for which Edison put aside the work of his phonograph. He believed that a number of lights could be supplied from one distributing wire, and he believed that the light could be improved so that its use would be a common thing, so he invented the incandescent lamp. He spent a couple of years over this work, and to perfect his system improved dynamo machines, and invented a whole scheme of distributing electricity so that it might be used for light, heat and power. The result is that you may read by a lamp lighted by electricity, the power for which had been generated perhaps at a waterfall miles away. The same power sends electricity to work and light offices and factories that would otherwise be dark.

Now we come to the moving pictures, where again Edison took up an idea which others had had before him. While it cannot be said that he invented the moving pictures, the invention on which the moving pictures are based is his.

These inventions are only a small part of the work done by this wonderful man. He has invented a new storage battery, giant rolls to crush rocks, a kiln for use in making Portland cement, and numbers of other things which he needed to help him in the larger work in hand.

When the World War broke out he found himself in danger of being cut off from his supply of carbolic acid for his factories at West Orange, New Jersey, so he devised a way of making it for himself, and also for making the benzol from which the carbolic acid is produced. For two years he gave his services to the United States Government and experimented and reported on many problems.

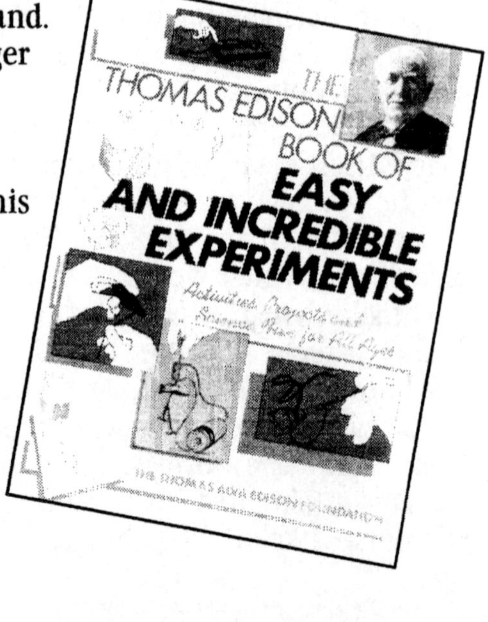

After reading the information on Thomas Alva Edison fill in the following web. Illustrate the most important events in his life. For more projects relating to Edison's work, consult the The Thomas Edison Book of Easy and Incredible Experiments.

WRIGHT BROTHERS AND OTHER INVENTORS

Project 3, Page 4

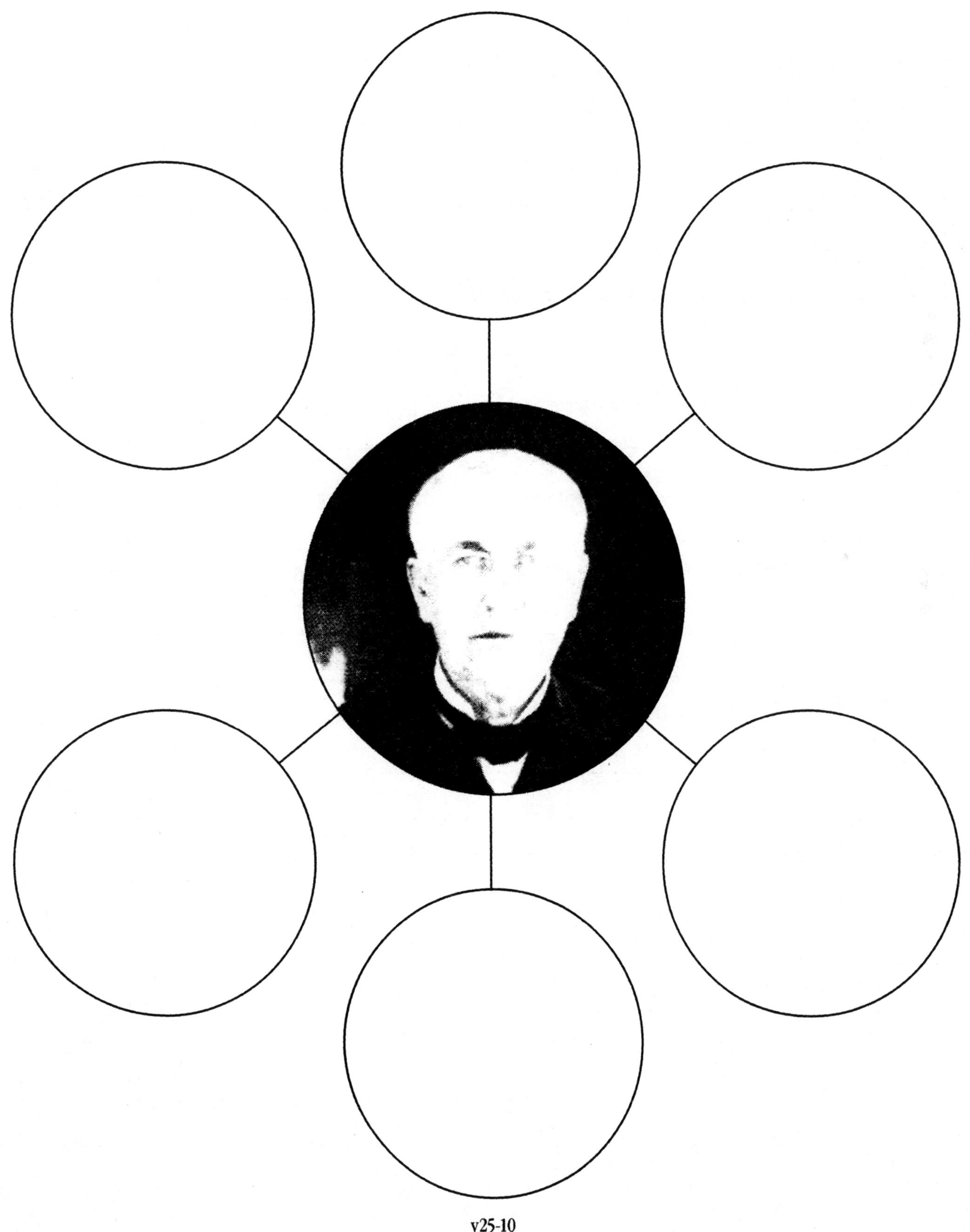

Wright Brothers and Other Inventors
Test

1. What is the date for the Wright Brothers and Other Inventors?

____

____

2. The late________ and early ________ saw many Americans inventing wonderful things we take for granted today.

3. Who was America's most famous inventor? Name two things he invented.

____

____

____

____

____

4. Who flew the first manned airplane? Where did they do this?

____

____

5. When did the airplane first gain popularity?

____

____

6. Who is responsible for the first massed produced automobile?

____

____

7. Who built the first telephone?

____

____

____

Wright Brothers and Other Inventors

Test, Page 2

Review

1. Who invented the cotton gin?

2. On which side of the War between the States did Robert E. Lee fight?

   What was his office?

3. On which side of the War between the States did Ulysses S. Grant fight?

4. Who was George Washington Carver?

5. In chronological order list the events studied to date.

   Next to each place the approximate date.

THE GREAT WORLD WAR
Worksheet

1. What are the dates of the Great World War?

2. What is nationalism?

3. What is imperialism?

4. What is militarism?

5. What are alliance systems?

6. When did the Great World War begin?

7. Name the Central Powers.

8. Name the Allied Powers.

THE GREAT WORLD WAR

Worksheet, Page 2

9. Where was the Great World War mostly fought?

____

____

10. What new weapons were used in this war?

____

____

11. The United States was initially ____________, but by 1917 entered on the side of the __________.

12. What was the Fourteen Points?

____

____

13. When did the Central Powers surrender?

____

____

14. What was the Treaty of Versailles?

____

____

15. Millions of ______________ lost their lives in the war.

The Great World War
Project

The Great War Trivia Game

Using the resources listed on the cards create a Great World War trivia game. Write the question on the side with the picture and the answer on the back. You should have at least twenty cards.

The Great World War
Project 2

Below you will read a first hand acount of Private Lowell R. Hollingshead. He was an eighteen year old American soldier during WWI, who was captured. He then delivered to Lieutenant Col. Chas W. Whittlesey the famous "Demand for Surrender."

Lowell R. Hollingshead.

On the morning of October 7, 1918, we were lying on a bleak and barren war scarred hillside in the Argonne Forest, having been separated from the rest of our command for a period of five days, all of us weakened from lack of food and continuous fighting. About ten o'clock a Sergeant came over to where myself and several comrades were lying in our funk-holes and told us the Major (meaning Major Whittlesey) had asked that eight men volunteer to try and get through to our support lines, to report our condition and get rations. I, among others, having visions of food and rest, volunteered to go. I did not at the time know the Seargeant's name nor have I ever been able to find out what Company he was with or from whom he received his orders to start us on this fool's errand. I only know that I had one driving thought, and that was the desire for food and anything that would help me secure it was all the incentive needed.

Through a light fog and mist myself and seven comrades started in the general direction of our support lines and crept down the hillside leading away from the beleagured battalion. We crossed a narrow valley and some of us waded and some of us stepped across a small stream of water known as Charlevaux Creek. Though we were badly in need of water none of us dared stop for even the smallest fraction of a second, so went hurrying on to the shelter of the forest which lay the other side of the valley. In a few minutes we were at the edge of the forest, and with a silent prayer of thanks all huddled down for a brief rest. We were very weak from lack of food as we had gone five days in this second "pocket" or trap without any. Prior to that we had been in the first "pocket" or trap for a period of three days and as there was only one day intervening between the two traps we were virtually without stimulant for a period of a week.

Imagine yourself in your own home, even with all modern twentieth century conveniences, going without food for a like period and make your own comparision between this and our little gang who had not only gone without food and water, but who for the greater part of that time had been lying out in the cold October rain in muddy funk-holes with wounded and dead lying all around us, fighting off attack after attack from the enemy and thinking each minute our last. But to go on with what happened, there was one man among the eight of us who was a full-blooded Indian from Montana and we delegated him as our leader and guide, as several times while crossing that little valley he had kept us from taking wrong paths or trails. Our very living hinged on every

The Great World War
Project 2, Page 2

wrong or right move that was made and it was only quite natural that we had a great deal of confidence in him and requested him to take the lead and guide us the rest of the way.

After resting awhile we started up a path in the forest with the Indian now leading us. He only permitted us to go short distances and them take rests to preserve what little strength we had left. We moved very carefully, going quite a bit of the way on our hands and knees. It was right after one of these rest periods when we were again moving that the Indian stopped short and motioned for the rest of us to halt by raising his hand high above his head, and I knew then the Indian had scented danger. We stopped dead in our tracks and in silence so dense you could hear your own heart beat, the machine guns suddenly started their deadly "rat-tat-tat" and we all dropped flat to the ground. We did not know where the firing was coming from, we only knew if was close and as the bullets began to cut away the brush and twigs around us, knew they had our range, yet we dared not move.

For the next few minutes we were in the midst of a terrific machine gun barrage, it fairly rained lead. As the bullets came closer and closer I noticed little spurts of dirt kicking up ahead of and around me and wondered to myself "What will happen next?" Then wondered how the other boys were faring, and even had a despairing wish that I was back with the rest of the battalion on the hill. Just about that time a peculiar feeling or chill came over me and I thought "this is the last" and fell into a sort of comma or daze. I have no idea how long that deadly "rat-tat-tat" of the machinery guns kept up, it way have been for only a few minutes or longer but it seemed like eternity to me. In my half dazed condition with every shot I felt some riveter of rivets was using the back of my head to drive his rivets in. I had no idea how many of the other fellows were alive, but I did know that the boy directly in front of me was dead as I had seen the jagged bullet holes in his head, although I do not remember him stirring or even uttering a sound.

Then came the thing that came into my mind was "what shall I do now?" I was afraid to move for fear the Germans would start their murderous fire again, but just about that time a German appeared from behind a bush not six feet from me and held a long Luger revolver leveled at my head. It is an actual fact that the barrel of it looked to me at that time as large as a shot gun.

THE GREAT WORLD WAR

Project 2, Page 3

The German half smiled, half sneered and I instinctively raised my hands and said the only German word I knew, "Kamerad." Perhaps a second passed between the time I said "Kamerad" until he slowly lowered his gun, but it seemed several lifetimes to me and I can never tell you all the thoughts that passed through my mind in that brief space of time. I do however, distinctly remember that my first thoughts were of my Mother, Dad and home and then a review of all my kid days and a multitude of thoughts too numerous to mention flooded through my mind and a whole pantomine of my life paraded through my brain like a swift moving motion picture. After the German lowered his gun he smiled a great smile, and what a lovely looking German he was. As he stood there in his gray uniform fully six feet tall, his smile seemed to broaden and broaden then he started walking toward me. I suppose the reason his smile is still in my mind is because it was so unexpected, as I had been taught to hate and expect fearful things from the Germans, should they ever capture me. I do not honestly believe there was ever any real hatred in my heart for the Germans or anyone else, and I have yet to hear any man who was actually "IN IT" say he ever had hatred in his heart. I have, however, heard many men who went through it all say that their outstanding feeling was one of self pity rather than anything else.

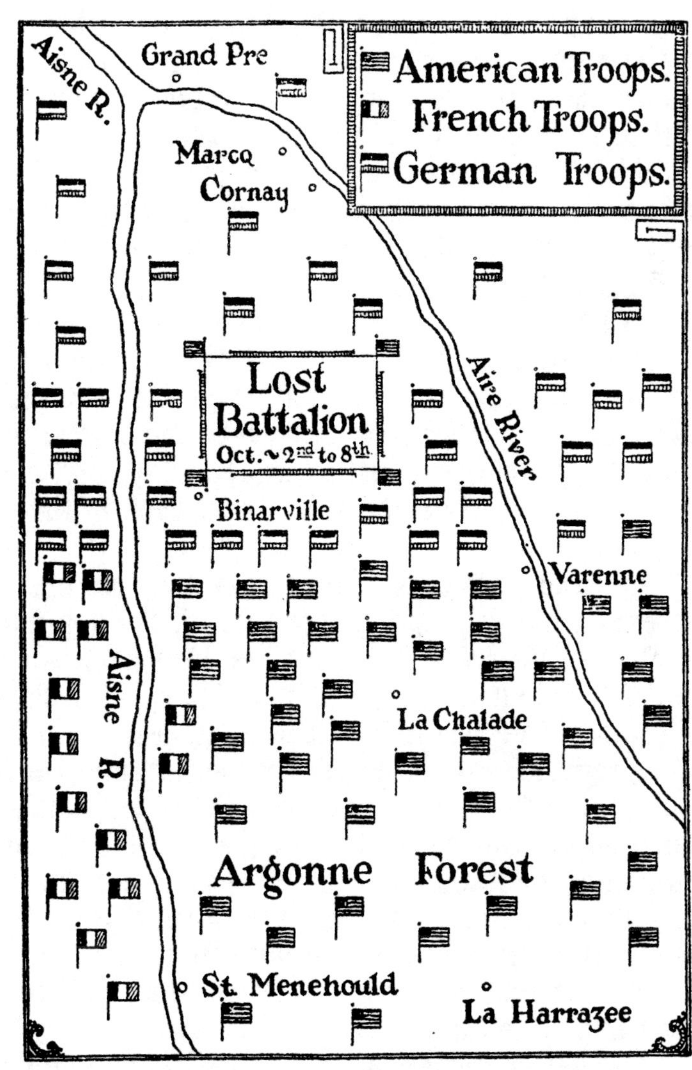

The German stepped over to me and started talking in his own language and pointed at my leg. I half turned and looked to where he was pointing and saw blood spouting from my leg near the knee. For the first time I realized I had been hit. Then other Germans appeared and began looking at my comrades and then I knew how they had fared. Of my seven Buddies I found four had been killed outright and all the rest wounded. Our Indian guide was one of those who had been killed. With this realization a sickening sensation came over me and I thought to myself "this is not real, it is just a dream."

My three comrades were more seriously injured than I and the same German who captured me put my arm around his shoulder and I half hobbled and was half carried over to where the machine gun sat which had played such havoc with us. The other Germans

carried my comrades over. They held a consultation and finally sent one of their men back to get instructions as to what to do with us. While he was gone I had an experience that I believe no other American prisoner had, and that was to have the gunner who had shot me down show me how they worked their machine guns, even going so far as to demonstrate by shooting in the general direction of the hillside where our Battalion lay. By this time the German Runner had returned and motioned for me to get up and started walking back through the forest with me, while other Germans carried my three comrades on improvised stretchers. Having to be carried it was necessary for them to stop often, and as I was able to make better progress went on ahead and did not see them any more. I felt more God-forsaken than ever without my Buddies. After we had gone a short distance I was turned over to another guide and a little farther on another, and in this way was relayed back to the German headquarters. The first thing each new guide would do was go through my pockets but none of them took any of my belongings. I was duly thankful for this as we all carried some little insignificant things which we treasured highly.
The one thing that interested all these different guides was my Gillette razor and they all wanted it. Two of them offering to buy it and another to trade his straight razor for it, but when I made known by gestures that I had declined, he put it back in my pocket.

Quite a distance from German Headquarters I was blindfolded and the bandage was not taken from my eyes until I arrived there. I entered what was apparently an ordinary dug-out and very completely furnished, being divided into small rooms having board floors and walls. I was taken to the best furnished of all the rooms. On a beautifully carved table was a typewriter, a phonograph, several chairs and a comfortable couch in the room all went to make the place as cozy and homelike as a front line dug-out could be made. As I was greeted by a well-dressed and handsome German Officer I could not help but make a comparison in my mind between this comfortable dug-out and immaculately clothed Officer and our Officers lying out on that cold war-strafed hillside, and for the first time I had a feeling of deep resentment.

This officer turned out to be Lieutenant Heinrich Prinz and addressing me in perfect English, his first question was, "How long since you have eaten?" and I replied, "five days." He said, "Poor devil, you must be starved." And I answered, "I certainly am." He then called an orderly to whom he spoke and who hurriedly disappeared. Prinz told me to lie down, but before doing so he gave me a gold tipped cigarette from a box which sat on his table and we were for all the world like host and guest rather than an officer and captured enemy soldier.

While I was resting a Doctor appeared from an interlocking dug-out and dressed my wound, and just as he was finishing, the orderly whom Prinz had previously sent out returned with a pail full of vegetables, meat and what-not swimming in vinegar. Also he had a large loaf of dark German war bread. He laid all this on the table before me and without any more adieu I went to it.

While I was eating Prinz and two other officers started asking me questions about our outfit, but finding it of no avail as I was still hungrily gulping down the food and between bites told them I was too busy to talk to them. In the meantime my leg started bleeding terribly and paining me so that I hardly cared what happened. Prinz called the medical officer again who undressed the wound, placed something on it that seemed to stop the bleeding and then placed a turniquet above the wound, bade me lie down on the couch again.

Then Prinz started asking me questions in earnest. He was very kind about the whole affair and at no time did he or any of the Germans with whom I came in contact treat me roughly or in any way abuse me. Prinz asked me what State I was from and I said "Ohio," he said, "Oh yes, I have been there to Cincinnati." And then he told me he had been in business for six years in Seattle, Washington. He said that he greatly admired the courage of our men on the hill and felt sorry for them. He then tried to find out how much ammunition we had, the number of men, etc., but I would not answer any of the questions and could not if I would. He then told me to come with him and led me to the mouth of the dug-out and handed me a powerful pair of glasses and asked me if I could locate our men on the hillside, all of which appeared very clearly through the glasses to me; but I said I could not as I was mixed up in my directions and he laughed and said, "Oh, I see, as you Americans say, you are a little entangled." Then he led me back into the dug-out again, by this time my head was beginning to go round in a whirl as I was quite weak from the loss of blood. Noting my condition he asked me to lie down again and rest, which I did. It was then about two or three o'clock in the afternoon.

He went to his typewriter and started typing and when he had finished he asked if I would take a letter back to my commanding officer. I told him I would like to read it first and he handed it to me. This letter was the "Demand for Surrender." Then I told him that I would go after I was rested. I do not know what possessed me to say that, except that I wanted to turn it over in my mind and for reasons unknown even to myself was stalling for time. It seemed like a dream to me to be sitting there captured and having this German Officer ask me to take back to my own Commander this request for surrender. I was just dozing off to sleep when Prinz touched me on the shoulder and said, "If you are to get the message back before dark you must start now." And I replied, "I am ready."

THE GREAT WORLD WAR
Project 2, Page 6

He then placed the letter securely in my pocket and going to a corner of the dug-out brought forth a cane which he handed me saying, "This will aid you in walking." (That cane is still one of my dearest treasures). Next he went to the Doctor's dug-out and came back with a white cloth which he tied to a stick and said it would be my protection while crossing No-Man's Land. It was to serve as a flag of truce. Then he called one of his men telling me this man would guide me through the German Lines to their farthest outposts to look out for me and not shoot at me, then giving me two packages of his cigarettes and what was left of the bread that had been brought for me to eat, he again placed the bandage over my eyes and bade me good-bye. I started out with my guide leading me. I liked this guide because he was very careful that I did not stumble over any rocks or other obstacles, and he tried to talk to me but I could not understand him.

In a little while we stopped and I was standing alone. Being very much exhausted I lay down and soon a German soldier came and threw and overcoat over me. I was thankful for this as I was really chilly but I do not know whether this was done to protect me from the cold wind or to conceal me from the sight of any of our planes that might happen that way at any time.

After I had lain there a few minutes I heard several Germans talking excitedly and then very suddenly and very near me a machine gun broke loose and for a short space of time I thought I was being murdered. However, I soon discovered the bullets were not coming my way and once more life seemed sweet, even to a wounded prisoner in the German Lines. I never knew at what they were firing but soon the firing ceased and my guide came and helped me to my feet and we continued on our way.

I have no idea how far we walked but at last we came to a halt and my guide removed the bandage from my eyes. I was much surprised to find that we were on a road as I remembered no road in that part of the forest. He pointed straight down the road and I knew he meant for me to travel that way. He smiled and spoke a few words in German to me and we shook hands. Then I started across No-Man's Land alone, limping along on my cane, blood soaking through the bandage on my leg, almost at the point of exhaustion, exposed to plain sight of both armies, I could not drive away the thought, "This is the end of my world."

I had not gone far when I came to our own outpost and was halted by one of our sentinels who asked me who I was and where I had been. I told him I had come from the German Lines and had a letter for Major Whittlesey. He called a Lieutenant who took me to Major Whittlesey to whom I presented my letter, after reading it and hearing what had happened to me, Major Whittlesey told me to go lie down and rest, so I went to my funk-hole and immediately fell unconscious.

Lt. Col. Charles W. Whittlesey

The Great World War

Project 2, Page 7

Below you will find the letter written from the German Officer to Major Whittlesey.

The Demand for Surrender

To the Commanding Officer-Infantry, 77th Division.

"Sir:-The bearer of this present, Private Lowell R. Hollingshead, has been taken prisioner by us. He refused to give the German Intelligence Officer any answer to his questions, and is quite an honorable fellow, doing honor to his Fatherland in the strictest sense of the word.

"He has been charged against his will, believing that he is doing wrong to his country to carry forward this present letter to the officer in charge of the batttalion of the 77th Division, with the purpose to recommend this commander to surrender with his forces, as it would be quite useless to resist any more, in view of the present conditions.

"The suffering of your wounded men can be heard over here in the German lines, and we are appealing to your human sentiments to stop. A white flag shown by one of your men will tell us that you agree with these conditions. Please treat Private Lowell R. Hollingshead as an honorable man. He is quite a soldier. We envy you.

The German Commanding Officer."

Under command of Major Charles W. Whittlesey, 550 men were cut off from the remainder of the Seventy-seventh Division and surrounded by a superior number of the enemy near Charlevaux, in the Forest d'Argonne, from the morning of October 3, 1918, to the night of October 7, 1918. Without food for more than one hundred hours, harassed continuously by machine gun, rifle, trench mortar, and grenade fire, Major Whittlesey's command, with undaunted spirit and magnificent courage, successfully met and repulsed daily violent attacks by the enemy. They held the position which had been reached for an advance, until communication was re-established with friendly troops. When relief finally came, approximately 194 officers and men were able to walk out of the position. Officers and men killed numbered 107.

On the fourth day a written proposition to surrender received from the Germans was treated with the contempt which it deserved.

The officers and men of these troops during their five days of isolation continually gave unquestionable proof of extraordinary heroism.

After reading the information on the Lost Battalion pretend that you were a news correspondent covering this story for your paper back home. Write an article about the Lost Battalion for your readers at home.

The Great World War

Project 2, Page 8

The Great World War

Project 3

The instructions for this project can be found in Appendix 2-1.

Enter the U.S.

I

When the United States decided to enter the rank of the great world powers, it did so almost overnight. To some degree, this wasn't so surprising, as the U.S. had been one of the great industrial giants for some time and easily had the population and resources that were necessary. The US had historically been fairly isolationistic, however, and had only raised large armies during the brief period in which it had fought a civil war. The man who, more than any other, was responsible for changing this situation was a naval historian named Alfred Thayer Mahan. Mahan isn't too well known today, but in his day, he was one of the most influential and well-known historians. The basic lesson that he drew from his studies of military and naval history were that countries that controlled the sea usually won and went on to dominate their opponents that ignored the importance of sea power.

II

Mahan's influence did not just effect the U.S. In fact, the naval officers' training schools in practically every major country made him required reading. His effect was greatest in England, Germany and Japan. In England, his ideas wouldn't be too surprising, because England had long depended on its naval power, but this marked a change that was very dramatic in the U.S., Germany and Japan. From the time that Germany was unified, in 1871, it had aspired to world leadership and Mahan's theories seemed to indicate that they needed a navy to do this. Wilhelm II, the second Kaiser of Germany agreed with Mahan wholeheartedly. His decision to start building a large navy was one of the main things which scared England into allying itself with the French against the Germans, a major turning point which prepared the world for World War I. In Japan, which had recently had a revolution called the Meiji Restoration and had been working very hard to modernize itself, Mahan's ideas found much support and it began embarking on a very ambitious naval program. When Mahan began writing, England was the world's foremost naval power with France a distant second. Though when he died England was still number one, Germany, Japan and the U.S. had all surpassed France.

III

One of Mahan's most enthusiastic fans was Theodore Roosevelt. The two men wrote each other and discussed their ideas for many years. The U.S. actually began building a world-class fleet in the last decade of the nineteenth century, which was just in time to

THE GREAT WORLD WAR

Project 3, Page 2

help the U.S. win an easy victory over Spain in the Spanish-American War. Roosevelt's dashing leadership during that war actually helped to bring him into the national spotlight. When Roosevelt became president himself, he announced to the world that the US had arrived as a world power when he sent the "Great White Fleet" around the globe on a world-wide tour. He also was instrumental in the creation of the Panama Canal, which made it much easier for the U.S. to make use of its naval power. Finally, he brokered a peace deal between the humbled Russian empire and the new, up-and-coming naval power in the Pacific, Japan in the Russo-Japanese War.

Vocabulary

1. *industrial:* ______________________________

____

2. *isolationistic:* ______________________________

____

3. *Kaiser:* ______________________________

____

4. *dashing:* ______________________________

____

5. *instrumental:* ______________________________

____

6. *brokered:* ______________________________

____

Key Word Outline

I ______________________________

1 ______________________________

2 ______________________________

3 ______________________________

The Great World War

Project 3, Page 3

4 ______________________________

5 ______________________________

6 ______________________________

II ______________________________

1 ______________________________

2 ______________________________

3 ______________________________

4 ______________________________

5 ______________________________

6 ______________________________

7 ______________________________

8 ______________________________

9 ______________________________

10 ______________________________

III ______________________________

1 ______________________________

2 ______________________________

3 ______________________________

4 ______________________________

5 ______________________________

6 ______________________________

7 ______________________________

The Great World War

Project 3, Page 4

Answers

Vocabulary

1. *industrial:* having to do with the production of machine-made goods
2. *isolationistic:* unwilling to interfere with what is happening in the rest of the world.
3. *Kaiser:* a term used to describe the emperor of Germany; it is basically German for "Caesar".
4. *dashing:* brave and courageous like a story-book hero; gallant
5. *instrumental:* having a great influence
6. *brokered:* negotiated a deal or compromise

Key Word Outline

I Mahan and the dawn of U.S. sea power

1. US, decided, overnight
2. Industrial, giant, resources
3. Historically, isolationistic
4. Responsible, historian, Mahan
5. One, most, influential
6. Lesson: importance, sea

II Mahan's influence abroad

1. Not, just, US
2. Made, required, reading
3. Effect, Germany, Japan
4. England, not, surprising
5. Germany, aspired, leadership
6. Wilhelm II, agreed, Mahan
7. decision, scared, England
8. Japan, ambitious, program
9. Began, France, second
10. All, surpassed, France

III Teddy Roosevelt and the New U.S. Muscle

1. Enthusiastic, fans, Roosevelt
2. Two, wrote, discussed
3. Began, building, 19th Century
4. Dashing, leadership, war
5. Announced, U.S., power
6. Instrumental, creation, Canal
7. Brokered, peace, Russo-Japanese War

The Great World War
Test

1. What are the dates of the Great World War?

2. In Europe what set the stage for the Great World War?

3. When did the Great World War begin?

4. Who were the Central Powers?

5. Who were the Allied Powers?

6. What new weapons were used during the Great World War?

7. When did the United States enter the war?

The Great World War
Test, Page 2

8. What was the Fourteen Points?

9. Who finally surrendered?

10. What was the Treaty of Versailles?

Review

1. For what is George Washington Carver best known?

2. What was the 13th amendment to the Constitution?

3. What was the 15th amendment to the Constitution?

4. In chronological order list all the events studied to date.
   Next to each place the approximate date.

Roaring Twenties
Worksheet

1. What is the date given on your card for the Roaring Twenties?

2. What was Prohibition?

3. Why did people break the law during Prohibition?

4. What evidence of moral decay did we see during the Roaring Twenties?

5. What was the cause of the Great Depression?

6. What was the most popular sport during the twenties?

Roaring Twenties
Worksheet, Page 2

7. Who was Babe Ruth?

____

____

8. Charles Lindbergh flew his plane, the ______________________, across the Atlantic Ocean by himself.

9. What theory was a teacher arrested for teaching in 1925?

____

____

____

Roaring Twenties
Project

Fashion Trends

After looking at the pictures below of clothing from the 1890's, 1900's, 1920's, 1930's and 1940's write a paragraph or two comparing the different styles.

Roaring Twenties
Project 2

Movie

Times were changing and rapidly. Young people were flocking to the movies which were making changes themselves. In 1927 the first talking picture, *The Jazz Singer*, starring Al Jolson aired. Its hard for us to imagine, but imagine the delight and surprise to be able to see people talking on stage. *The Jazz Singer* can be rented at most local video stores. View this movie and see how times have changed.

Roaring Twenties
Project 3

Prohibition—Making Root Beer

The United States Congress amended the Constitution in 1919 and made alcohol illegal. This amendment was called Prohibition. Prohibition made alcohol even more attractive to some and gangsters like Al Capone produced alcohol illegally. He brewed beer and would sell it in nightclubs and other places. If you want to see how it was made you can make ROOT BEER which is a similar process.

Ingredients

9 cups sugar
4 3/4 gallons warm water
1/2 teaspoon fresh dry yeast
1 bottle Shank's Root beer extract
bottles

Dissolve 9 cups sugar in 4 3/4 gallons of warm water. Stir in one bottle of Shanks Root Beer Extract (Shanks Extracts, Inc., Lancaster, Pa 17603). Mix in 1/2 teaspoon fresh dry yeast in 2 cups warm water. Let stand for 5 minutes. Then add yeast mixture to sugar solution; stir and bottle immediately. Fill bottles to within 1/2 inch from top. Store bottles in a warm place for six to ten days and refrigerate before serving.

Roaring Twenties
Test

1. What are the dates given for the Roaring Twenties?

2. What was the amendment to the Constitution in 1919 making alcohol illegal called?

3. Who was the most famous gangster in the twenties?

4. What was one of the ways gangsters made money during prohibition?

5. How was moral decay evident in the twenties?

6. How did popular music change during the twenties?

7. Businessmen forsook sound business practices and tried to make money quickly and with ______________ money.

8. What was the cause of the Great Depression?

Roaring Twenties
Test, Page 2

9. In the twenties what was the most popular sport? Who was its most famous player?

10. Who was Charles Lindbergh?

11. What theory became more popular to teach in public schools?

Review

1. Who was our sixteenth president?

2. What replaced the Pony Express?

3. Who were the '49ers?

4. What was the Cherokee Trail of Tears?

5. On the back list in chronological order all the events studied to date.

   Next to each place the approximate date.

THE GREAT DEPRESSION
Worksheet

1. What are the dates given for The Great Depression?

2. What triggered the Great Depression?

3. What happened during the Great Depression?

4. What one person do many people blame for the Great Depression?

5. Who was elected president in 1932?

6. What was the New Deal?

7. What occured in 1932 that helped to bring an end to the Depression?

The Great Depression
Project

The Crisis of the Early 1930's

The Boom

In the summer and early autumn of 1929, the United States looked like a very prosperous country except in the farming regions. Many mills were working night and day; stores were crowded with eager buyers; prices were high; new factories new homes, new roads were being built; on the stock exchanges in the big cities, stocks and bonds were selling at far more than they were worth. It was a "boom" time.

A few business men, a few economists, looked grave. They remembered that boom times had often before been followed by a bad crisis and depression. But others said that a new era had come to the earth, in which everyone would have plenty of money. They said that the old rules which had held in former times, when wealth was limited, no longer held. The United States government tried to reduce the feverish activity by having the Federal Reserve banks charge higher interest on loans. But this did not check the boom, for there was so much wealth and credit that borrowers could easily find money elsewhere. Every day there seemed to be more buying and selling, more building, more jobs, more business. Wages were high, and people were buying furniture, houses, automobiles, even stocks and bonds, on the installment plan.

The Crash and the Depression

Then suddenly, in October, prices went down and business almost stopped. Stocks and bonds could not be sold; people began to save their money, to dismiss their employees, and to buy as little as possible. Things went from bad to worse; factories and mines closed, farmers lost their farms when mortgages were foreclosed, and little shops had to be given up. People who could not pay their rent went to live with relatives. In all the towns one saw rows of empty stores, and tall chimneys from which no smoke came. Taxes failed. People who had always paid their own way had to be helped by charity, and people who usually gave to charity had little money left to give. People were worried, hungry, and miserable.

Causes of the Depression

1. Some laid the blame for the depression on the World War, and called attention to the billions of dollar's worth of property that had been destroyed and the millions of men that had been killed or wounded.
2. Some pointed to the invention of new machinery and said that every new machine put men out of work.
3. Other people thought that the tariffs between counties had been so high as to shut off international trade, and they claimed that tariffs were partly to blame.
4. Still others believed that people everywhere had been living beyond their incomes, and that the depression was the result of their folly.

The Great Depression
Project, Page 2

5. Many students claimed that such depressions come because the business system and control in the modern business world are formed on wrong principles. They said that such depressions will continue until better principles are adopted.

Nobody, however, was wise enough to be sure which of these causes was most important. Nor could anyone be sure that he knew just what changes should be made or how they could be made.

With business so bad, employers had to turn away more and more of their workmen. By October, 1931, it was roughly estimated that ten million people were out of work. Every town and state, as well as the United States government, tried to find ways of helping the unemployed. Public buildings and roads were built, so as to keep busy as many as possible. Wealthy people gave millions of dollars; colleges gave part of the money which they received from athletic games; everybody tried to relieve the distress caused by the lack of work. But as the months passed, things grew worse instead of better. The value of American exports fell about two billions of dollars in the two years after 1929. Business men found their profits growing smaller and smaller; such workers as still had jobs were very poorly paid. The American people had not for many years known such poverty and want.

"UNCLE SAM" IN TROUBLE

The Federal government is merely the representative of all of us. And so when the people are in financial trouble the government at Washington also suffers. The larger part of the money with which the government is run comes from income taxes. Of course when incomes grow smaller the government receives less money. In writing to Congress on December 9, 1931, President Hoover said that Uncle Sam's expenses for the next year would be over two billion dollars more than his income.

Not even the Federal government can afford not to balance its budget—that is, not to raise enough money each year to pay its expenses. Hence, upon getting this message from President Hoover, Congress levied new taxes. It increased postage rates, and taxed theater tickets, gasoline, and tickets to athletic games. Income taxes were made higher. And still the budget was not balanced. It was no wonder that there arose all over the country a demand that the costs of government be reduced.

Other nations were also in deep trouble; they too could not balance their budgets. Germany had been paying for reparation debts, but she had paid them out of borrowed money. Everywhere there was unemployment and depression and poor crops and business failures. At the beginning of 1932, this world wide depression had lasted over two years and was growing worse every day.

THE GREAT DEPRESSION

Project, Page 3

THE ELECTION OF 1932

The election of a president and a Congress in 1932 took place under unusual conditions. The depression made many people restless and dissatisfied, and eager for a change. The prohibition amendment had not worked so well as had been hoped. Moreover people were not agreed on what ought to be done about the debts which foreign nations owed us. President Hoover was again the Republican nominee. The election was held on November 8, 1932, and resulted in the choice of Franklin D. Roosevelt, a Democrat, as president. With him the people elected enough Democrats to control the Senate and House of Representatives.

The United States was in the midst of the depression when President Roosevelt was inaugurated on March 4, 1933.

THE BANKING CRISIS

Since 1922, many banks in the farming regions of the country had failed, but in 1932 most of the banks in the cities and in the East were still carrying on business. In January and February of 1933, however, people began to fear that even these banks would fail. In February there was a frightened rush by the people who had money in the banks to take it out. Just before March 4, people were wondering if all the suffering they had endured was only the beginning, and if things would soon be far worse than ever.

President Roosevelt acted at once. He did two things: He ordered all the banks in the country to close for a few days: They were not to open until the fright was over and their affairs were in good order. He called an extra session of Congress to pass laws to help the country recover from the depression.

THE NEW DEAL

President Roosevelt promised the people a "New Deal." No one knew just what this new deal was to be, and Mr. Roosevelt himself said that he did not know. He said that new conditions had come, and that men and governments must try new ways of dealing with them; they must experiment. He gathered around him the economists and scholars who had studied these conditions, and after the conferences with these men he advised Congress.

Congress passed a series of eighteen laws between March 9 and June 16, 1933, which taken together form the basis for the New Deal. Some of the most important of these laws are:

The Emergency Banking Law, which was passed to bring back confidence of the people to the banks. The president was given power to control money and banking through the Federal Reserve system. He was also to forbid the people to hoard money, especially gold, where it would do no good. Another law, the Glass-Steagall Act, made the government insure the money that its citizens placed in the banks, and provided other ways of making the banks safer.

An *Economy Act* stopped the payment of great sums of money to World War soldiers who had not been wounded in the war, and reduced the salaries of government employees.

The Great Depression
Project, Page 4

A *Prohibition Modification Act* placed a tax upon beer and wine, which was not permitted to be sold. (A movement against the Eighteenth Amendment itself was going on at this time, which resulted in its repeal on December 5, 1933. Since that time the control of liquor traffic has been mainly in the hands of the states.)

An unemployment *Relief Act* and a *Federal Emergency Relief Act* directed that idle workers be used by the government in various conservation projects. They were to plant trees, prevent forest fires, control floods, guard against erosion, fight insect pests and plant diseases. Thousands of men and boys were put to work out of doors under this act, with good food and warm clothing.

The Agricultural Adjustment Act was aimed at the raising of prices of farm products. The Secretary of Agriculture was to regulate the amount of cotton, wheat, and other crops. Since the prices usually go higher when there is a smaller crop, he tried to reduce the amount raised. If, for instance, a farmer reduced his wheat crop from forty to thirty-three acres, the Agricultural Administration paid him about what he would lose by not planting seven acres. The money to pay this fee to the farmer came from the miller who made the wheat into flour; he had to pay a "processing tax" on the flour he made. The Thomas Amendment to this bill gave the president the power to reduce the value of the dollar, as measured by the value of the standard gold dollar as much as half. Another law, the *Farm Credits Act,* offered a plan to help farmers whose land was mortgaged.

The Home Owners Loan Act was passed to help the people who could not pay the mortgages on their homes because of the hard times. The government borrowed money from people by selling them bonds. Then the government loaned this money to home-owners who needed it.

The Emergency Railway Act created the office of a Federal Coordinator of Transportation, with three committees to help him. They were to advise the railroads what to do to save expenses. In this way Uncle Sam tried to save the poorer railroads from bankruptcy.

The Tennessee Valley Authority did something that was new and different; it actually put the United States into business. Uncle Sam was directed to make electric power from the valuable falls at and near Muscle Shoals, in Tennessee and Alabama, and to sell it to farms, towns, and cities. The nation watched this new venture carefully to see whether it could succeed or not.

The National Industrial Recovery Act was commonly known as the *NIRA* or the *NRA.* Its purpose was to help revive business and to regulate it so as to prevent the conditions that had helped to bring on the crisis and the hard times. Each trade and industry was asked to draw up a set of rules, called a code, which were to list what it was fair to do in that particular business. Minimum wages were set for the lowest-paid workers. All workers might form unions, which could bargain for wages with employers. The effect of this law was to stimulate business and to put it under national control, to raise the pay of the lowest-paid workers, and to start a fresh struggle between the employers and the unions. In May, 1935, the Supreme Court declared the most important parts of the NRA to be unconstitutional. Some of its results had been so good, however, that many large companies decided, of their own free will, to continue to observe the codes.

The Great Depression

Project, Page 5

General Results of the New Deal

At once after the passing of these new laws, many people felt more cheerful. They felt that their government was trying to help them, and they were encouraged to help themselves. By July 1, 1934, about a year after the laws were passed, it was clear that things were better. More men were at work, many more people were able to buy food and clothing, and more banks were open. Sometimes things became worse for a short time, and then better again. Recovery was halting and slow, and the recovery laws were bitterly criticized all over the country. While this was going on, thoughtful people were trying to think how terrible depressions like that of 1929-1935 might be prevented in the future. They said that:

1. People and nations must find out what causes such hard times as came to the United States in 1837, 1857, 1873, 1893, and 1929.
2. When the causes are found, they should be removed. The bad effects can never be remedied if the causes remain.

Most of the original New Deal laws were greatly changed after their passage, as parts of them were found to be mistaken or inadequate, or the need for them no longer existed. President Roosevelt followed the custom first begun by Wilson, of talking to the people at intervals about the government and its problems, over the radio. His simple and earnest talks pleased the nation and made the complicated problems of recovery clearer to his listeners. In 1934 an election of state officers, and of members of Congress showed that a great majority of the people trusted the President and believed that the New Deal would improve their condition. It was noticed that a great many people were now asking if things were right instead of asking only if they were successful. As the year 1935 closed, it recorded so many changes for the better since 1932 that the nation entered upon 1936 with hope, with sober questioning as to what is right and just and wise, and with courage to keep trying new ways until the best ways of living together, both within the United States and with other peoples, shall be found and put into practice.

After reading this, list the more important separate acts in the New Deal legislation enacted by the special session of Congress called by President Roosevelt. Show what each act was intended to do.

THE GREAT DEPRESSION
Test

1. What are the dates given for The Great Depression?

____

____

2. What triggered The Great Depression?

____

____

3. What was The Great Depression?

____

____

____

4. Why did businesses quit making products during The Great Depression?

____

____

5. Farmers received less and less money for their _______________.
6. What one person did many people blame for The Great Depression?

____

____

7. What was the New Deal and who enacted it?

____

____

8. What finally brought an end to The Great Depression?

____

____

THE GREAT DEPRESSION
Test, Page 2

Review

1. Who was Thomas Edison?

2. What was the Spanish-American War?

3. Why was the cotton gin such an important invention?

4. What was Andrew Jackson's nickname?

5. List in chronological order all those events studied to date.

   Next to each place the approximate date.

World War II, the Biggest War
Worksheet

1. What are the dates given for World War II?

____

____

2. When did World War II begin?

____

____

3. Who were the Axis Powers?

____

____

____

4. Who were the Allied Powers?

____

____

____

5. When did the U.S. declare war on Japan?

____

____

6. Hitler set up ______________________ for Jews and POW's.
7. About how many Jews did Hitler have killed?

____

____

8. What was D-Day?

____

____

____

World War II, the Biggest War
Worksheet

9. When did Germany surrender to the allies?

____

____

10. What ultimatum did President Truman give to the Japanese? Because of their response what did President Truman do?

____

____

____

____

11. Japan surrendered on ________________________________.

World War II, the Biggest War

Project

Movie and Radio Newscast

Watch one or both of the following movies: *Tora! Tora! Tora!* ("Tora! Tora! Tora! is the Japanese signal to attack—and the movie meticulously recreates the attack on Pearl Harbor and the events that leading up to it.), or *The Longest Day* ("On June 6, 1944, the Allied invasion of France marked the beginning of the end of Nazi domination over Europe. The attack involved 3,000,000 men, 11,000 planes and 4,000 ships, compromising the largest armada the world has ever seen. Presented in its original black and white version, *The Longest Day* is a vivid, hour-by-hour re-creation of this historic event.)

After watching one of these movies pretend that you are a journalist covering these events. Make a tape recording for a radio broadcast.

World War II, the Biggest War

Project 2–Literature Unit

The Hiding Place

After reading *The Hiding Place,* complete the following book report.

Title of book: ______________________

Author: ______________________

Is this book fiction or non-fiction?

____

____

Describe the three main characters in the book.

Be sure to give as much detail as possible.

1. ______________________

____

____

____

____

2. ______________________

____

____

____

____

3. ______________________

____

____

____

____

____

World War II, the Biggest War

Project 2, Page 2—Literature Unit

What time in history does this story take place?

Write a two paragraph summary of the book.

What do you believe is the theme of The Hiding Place?

Read Betsie's final word on page 197. Do you think "there is no pit so deep that He is not deeper still" is an appropriate theme?

WORLD WAR II, THE BIGGEST WAR

Project 2, Page 3—Literature Unit

Activities

1. Estimate and research the size of the hiding place. Use boxes to re-create Corrie's room and the hiding place.

2. Write a letter with a hidden message under the stamp.

World War II, the Biggest War
Project 3

Navajo Code Talkers

Navajo Indians were a key element in U.S. Marine Communications during World War II. The Navajo language was the code used to send messages. Even though the Japanese were skilled in breaking codes, the Navajo Code baffled them. The language was very complex, did not have a written alphabet and was spoken only on Navajo lands of the American Southwest. Navajo Marines were sent to boot camp to perfect the code and used it very successfully to aid the American war effort in th Pacific Theater.The Pacific Theater refers to the fighting in the Pacific during the second World War.

The idea to use Navajo for secure communications came from Philip Johnston, the son of a missionary to the Navajos and one of the few non-Navajos who spoke the language fluently. Johnston was a WWI veteran who knew of the military's use of the Native American lnguage of Choctaw in the first World War.

Johnston believed Navajo answered the military's requirement for an undecipherable code. Its syntax and tonal qualities, not to mention dialects, make it unintelligible to anyone without extensive exposure and training.

The code was created in May 1942. They developed a dictionary and numerous words for military terms, all of which were memorized during training. Once a Navajo code talker was trained, he was sent to a Marine unit in the Pacific Theater.His primary task was to talk, transmitting information on tactics, troop movements, and vital battlefield communications over telephone lines and radios. At Iwo Jima, Major Howard Connor praised their efforts, "Were it not for the Navajos, the Marines would never have taken Iwo Jima." Connor had six talkers working round the clock during the first two days of the battle, sending over 800 messages, all without error.

When a Navajo code talker received a message, what he heard was a string of seemingly unrelated Navajo words. The words were then translated into its English equivalent. Then only the first letter of the English equivalent wasused to spell the English word. For example, to say the word "Navy" in Navajo code could be "tsah" (Needle), "wol-la-chee" (Ant), "ah-keh-di-glini" (Victor), and "tash-ah-dzoh" (Yucca).

Most letters had more than one Navajo word representing them. Thus, the Navajo words "wol-l-chee" (ant), "bel-la-sana" (apple) and "tse-nill" (axe) all stood for the letter "a." Not all words had to be spelled out letter by letter. The code's developers assigned Navajo words to represent 450 frequently used military terms. For example, "besh-lo" (iron fish) meant "submarine" and "dah-he-tih-hi" (hummingbird) meant "fighter plane."

The following pages contain a portion of the dictionary the Navajo Marines developed. Using this dictionary, crack the message below. Or better yet, write a message to a friend in code and then "crack" their encoded response.

Sample messgae for decoding–

DI HA-NEH-AL-ENJI SEIS BILH-BIGIH BAH-HAS-TKIH YIL-TAS –
CHA-GEE NE-HE-MAH NAL-DEH-HI GLOE-IH-DOT-SAHI WOLTAH-AL-KI-GI-JEH
CHA-GEE BEH-NA-ALI-TSOSIE TKAL-KAH-O-NEL

WORLD WAR II, THE BIGGEST WAR

Project 3, Page 2

Navajo Code Talkers' Dictionary

Following is a portion of the dictionary used by the U.S. Marines in the Pacific Theater during World War II for confidential communications. Revised as of 15 June 1945. Declassified under Department of Defense Directive 5200.9.

WORD	NAVAJO WORD	LITERAL TRANSLATION
Organizations		
CORPS	DIN-NEH-IH	CLAN
DIVISION	ASHIH-HI	SALT
REGIMENT	TABAHA	EDGE WATER
BATTALION	TACHEENE	RED SOIL
COMPANY	NAKIA	MEXICAN
PLATOON	HAS-CLISH-NIH	MUD
SECTION	YO-IH	BEADS
SQUAD	DEBEH-LI-ZINI	BLACK SHEEP
Officers		
COMMANDING GEN.	BIH-KEH-HE	WAR CHIEF
MAJOR GEN.	SO-NA-KIH	TWO STAR
BRIGADIER GEN.	SO-A-LA-IH	ONE STAR
COLONEL	ATSAH-BESH-LE-GAI	SILVER EAGLE
LT. COLONEL	CHE-CHIL-BE-TAH-BESH-LEGAI	SILVER OAK LEAF
MAJOR	CHE-CHIL-BE-TAH-OLA	GOLD OAK LEAF
CAPTAIN	BESH-LEGAI-NAH-KIH	TWO SILVER BARS
LIEUTENANT	BESH-LEGAI-A-LAH-IH	ONE SILVER BAR
C.O.	HASH-KAY-GI-NA-TAH	WAR CHIEF
X.O.	BIH-DA-HOL-NEHI	THOSE IN CHARGE
Countries		
AFRICA	ZHIN-NI	BLACKIES
ALASKA	BEH-HGA	WITH WINTER
AMERICA	NE-HE-MAH	OUR MOTHER
AUSTRALIA	CHA-YES-DESI	ROLLED HAT
BRITAIN	TOH-TA	BETWEEN WATERS
CHINA	CEH-YEHS-BESI	BRAIDED HAIR
FRANCE	DA-GHA-HI	BEARD
GERMANY	BESH-BE-CHA-HE	IRON HAT
ICELAND	TKIN-KE-YAH	ICE LAND
INDIA	AH-LE-GAI	WHITE CLOTHES
ITALY	DOH-HA-CHI-YALI-TCHI	STUTTER
JAPAN	BEH-NA-ALI-TSOSIE	SLANT EYE
PHILIPPINE	KE-YAH-DA-NA-LHE	FLOATING ISLAND
RUSSIA	SILA-GOL-CHI-IH	RED ARMY
SOUTH AMERICA	SHA-DE-AH-NE-HI-MAH	SOUTH OUR MOTHER
SPAIN	DEBA-DE-NIH	SHEEP PAIN
Airplanes		
PLANES	WO-TAH-DE-NE-IH	AIR FORCE
DIVE BOMBER	GINI	CHICKEN HAWK
TORPEDO PLANE	TAS-CHIZZIE	SWALLOW
OBS. PLAN	NE-AS-JAH	OWL
FIGHTER PLANE	DA-HE-TIH-HI	HUMMING BIRD
BOMBER PLANE	JAY-SHO	BUZZARD
PATROL PLANE	GA-GIH	CROW
TRANSPORT	ATSAH	EAGLE

WORLD WAR II, THE BIGGEST WAR

Project 3, Page 3

Ships

SHIPS	TOH-DINEH-IH	SEA FORCE
BATTLESHIP	LO-TSO	WHALE
AIRCRAFT	TSIDI-MOFFA-YE-HI	BIRD CARRIER
SUBMARINE	BESH-LO	IRON FISH
MINE SWEEPER	CHA	BEAVER
DESTROYER	CA-LO	SHARK
TRANSPORT	DINEH-NAY-YE-HI	MAN CARRIER
CRUISER	LO-TSO-YAZZIE	SMALL WHALE
MOSQUITO BOAT	TSE-E	MOSQUITO

Vocabulary

ABANDON	YE-TSAN	RUN AWAY FROM
ABOUT	WOLA-CHI-A-MOFFA-GAHN	ANT Fight
ACTION	AH-HA-TINH	PLACE OF ACTION
ACTIVITY	AH-HA-TINH-Y	ACTION ENDING IN Y
AFTER	BI-KHA-DI	AFTER
AGAINST	BE-NA-GNISH	AGAINST
AID	EDA-ELE-TSOOD	AID
AIR	NILCHI	AIR
ALERT	HA-IH-DES-EE	ALERT
ALL	TA-A-TAH	ALL
ALSO	EH-DO	ALSO
AMMUNITION	BE-ELI-DOH-BE-CAH	AMMUNITION
AMPHIBIOUS	CHAL	FROG
AND	DO	AND
ANY	TAH-HA-DAH	ANY
APPEAR	YE-KA-HA-YA	APPEAR
APPROACH	BI-CHI-OL-DAH	APPROACH
ARE	GAH-TSO BIG	RABBIT
AREA	HAZ-A-GIH	AREA
ARMY	LEI-CHA-IH-YIL-KNEE-IH	ARMY
ARRIVE	IL-DAY	ARRIVE
AS	AHCE	AS
AT	AH-DI	AT
ATTACK	AL-TAH-JE-JAY	ATTACK
ATTEMPT	BO-O-NE-TAH	TRY
AVAILABLE	TA-SHOZ-TEH-IH	AVAILABLE
BASE	BIH-TSEE-DIH	BASE
BATTLE	DA-AH-HI-DZI-TSIO	BATTLE
BAY	TOH-AH-HI-GHINH	BAY
BAZOOKA	AH-ZHOL	BAZOOKA
BE	TSES-NAH	BEE
BEEN	TSES-NAH-NES-CHEE	BEE NUT
BEFORE	BIH-TSE-DIH	BEFORE
BEGIN	HA-HOL-ZIZ	COMMENCE FROM
BELONG	TSES-NAH-SNEZ	LONG BEE
BETWEEN	BI-TAH-KIZ	BETWEEN
BEYOND	BILH-LA DI	DOWN BELOW
BOMB	A-YE-SHI	EGGS
BOOBY TRAP	DINEH-BA-WHOA-BLEHI	MAN TRAP
BUT	NEH-DIH	BUT
BY	BE-GHA	BY
CAN	YAH-DI-ZINI	CAN
CARRY	YO-LAILH	CARRY
CLEAR	YO-AH-HOL-ZHOD	CLEAR
COAST GUARD	TA-BAS-DSISSI	SHORE RUNNER
CODE	YIL-TAS	PECK
COME	HUC-QUO	COME
COMMUNICATION	HA-NEH-AL-ENJI	MAKING TALK
CONCEAL	BE-KI-ASZ-JOLE	CONCEAL
CONCENTRATION	TA-LA-HI-JIH	ONE PLACE
CONCUSSION	WHE-HUS-DIL	CONCUSSION

WORLD WAR II, THE BIGGEST WAR

Project 3, Page 4

CONDITION	AH-HO-TAI	HOW IT IS
CONSIDER	NE-TSA-CAS	THINK IT OVER
CONSIST	BILH	CONSIST
CONVOY	TKAL-KAH-O-NEL	MOVING ON WATER
COORDINATE	BEH-EH-HO-ZIN-NA-AS-DZOH	KNOWN LINES
COUNTER ATTACK	WOLTAH-AL-KI-GI-JEH	COUNTER ACT
CROSS	AL-N-AS-DZOH	CROSS
DAWN	HA-YELI-KAHN	DAWN
DO	TSE-LI	
DOCUMENT	BEH-EH-HO-ZINZ	
DRIVE	AH-NOL-KAHL	
DUD	DI-GISS-YAHZIE	
DUMMY	DI-GISS-TSO	
ESCAPE	A-ZEH-HA-GE-YAH	ESCAPE
EXCEPT	NEH-DIH	EXCEPT
EXECUTE	ALH-NAHL-YAH	EXCHANGE
EXPLOSIVE	A-DO-NIL	EXECUTE
FAIL	CHA-AL-EIND	EACH END
FORCE	TA-NA-NE-LADI	WITHOUT CARE
FORM	BE-CHA	FORM
FRIENDLY	NEH-HECHO-DA-NE	FRIENDLY
FROM	BI-TSAN-DEHN	FROM
GASOLINE	CHIDI-BI-TOH	GASOLINE
GRENADE	NI-MA-SI	POTATOES
GUARD	NI-DIH-DA-HI	GUARD
GUIDE	NAH-E-THLAI	GUIDE
HAVE	JO	HAVE
HEADQUARTER	NA-HA-TAH-TA-BA-HOGAN	HEADQUARTER
HOLD	WO-TKANH	HOLD
HOSPITAL	A-ZEY-AL-IH	PLACE OF MEDICINE
HOSTILE	A-NAH-NE-DZIN	NOT FRIENDLY
IMPORTANT	BA-HAS-TEH	IMPORTANT
INFANTRY	TA-NEH-NAL-DAHI	INFANTRY
INFILTRATE	YE-GHA-NE-JEH	WENT THROUGH
INTELLIGENCE	HO-YA (I)	SMART
IS	SEIS	SEVEN
ISLAND	SEIS-KEYAH	SEVEN ISLAND
JUNGLE	WOH-DI-CHIL	JUNGLE
KILL	NAZ-TSAID	KILL
LABOR	NA-NISH (L)	LABOR
LAND	KAY-YAH	LAND
LEFT	NISH-CLA-JIH-GOH	LEFT
LESS	BI-OH (L)	LESS
LOSS	UT-DIN	LOSS
MACHINE GUN	A-KNAH-AS-DONIH	RAPID FIRE GUN
MAP	KAH-YA-NESH-CHAI	MAP
MESSAGE	HANE-AL-NEH	MESSAGE
MILITARY	SILAGO-KEH-GOH	MILITARY
MINE	HA-GADE	MINE
MORE	THLA-NA-NAH	MORE
NAVY	TAL-KAH-SILAGO	SEA SOLDIER
NOT	NI-DAH-THAN-ZIE	NO TURKEY
NOTICE	NE-DA-TAZI-THIN	NO TURKEY ICE
NOW	KUT	NOW
OF	TOH-NI-TKAL-LO	OCEAN FISH
ONLY	TA-EI-TAY-A-YAH	ONLY
OR	EH-DO-DAH-GOH	EITHER
OTHER	LA-E-CIH	OTHER
OUT	CLO-DIH	OUT SIDE
PHOTOGRAPH	BEH-CHI-MA-HAD-NIL	PHOTOGRAPH
PLANE	TSIDI	BIRD
PREPARE	HASH-TAY-HO-DIT-NE	PREPARE
PRESENT	KUT	PRESENT

WORLD WAR II, THE BIGGEST WAR

Project 3, Page 5

PROBABLE	DA-TSI	PROBABLE
PROBLEM	NA-NISH-TSOH	BIG JOB
QUESTION	AH-JAH	EAR
QUICK	SHIL-LOH	QUICK
RADAR	ESAT-TSANH	LISTEN
RAID	DEZJAY	RAID
RAILROAD	KONH-NA-AL-BANSI-BI	RAILROAD
REACH	IL-DAY	REACH
READY	KUT (R)	READY
ROCKET	LESZ-YIL-BESHI	SAND BOIL
SABOTAGE	A-TKEL-YAH	HINDERED
SAILOR	CHA-LE-GAI	WHITE CAPS
SEAMAN	TKAL-KAH-DINEH-IH	SEAMAN
SECRET	BAH-HAS-TKIH	SECRET
SHELL	BE-AL-DOH-BE-CA	SHELL
SQUADRON	NAH-GHIZI	SQUASH
STORM	NE-OL	STORM
STRATEGY	NA-HA-TAH (S)	STRATEGY
STRIKE	NAY-DAL-GHAL	STRIKE
SUCH	YIS-CLEH	SOX
TAKE	GAH-TAHN	TAKE
TANK	CHAY-DA-GAHI	TORTOISE
TANK DESTROYER	CHAY-DA-GAHI-NAIL-TSAIDI	TORTOISE KILLER
TARGET	WOL-DONI	TARGET
TASK	TAZI-NA-EH-DIL-KID	TURKEY ASK
TEAM	DEH-NA-AS-TSO-SI	TEA MOUSE
THAT	TAZI-CHA	TURKEY HAT
THE	CHA-GEE	BLUE-JAY
THEIR	BIH	THEIR
THEREAFTER	TA-ZI-KWA-I-BE-KA-DI	TURKEY HERE AFTER
THESE	CHA-GI-O-EH	THE SEE
THEY	CHA-GEE (Y)	THE Y
THIS	DI	THE
TOGETHER	TA-BILH	TOGETHER
TORPEDO	LO-BE-CA	FISH SHELL
TROOP	NAL-DEH-HI	TROOP
UNDER	BI-YAH	UNDER
UNTIL	UH-QUO-HO	UNTIL
VICINITY	NA-HOS-AH-GIH	THERE ABOUT
VILLAGE	CHAH-HO-OH-LHAN-IH	MANY SHELTER
VISIBILITY	NAY-ES-TEE	VISIBILITY
VITAL	TA-EH-YE-SY	VITAL
WARNING	BILH-HE-NEH (W)	WARNING
WAS	NE-TEH	WAS
WATER	TKOH	WATER
WAVE	YILH-KOLH	WAVE
WEAPON	BEH-DAH-A-HI-JIH-GANI	FIGHTING WEAPON
WELL	TO-HA-HA-DLAY	WELL
WHEN	GLOE-EH-NA-AH-WO-HAI	WEASEL HEN
WHERE	GLOE-IH-QUI-AH	WEASEL HERE
WHICH	GLOE-IH-A-HSI-TLON	WEASEL TIED TOGETHER
WILL	GLOE-IH-DOT-SAHI	SICK WEASEL
WITH	BILH (W)	WITH
WITHIN	BILH-BIGIH	WITH IN
WITHOUT	TA-GAID	WITHOUT
WOOD	CHIZ	FIRE WOOD
WOUND	CAH-DA-KHI	WOUND
YARD	A-DEL-TAHL	YARD
ZONE	BIH-NA-HAS-DZOH	ZONE

WORLD WAR II, THE BIGGEST WAR

Test

1. When did WWII begin?

____

____

2. What was the blitzkrieg?

____

____

3. List the Axis powers.

____

____

____

____

4. List the Allied powers.

____

____

____

____

5. What occurred at Pearl Harbor on December 7, 1941?

____

____

6. Hitler set up concentration camps for ____________ and ____________.

7. How many people were killed in the concentration camps? Who were these people?

____

____

____

World War II, The Biggest War

Test, Part 2

8. Describe D-Day.

9. When did Germany surrender?

10. What president issued the ultimatum that eventually caused the U.S. to drop the atomic bomb on Hiroshima and Nagasaki Japan.

11. When did Japan finally surrender?

Review

1. Why was Abraham Lincoln referred to as the "Log cabin president?"

2. What was the Monroe doctrine?

World War II, The Biggest War

Test, Page 3

3. What was the transcontinental railroad?

4. Who invented the cotton gin?

5. List in chronological order those events studied to date.

   Next to each place the approximate date.

THE COLD WAR, KOREA AND VIETNAM
Worksheet

1. What are the dates given for the Cold War, Korea and Vietnam?

___

___

2. What was the "Cold War?"

___

___

3. Where did the most important and deadly battles of the "Cold War" take place for the U.S.?

___

___

4. What caused the conflict in Korea in the 1950's? What brought it to an end?

___

___

___

___

5. What happened to Vietnam in the 1960's?

___

___

6. Unlike other wars, the Korean and Vietnam wars had "rules." What were these "rules?"

___

___

7. When did the "Cold War" end?

___

___

___

THE COLD WAR, KOREA AND VIETNAM
Project

Political Comparison

Using the space provided below, write a paper comparing and contrasting Democracy and communism.

THE COLD WAR, KOREA AND VIETNAM
Project 2

Find a Vietnam Veteran and conduct an interview using the following questions.

1. How old were you when you went to Vietnam?
2. What are your best memories of your experience there?
3. What are your worst memories that you are comfortable talking about?
4. Describe the geographic conditions in which you fought. How did these impact the outcome?
5. If you had been in control of the American armed forces would you have done anything differently? If so, what?

The Cold War, Korea and Vietnam

Test

1. What are the dates given for the Cold War, Korea and Vietnam?

2. What was the "Cold War?" What countries were involved?

3. Where did the most important and deadly battles of the "Cold War" take place for the U.S.?

4. What was the cause of the Korean War? What countries were involved?

5. What happened to Vietnam in the 1960's? What did the U.S. have to do with this?

6. Unlike other wars, the Korean and Vietnam wars had "rules." What were these "rules?"

THE COLD WAR, KOREA AND VIETNAM

Test, Page 2

7. When did the "Cold War" end?

Review

1. How was the moral decay evident in the 1920's?

2. What were Wilbur and Orville Wright best known for?

3. What happened at the Battle of Little Big Horn?

4. What is George Washington Carver best known for?

5. List in chronological order all the events studied to date.

   Next to each place the approximate date.

THE SPACE RACE
Worksheet

1. What are the dates given for the Space Race?

2. During the ______________ ______________ the USSR (Soviet Union) and the United States competed against each other in almost every way, even in science and inventions.

3. What country put the first satellite into space? What was its name?

4. What was the "Space Race?"

5. In 1961 what did President Kennedy announce regarding space exploration?

6. Who was the first man that the U.S. put into space?

7. Who was the first man to orbit the earth?

8. What was Apollo 11?

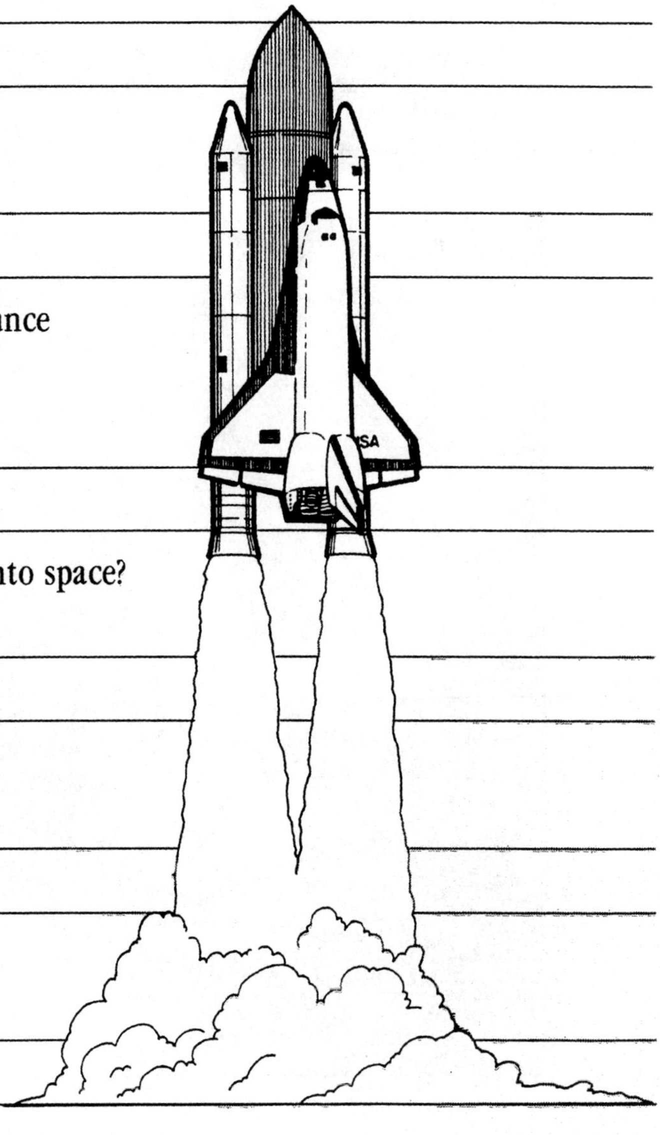

The Space Race
Worksheet, Page 2

9. What was the Lunar Rover?

10. After the moon mission what kind of space craft began to be used?

THE SPACE RACE

Project

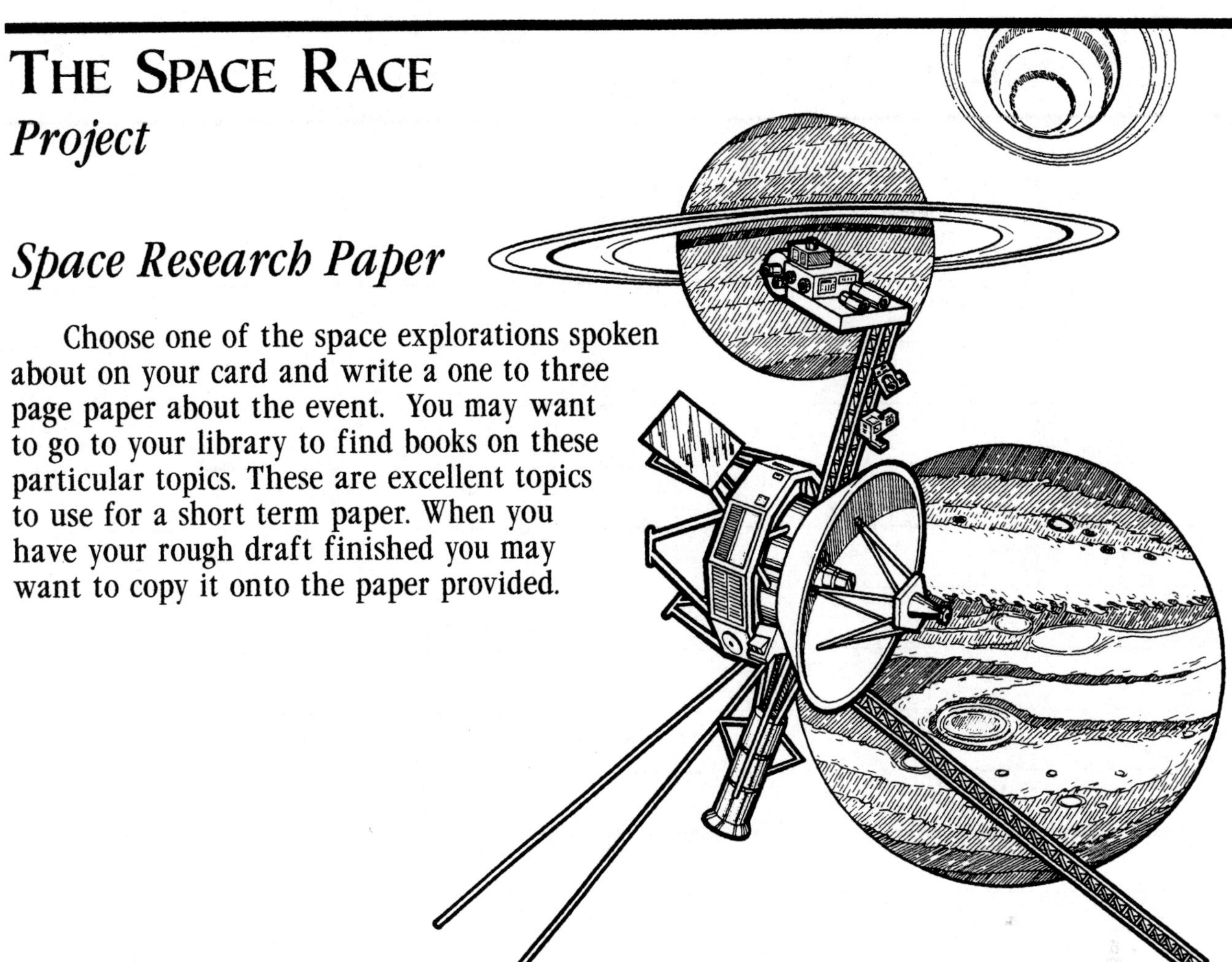

Space Research Paper

Choose one of the space explorations spoken about on your card and write a one to three page paper about the event. You may want to go to your library to find books on these particular topics. These are excellent topics to use for a short term paper. When you have your rough draft finished you may want to copy it onto the paper provided.

The Space Race

Project , Page 2

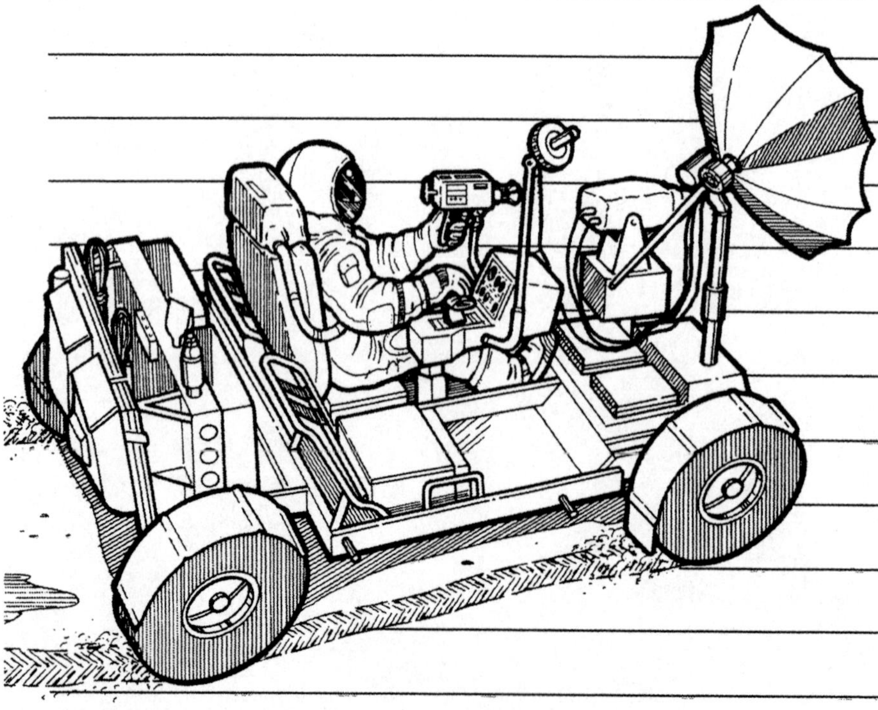

THE SPACE RACE
Project 2

Making a Rocket—Bottle Rockets

Supplies
1 one quart plastic soda bottle
1 cork to fit in the top of the bottle
1/2 cup of vinegar
1/2 cup water
1 teaspoon baking soda
4" square piece of paper towel
ribbon
thumbtacks

Make sure that the bottle is clean. Pour the water and vinegar into the bottle. Attach ribbon to the top of the cork with a thumbtack. Place all of the baking soda in the center of the paper towel, roll it up and twist the ends tight. ***Make sure you go outside before attempting the next step!!!*** Place the paper towel packet into the bottle and push the cork into the top of the bottle to close it. Place the bottle on a flat surface and **STAND AWAY FROM IT.** You should see the cork fly into the air.

THE SPACE RACE
Test

1. What are the dates given for the Space Race?

2. What occurred during the Cold War?

3. What was Sputnik?

4. What country in particular was the United Spaces competing against in the Space Race?

5. Who was the first man that the U.S. put into space?

6. Who was the first man to orbit the earth?

7. What was Apollo II's mission?

8. What was the Lunar Rover?

The Space Race
Test, Page 2

9. What are the vehicles called that we now use to do the work in space?

____

____

Review

1. When did WWII begin?

____

____

2. What president is remembered for starting the Panama Canal?

____

____

3. Why were cowboys first needed?

____

____

4. What was the period referred to in history as "Reconstruction" about?

____

____

5. List in chronological order all the events studied to date.

   Next to each place the approximate date.

____

____

____

____

____

____

Modern America Today

Worksheet

1. Why did the United States become the greatest manufacturer of goods in the entire world?

   ____

   ____

2. The US supplied many goods to even our former enemies, ____________ and ____________, during the 1950s.

3. What event stimulated the United States to work hard at military defense and technology?

   ____

   ____

4. After WWII the US Navy quickly made its ships ____________ powered.

5. What allowed us to grow and enjoy the best standard of living in the entire world?

   ____

   ____

6. When did the USSR finally fall apart?

   ____

   ____

7. Name two positive and two negative areas in which the United States is the world leader?

   ____

   ____

   ____

8. What is the only complete answer to the problems in America today?

   ____

   ____

Modern America Today

Project

Interview

Using this information sheet interview a local politician (Mayor, State Representative, Congressman, Police chief or Councilman) to see what they think about modern America.

Name of person contacted: ______________________

Date: ______________________

Title: ______________________

1. What problems do you consider most needing to be addressed today?

____

____

____

2. How do you plan to address the problems?

____

____

____

3. What impact does Scripture have on how you will address them?

____

____

____

4. If Scripture is not the standard, by what do you judge what is right, what is the standard and why?

____

____

____

____

Modern America Today
Project 2

The instructions for this project can be found in Appendix 2-1.

20th Century Conflicts, 20th Century Ideas

I

From 1919 to the end of World War II, there were three main political ideologies competing with each other: "fascism", "communism" and "liberal democracy". An "ideology" is a set of ideas that all fit together. Thus you might be able to guess that a political ideology is a set of ideas that explains what the role of government should be. "Liberal democracy", which has been the view of most Americans since the founding of the country, basically says that government should be elected by the people on the one had, while on the other hand it should respect private property and not interfere too much with private businesses. "Communism", which traces much of its inspiration to Karl Marx's writings in the 19th Century, says that big businesses oppress ordinary workers, and so the workers should take over the state in a revolution and use its power to take over the businesses for the sake of those oppressed workers. "Fascism" said that only the nation and its interests were important and that a strong leader was needed to guide the state and mobilize its businesses and people to win wars against other countries.

II

World War II completely discredited fascism. Not only were the fascist regimes of Germany, Japan and Italy incredibly harsh and cruel, but they failed to achieve their own standard of greatness by not winning the victory! In the end, they were unable to mobilize their countries' resources as successfully as the liberal democracies did. Russia's communist government, on the other hand, seemed to come out of the war far stronger than anyone expected. They produced more tanks, for example, than all of the axis combined! The long war of ideas known as the "Cold War", however, showed the weakness of the communist system. While Russia's government economic planning was very good at producing war materials, it was far less effective at meeting the needs of ordinary people. While the willingness of the communist leaders to persecute any who dared disagree with them helped them stay in power for a long time, eventually the economic problems got worse until, in 1989 and 1990, a series of (mostly non-violent) revolutions overthrew most of the communist governments in Europe.

MODERN AMERICA TODAY

Project 2, Page 2

III

If, in profound irony, fascism was weak in war and communism weak in economics, does liberal democracy have a weakness? If it does, it is the fact that democracy rests on the will of the people. If the people ever stop being willing to sacrifice for democratic government, democracy will die. If they stop being willing to boldly stand up for the rights of those that they may not agree with, democracy can turn ugly, like it has in Iran, or, to use a fictional example, like it did in Fahrenheit 451. That's why democracy hasn't worked too well in some countries where it's been tried. In some places, either the people put up with being ruled by a small group of people or they don't allow enough freedom to those who are in the minority.

Vocabulary

1. *discredited:* ______________________________

2. *mobilize:* ______________________________

3. *profound:* ______________________________

4. *irony:* ______________________________

5. *oppress:* ______________________________

Modern America Today

Project 2, Page 3

Key Word Outline

I ________________________________

1 ________________________________

2 ________________________________

3 ________________________________

4 ________________________________

5 ________________________________

6 ________________________________

II ________________________________

1 ________________________________

2 ________________________________

3 ________________________________

4 ________________________________

5 ________________________________

6 ________________________________

7 ________________________________

8 ________________________________

III ________________________________

1 ________________________________

2 ________________________________

3 ________________________________

4 ________________________________

5 ________________________________

6 ________________________________

Modern America Today

Project 2, Page 4

Vocabulary

1. *discredited:* shown to be not worthy of belief or trust
2. *mobilize:* to organize and bring to bear all available forces for a conflict
3. *profound:* deep or great
4. *irony:* something that is oddly the opposite of what one might expect initially
5. *oppress:* to deny others fundamental rights or needs, usually by force

Key Word Outlines

I The Three Competing World Ideologies
1. Three, main, ideologies
2. Political government
3. Idea, fit, together
4. "Liberal Democracy", elected, private
5. "Communism", revolution, oppressed
6. "Fascism", nation, leader

II The Debunking of Fascism and Communism
1. World War II, discredited, fascism
2. Failed, achieve, greatness
3. Unable, mobilize, resources
4. Communist, stronger, expected
5. Produced, more, tanks
6. "Cold War", showed, weakness
7. Less, effective, ordinary
8. Problems, worsened, revolutions

II The Weakness of Democracy?
1. Democracy, weakness ?
2. Rests, on, will
3. People, stop, sacrifice
4. Stop, stand up, rights
5. Why, hasn't, worked

Modern America Today

Project 3

Following is an excerpt from an address given by President George Bush, May 31, 1989 in Mainz, West Germany.

THE END OF THE COLD WAR AND THE VICTORY OF FREEDOM AND DEMOCRACY

UNLEASHING THE FORCE OF FREEDOM

I said recently that we're at the end of one era and at the beginning of another. And I noted that in regard to the Soviet Union, our policy is to move beyond containment.

For 40 years, the seeds of democracy in Eastern Europe lay dormant, buried under the frozen tundra of the Cold War. And for 40 years the world has waited for the Cold War to end. And decade after decade, time after time, the flowering human spirit withered from the chill of conflict and oppression. And again the world waited. But the passion for freedom cannot be denied forever. The world has waited long enough. The time is right. Let Europe be whole and free.

In the East, brave men and women are showing us the way. Look at Poland, where solidarity and the Catholic Church have won legal status. The forces of freedom are putting the Soviet status quo on the defensive. In the West, we have succeeded because we have been faithful to our values and our vision. And on the other side of the rusting Iron Curtain, their vision has failed. The Cold War began with the division of Europe. It can only end when Europe is whole.

And today, it is this very concept of a divided Europe that is under siege. And that is why our hopes run high, because the division of Europe is under siege, not by armies, but by the spread of ideas that began here, right here. It was a son of Mainz, Johannes Gutenburg, who liberated the mind of man through the power of the printed word. And that same liberating power is unleashed today in a hundred new forms.

The Voice of America, Deutche Welle, allow us to enlighten millions deep within Eastern Europe and throughout the world. Television satellites allow us to bear witness from the shipyards of Gdansk to Tiananmen Square. But the momentum for freedom does not just come from the printed word or the television screen. It comes from a single powerful idea —Democracy.

This one idea is sweeping across Eurasia. This one idea is why the Communist world, from Budapest to Beijing, is in ferment. And of course, for the leaders of the East it is not just freedom for freedom's sake. But whatever their motivation, they are unleashing a force they will find difficult to control, the hunger for liberty of oppressed peoples who have tasted freedom.

The nations of Eastern Europe are rediscovering the glories of their national heritage, so let the colors and hues of national culture return to these gray societies of the East. Let Europe forego a peace of tension for a peace of trust, one in which the peoples of the East and West can rejoice, a continent that is diverse, yet whole. Together we shall answer the call.

The world has waited long enough.

MODERN AMERICA TODAY

Project 3

Berlin Wall Timeline

1948	The Soviet Union cuts off all rail water, and highway routes to West Germany.
1949	The west becomes known as West Berlin, and East Berlin as The Soviet Sector.
1950's	West Germany expands and modernizes rapidly.
1955	West Germany joins NATO.
1958	The Soviets demands that West Berlin become a "Free City."
1961	Communists build Berlin Wall
1969	Willy Brandt becomes West Germany's first Social Democratic chancellor.
1970's	Standard living in East Germany now improved and is catching up with West Germany.
1976	The 12 members of NATO pledge military support to one another in case of attack.
1982	Coalition government collapses.
1983	Christian Democrat returns to power, Helmut Kohl.
1989	The Berlin Wall opens, allowing East and West Germans to unite.
1990	Germany reunites, the Unification Peace Treaty is signed, and Berlin is named the capitol.
1991	Soviet Government officially grants independance.
1997	A red line is painted, marking the place where the Berlin Wall stood.

Modern America Today
Test

1. Why did the United States become the greatest manufacturer of goods in the entire world?

   ____

   ____

2. What two former enemies did the U.S. supply goods to during the 1950's?

   ____

   ____

3. The Cold War stimuated the United States to work hard at ______________ and ______________.

4. What kind of improvements did the space race bring about?

   ____

   ____

5. What allows us to grow and enjoy the best standard of living in the entire world?

   ____

   ____

6. What happened to the USSR in 1989?

   ____

   ____

7. Name two areas in which the United States became the world leader?

   ____

   ____

   ____

8. What is the only complete answer to the problems in America today?

   ____

   ____

MODERN AMERICA TODAY

Test, Page 2

Review

1. President Monroe did not want ____________ nations to control countries in this hemisphere.
2. For what is George Washington Carver best known?

____

____

____

3. What was the 13th amendment to the Constitution?

____

____

____

4. Unlike other wars, the Korean and Vietnam wars had "rules." What were these "rules?"

____

____

____

5. In chronological order list all the events studied to date.
   Next to each place the approximate date.

____

____

____

____

____

____

____

____

Cumulative Review

Test

Card:

Date:

Two Facts:

Card:

Date:

Two Facts:

Card:

Date:

Two Facts:

Card:

Date:

Two Facts:

READING PROJECTS
Instructions

Teacher's Instructions for Integrating History and Writing

1. Vocabulary: Before giving the assignment the teacher should look at the vocabulary and make a judgement as to whether or not the students will be likely to know most of them. If the answer is yes, skip to step #2 and have them look up the vocabulary afterward. If not, have them look up the vocabulary words first.

2. Reading/Note-taking: have the students read the passage while taking notes using the "key-word method." In brief, this means ***no more than 3*** words from each sentence that will help the student remember what is said in it. Appropriate answers can, of course vary, but sample answers are given in the answer key. Two general rules can help these notes to be meaningful:
   a. Distilling the grammatical core—words that are part of the grammatical core of the sentence, particularly subjects, action verbs, direct objects, predicate nouns and adjectives.
   b. Note that *linking verbs* are not listed above. Though they are just as much a part of the grammatical core, they are easy to assume (i.e., instead of writing "Alexander was brutal," it is more effective to write, "Alexander brutal").

3. Title: have the students try to come up with a title for each paragraph. This forces them to try to look at each paragraph and try to understand its main point. Sample titles are given on the answer key.

4. Summary paragraph: Have the students turn the page and try to reconstruct, in brief, the essence of the original on a separate sheet of paper using only their notes.

5. Improved paragraph: have the students spruce up their paragraphs using a list of "modifiers", "power words" or grammatical constructions that can help the students to make their writing more interesting. (Andrew Pudewa's "Excellence in Writing" method is a good example of how to do this in practice.)

1850 TO THE PRESENT

Project—Example Grammar-History Sentences

DIRECTIONS FOR HISTORY-GRAMMAR INTEGRATION

We recommend the Shurley Grammar program as being the one which does the best job of teaching students the fundamental structure of the English sentence. Obviously, the sentences in the various sentences groups of Shurley are not all going to have any relationship with the content of their history, but we believe that making up extra practice sentences which have content culled from their history lessons can bring a beneficial "synergy" into the curriculum.

Several sentences derived from the content of the history lessons have been written and parsed as examples. Obviously, the possibilities are limitless.

It would also be worthwhile to have the children make up their own, history-related sentences. This could be done for the whole class to parse, or for their own, individual practice and improved sentences that are integral to the Shurley lessons.

LV SN A ADJ PN P A OP
1. SN LV PN P4 Was Teddy Roosevelt/a charismatic leader (during the Spanish-American War)? INT

1. Who was a charismatic leader during the Spanish-American War? Teddy Roosevelt/SN
2. What is being said about Teddy Roosevelt? Teddy Roosevelt was/V
3. Was What? Leader/verify the noun
4. Is leader the same thing as Teddy Roosevelt? yes
5. Teddy Roosevelt/PN
6. Was/LV
7. What Kind of leader? charismatic/Adj
8. A/A
9. During/P
10. During what? Spanish-American War/OP
11. The/A
12. SN LV PN P4 check
13. (during the Spanish-American War)/prepositional phrase
14. question mark, question, interrogative sentence
15. Go back to the verb; divide the complete subject from the complete predicate.
16. Is there an adverb exception? no
17. Is this sentence in a natural or inverted order? inverted.
18. Underline the subject parts once and the predicate parts twice.

1850 TO THE PRESENT

Project, Page 2—Example Grammar-History Sentences

SN V-T A IO A CADJ C CADJ
2. <u>SN V-t</u> Andrew Jackson gave the British a spectacular, but irrelevant,
DO P OP
IO DO P3 defeat (in New Orleans). D

1. Andrew Jackson gave the British a spectacular, but irrelevant, defeat in New Orleans.
2. Who gave the British a spectacular but irrelevant defeat in New Orleans? Andrew Jackson/SN
3. What is being said about Andrew Jackson? Andrew Jackson gave/V
4. Gave what? defeat/verify the noun
5. Does defeat mean the same thing as Andrew Jackson? no
6. Defeat/DO
7. Gave/V-t
8. Gave defeat to whom? British/IO
9. The/A
10. A/A
11. What kind of defeat? spectacular but irrelevant/ Cadj,Cadj
12. But/C
13. In/P
14. In Where? New Orleans/OP
15. SN V-t DO IO P3 check
16. (in New Orleans)/ prepositional phrase
17. period statement, declarative sentence
18. Go back to the verb; divide the complete subject from the complete predicate.
19. Is there an adverb exception? no
20. Is this sentence in a natural or inverted order? natural/no change.

A SN V-T DO P ADJ OP
3. <u>SN V-t</u> The Civilian Conservation Corps / provided jobs (for young men)
DO P1 P A OP
(during the depression).D

1. The Civilian Conservation Corps provided jobs for young men during the depression.
2. What provided jobs for young men during the Depression? the Civilian Conservation Corps/SN
3. What is being said about Civilian Conservation Corps? Civilian Conservation Corps provided/V
4. Provided What? jobs/verify the noun.
5. Does jobs mean the same thing as Civilian Conservation Corps? no
6. Jobs/DO
7. Provided/V-t
8. For/P

1850 TO THE PRESENT

Project, Page 3—Example Grammar-History Sentences

9. For what? men/OP
10 What kind of men? young/Adj
11. During/P
12. During what? Depression/OP
13. The/A
14. The/A
15. SN V-t DO P2 check
16. (for young men)/ prepositional phrase
17. (During the Depression)/ prepositional phrase
18. Period, statement, declarative sentence
19. Go back to the verb; divide the complete subject from the complete predicate.
20. Is there an adverb exception? no
21. Is this sentence in a natural or inverted order? natural/no change.

	A ADJ SN P OP
4. <u>SN LV</u>	The relentless attacks (of General Grant,
	OP C OP LV ADV PA P
PA P5	General Sherman and General Sheridan) /were too difficult (for
	A OP
	the Confederacy).D

1. The Relentless attacks of General Grant, General Sherman and General Sheridan were too much for the Confederacy.
2. What were too much for the Confederacy? attacks/SN
3. What is being said about attacks? attacks were/V
4. Were what? Difficult/PA
5. Were/LV
6. How difficult? too difficult/Adv
7. For/P
8. For what? Confederacy/OP
9. The/A
10. The/A
11. What kind of attacks? relentless/Adj
12. Of/P
13. Of what? General Grant, General Sherman, and General Sheridan/COP,COP,COP
14. And/C
15. SN LV PA P5 check
16. (of General Grant, General Sherman and General Sheridan)/prepositional phrase
17. (for the Confederacy)/prepositional phrase
18. Period, statement, declarative sentence

1850 TO THE PRESENT

Project, Page 4—Example Grammar-History Sentences

19. Go back to the verb; divide the complete subject from the complete predicate.
20. Is their and adverb exception? no
21. Is this sentence in a natural or inverted order? natural/no change.

```
             A      SN           HV  V       P   A          OP
5. SN V      The Panama Canal / was built (through the Isthmus of Panama).D
   PI
```

1. The Panama Canal was built through the Isthmus of Panama.
2. What was built through the Isthmus of Panama? Panama Canal/SN
3. What is being said about Panama Canal? Panama Canal was built/V
4. Was/HV
5. Through/P
6. Through what? the Isthmus of Panama/OP
7. The/A
8. The/A
9. SN V P1 check
10. (through the Isthmus of Panama)/prepositional phrase
11. Period, statement, declarative sentence
12. Go back to the verb; divide the complete subject from the complete predicate.
13. Is there an adverb exception? no
14. Is this sentence in a natural or inverted order? natural/no change.

CHAPTER SUMMARY

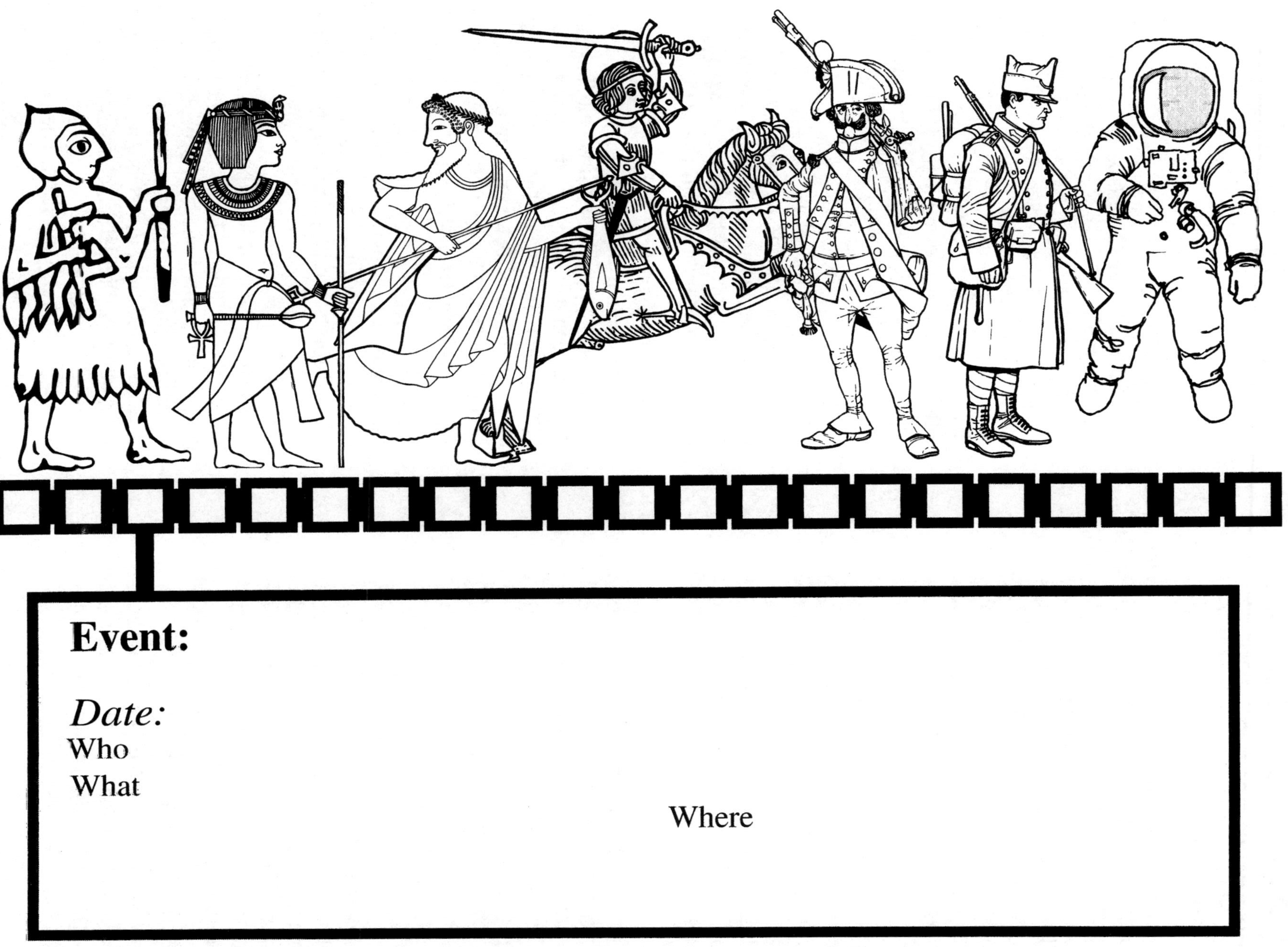

Event:

Date:

Who

What

Where

1850 TO THE PRESENT

Great Games for History Review

Make cards with names, dates, events and places to keep in a packet. Add to the cards as more topics are studied. On review days pull out the 3x5 cards for ready made clues. They can be helpful for many of the following games, especially when everyone's brains are tired and they just can't think of a word for *hangman* or a *charade* to act out.

Who Am I? (Where Am I? What Am I?)
A Student selects a person, place or thing from their history knowledge. The student who is "It" gives clues and calls on classmates (with their hands raised) to guess. The student with the correct guess gets the next turn to be "It."

Twenty Questions
The student chooses a history person, place or thing. They announce to the class whether they are a person, place or thing. The class can ask twenty questions. All questions must be worded so that a 'yes' or a 'no' answer is given. If after twenty questions no one has guessed the correct answer, "It" identifies the person, place or thing.

Charades
Play as individuals or as teams. One person or team acts out clues to an identity or event. The remaining students or team tries to guess. Set a time limit of several minutes.

Thumbs Up or Down
The teacher asks 'yes' or 'no' questions pertaining to history. The class responds with thumbs up for yes and thumbs down for no.

Knock-Knock
Teacher says, "Knock-Knock."
Student replies "Who's there?"
Teacher gives a fact as response. For example, "I had six wives." Student tells the name, "King Henry VIII."

Mixed-Up Story
Retell a historical event with a few facts incorrect. As the teacher tells the story, students raise their hands and correct the errors.

Chronological Order
Give the students one or two history flashcards. Have the students place their cards in the chronological order without looking at the numbers on the back.

A, B, C's of History
The first student begins by naming a history person, place or thing that begins with an A and telling a fact about it. The next student follows in turn with the next letter of the alphabet. For example, A-Aristotle was a philosopher. B-Botticelli was a Renaissance artist.

Ball Toss
Teacher tosses a small soft ball to a student who answers the question posed. The student tosses the ball back to the teacher.

Baseball
This can be adapted to paper for smaller groups or for quieter times. Chair baseball can be quite noisy, but will probably be the class' favorite review game. Set up chairs in a baseball diamond. Label home, 1st, 2nd, and 3rd bases. Divide the class into two teams. Player gets a hit when they correctly answer a question. They can move

1850 TO THE PRESENT

Great Games, Page 2

around the bases as their team mates correctly answer. A run is scored when the players advance to home. Incorrect answers are outs.

Tic Tac Toe
This can be played in pairs or by dividing into two teams. Students choose where to place the X or O when they correctly answer a question.

Secret Identity
One player selects a person and tells other players the initial of the selection's last name. Other players ask questions phrased so that the chooser has to identify other people with the same initial. If the initial is H for example, the first question could be "Are you a president of the United States?" The response may be, "No, I am not William Harrison." If the chooser is stumped for a response with the proper initial, then the asker can request other information: "Are you alive?" The "stumped" questions can only be answered by a 'yes' or a 'no.' The chooser continues answering questions until someone guesses the identity.

Boxes
Set up the game with a square grid made up of dots. Ask questions of the students. Correct answers earn a horizontal or vertical line connecting two of the dots. The student who closes in a box puts his initials inside and gets another turn. He may continue adding lines as long as each line forms a new box. The Student with the most boxes wins.

Categories
Select twenty categories ahead of time (colonies, items traded with England, Presidents, founding fathers, famous ships, items England taxed). Each student writes names of all the categories across the top of his paper. The players have 5-10 minutes to write as many items that fit the categories as they can. When time is up, trade lists for scoring. Each correct answer is one point. An answer no one else has gets two points. The player with the most points wins.

Drawing in the Dark
Retell a history event to the class. The class should draw the events with their eyes closed. Judges can choose the most accurate, funniest, etc.

Hangman
Choose words related to history. Each student guesses a letter in turn until someone has a guess or the stickman figure is hanged.

Magazing
Collect as many old magazines as feasible. Allow students several minutes to depict a historical event by cutting out pictures and words from magazines and gluing them to blank pages. They can even compile the pages into a book to show the flow of events.

Questions
The first player asks a question. The second player must respond with another related question, and then the first player with a question, etc. If a player pauses too long between questions, forgets to ask a question, or asks a nonsensical question, he is out. For example, "Did Paul Revere live in Boston?" "Didn't he look for a signal in the church tower?" "Was it one if by land, two if by sea?"

1850 TO THE PRESENT
Veritas Press History Song

Let's begin in history with the doctrine of James Monroe back in 1823 against European control.
Second came the travel on the Erie Canal across the state of New York.
Third, Jacksonian Democracy, he knew how to make it work.
Number four, the Cotton Gin. This established the South in the Industrial Revolution, Eli Whitney brought it about.
Number five, slavery in the South finally was outlawed. The 13th Amendment to the Constitution was passed to end it all.

Number six came the Cherokee Trail of Tears from Georgia to Oklahoma.
Number seven, remember the Alamo, defended itself against Mexico.
Eight came the westward expansion, Wagons Ho!
Nine came the war with the country of Mexico.
Number 10 came the California Gold Rush by the people called the "49er's."
11 came the split of Oregon by the United States and Great Britain.
12 came Lincoln, the 16th president.
His Emancipation Proclamation and the Gettysburg Address.

13 the War Between the States began. Eleven southern states seceded, Confederate states they became from 1861 to 1865. They finally surrendered to the North, the Union was kept alive.
14, the Confederates made their last invasion at the three day Battle of Gettysburg, defeated by the Union.
15, remember the Generals in the War Between the States. The South had Robert E. Lee and Jackson. The North, Ulysses Grant.

16, the completion of the Transcontinental Railroad. A trip to California took only 10 days all the way from the State of New York.
17, the mending of the broken Union, reconstruction of the South. President Lincoln was assassinated, so it never really came about.
18, the emergence of black leadership in the South.
19, the Age of Industry, new factories, new transportation.
20 came the Battle of the Little Big Horn.
Sitting Bull and Crazy Horse defeated General Custer and all of his men, the Union was surprised, of course.

21 came the cowboys and the West, famous for their cattle trails.
22 came the Spanish-American War.
The "roughriders" charged up San Juan Hill.
23 was Teddy Roosevelt. He cleared a path between the oceans with the Panama Canal.

24 came immigration round the world to America.
25 came a time of great inventors, Edison and the Wright Brothers.
26 was the Great World War from 1914 to 1918 and the U.S. joined in the Allied Force.

Number 27 came the Roaring 20's, a decade of greed and decadence which led to
Number 28. The Great Depression was triggered by the crash. People lost entire fortunes, it vanished in a flash.
29 came World War II. Hitler invaded Poland.
He persecuted six million Jews. The biggest war was waging from 1939 to 1945. And the US fought with the Allied Troops, victory was on their side.

30 came the Cold War about the spread of Communism.
31 was the race in space. The moon became our vision. And that brings us to
32, America today.
We've come so far, there's so much to do.
But only by God's grace.
We've come so far, there's so much to do.
But only by God's grace.